THE WRITER'S SURVIVAL MANUAL

THE MOST COMPLETE, UP-TO-DATE GUIDE TO PUBLISHING FOR THE WORKING WRITER.

Each year about 35,000 new books are published in the United States alone. But to make your book one of them takes the kind of insider's knowledge *The Writer's Survival Manual* can give you. It explains in step-by-step fashion everything from selling your manuscript to understanding the bottom line that will determine what your book will look like, how it will be marketed—and how much you will earn. Whether it's negotiating your contract or reading your royalty statement, this book will teach you everything you need to know about the writing and publishing business.

"The best and most inclusive introduction to the publishing process and the writing trade . . . Like most people in the writing business I get many requests for advice from apprentice writers. Now I will be able to say: Get *The Writer's Survival Manual*."

—Matthew Bruccoli, President, Bruccoli Clark Publishers

CAROL MEYER, a graduate of the University of Minnesota, has been working in New York publishing for more than twelve years. She was a subsidiary rights assistant at Random House. She then worked her way up from assistant to the director of the trade department, to managing editor and editor in Harcourt Brace Jovanovich's trade book division. She is currently a freelance writer, editor and consultant, and director of the Rice University Publishing Program in Houston, Texas.

The Writer's Survival Manual:

The Complete Guide to Getting
Your Book Published Right

by Carol J. Meyer

BANTAM BOOKS
TORONTO · NEW YORK · LONDON · SYDNEY · AUCKLAND

THE WRITER'S SURVIVAL MANUAL
*A Bantam Book / published by arrangement with
Crown Publishers, Inc.*

PRINTING HISTORY
*Crown edition published November 1982
A Main Selection of Writer's Digest Book Club, November 1982.*

*Statements in this book concerning contractual or legal issues
are general statements. This book does not purport to be a
substitute for the advice of an attorney in dealing with specific
situations or problems which may confront an author.*

*Special thanks to Random House, Inc., for the use of their trade
book contract form, to Mergenthaler Linotype for the use of the
linotype machine illustration, and to Graphic Arts
Technical Foundation for the illustration of a Lens System of a
Phototypesetter.*

Revised and updated Bantam edition / September 1984

ISBN 0-553-24108-7

Published simultaneously in the United States and Canada

*Bantam Books are published by Bantam Books, Inc. Its trade-
mark, consisting of the words "Bantam Books" and the por-
trayal of a rooster, is Registered in U.S. Patent and Trademark
Office and in other countries. Marca Registrada. Bantam
Books, Inc., 666 Fifth Avenue, New York, New York 10103.*

PRINTED IN THE UNITED STATES OF AMERICA

O   0 9 8 7 6 5 4 3 2 1

TO MY FAMILY

Acknowledgments

This book would not have been possible without the help of many people. I particularly want to thank the many colleagues at Harcourt Brace Jovanovich who generously answered my questions and extended my understanding of the publishing process. Richard Udell was particularly helpful in explaining contracts and literary law; Charles McDade was also of great assistance in untangling the intricacies of publishing contracts. Many other colleagues also provided their time and knowledge, including Kathleen Barco, Jess Brolier, Chris Christofis, Ron Coplen, Brian Dumaine, Ray Ferguson, Eugene Gordon, Judy Greissman, Stuart Harris, Carol Hill, Kristin Kliemann, Carol Kohlman, Barbara Knowles, Carol Lazare, Barbara Lucas, Georgia McCaughey, Frank McCormick, Margot Mabie, Amanda Mecke, Meyer Miller, Julian Muller, Maggie O'Brien, Rubin Pfeffer, B.J. Robbins, Michael Romano, Laura Schneider, Irene Skolnick, Rita Vaughan, Gloria Weiner, and Barbara Wood.

Beside these kind souls, I would like to acknowledge my editor, Daphne Abeel, and the staff of Crown Publishers—also the considerable assistance of Cynthia Blair, Ed Breslin, Matthew Bruccoli, Grace Budd, Jane Chambers, Richard Curtis, Mary Dorman, Jean Fiedler, Fred Graver, Elaine Jacobson, Susan Kamil, Denise LaVoie, Richard Layman, Wendy and Jonathan Lazear, Evan Marshall, Joyce Mitchell, Susan Moldow, Charles Myers, Daniel Okrent, Debbie Phillips, Felice Picano, Eileen Prescott, Linda Price, Kathy Robbins, Marcella Smith, Gene Stone, Nancy Stremmel, Mary Lou Thomas, Mark Washburn, Marjorie Williams, and Jonathan Yardley.

Finally, my thanks to several friends who supported me patiently during the long writing of this book. I particularly want to acknowledge Barbara Clark, Beverly Miller, and Madge Strickland in Minnesota, and Joanna Asperger, Cynthia Beer, Martha Goldstein, Anne MacKay, Sylvia Newman, and Freddie Wachsberger in New York.

Contents

Introduction to the Paperback Edition

Writing a book—or getting an idea for one and developing it to the point where a publisher might be interested—is one thing, but actually finding a publisher for it and signing a contract can be quite another. Each year nearly 35,000 new books and 10,000 new editions of previously published books are released in this country alone. Yet there are thousands of other manuscripts and proposals—some of them as good as the books that do get published—that never find a home. Why is that? Is there some sort of conspiracy against new writers?

The answer is—no, there is no conspiracy. In fact, publishers are eager for new talent, and editors spend a good deal of time looking for new writers and new projects. But much of what they review proves to be unsuitable for one of two reasons:

1. The manuscript or proposal is not well thought out and/or not well written. The writer has either not taken the time to carefully consider the *audience* for the book, or has not taken the trouble to write it so that it is as appealing to a potential purchaser as possible.

2. The manuscript or proposal has come to the wrong place or the wrong editor. Not all houses publish all kinds of books. And not all editors respond to material in the same way. They're human too, and can make decisions only on the basis of their own experience, judgment, and taste. If a project doesn't interest them, they're going to pass it by—even though the same project may be wildly exciting to someone

else. There are plenty of manuscripts that have travelled from house to house before finally finding a very happy home.

This suggests two things. One is that you as a writer must be responsible for making your project as relevant, as well written, and as excellently presented as possible. You still may fail to find a publisher for it, but at least it won't be because you sabotaged its chances from the beginning. The other thing is that looking for a publisher takes time, patience, and effort. If your book is truly of merit, and has a potential audience that exceeds your family and personal friends, you have a very good chance of getting it published—but only if you send it to places that are *likely* to be interested in it, and then persist until you find the right editor for it.

This manual is designed to show you not only how to find a publisher (or literary agent), but what to do once you've found one and received a publishing offer. It is based on my many years of experience as an editor and managing editor in a trade book house, and also on the hundreds of questions that writers have asked me over the years. It is as though an editor were taking you by the hand and leading you step-by-step through the publishing process, from the time you start putting your material together for submission to the time that you are trying to decipher your royalty statement and think about your next book. Furthermore, the manual has been completely revised and updated for this paperback edition, to make certain that you have the most current and useful information possible.

The Writer's Survival Manual is aimed at the writers of trade books and of mass market paperbacks. A trade book is a book of general interest sold primarily through the retail bookstore (as opposed to textbooks, professional books, etc., that are sold through other channels). A trade book can be on virtually any subject, and can be either a hardcover or a so-called "trade paperback." About 15,000 of the books published in the U.S. each year are trade books.

A mass-market paperback is a small format paperback sold primarily through nonbookstore outlets such as newsstands, drugstores, discount stores, and the like. These are somewhat different from trade paperbacks not only in the way they are distributed, but also in the fact that the size of mass-market paperbacks is fairly rigidly maintained (usually

4½ x 7 inches) and that they are usually considerably less expensive than trade paperbacks. Furthermore, they are published on a monthly cycle rather than a seasonal one as trade books are, and usually include a fair number of so-called "genre" or "category" novels such as historical and contemporary romances, mystery and detective stories, science fiction, westerns, and so on. However, the distinctions between trade paperbacks and mass-market paperbacks are becoming increasingly blurred, as both types of books are distributed to each other's markets, and the types of books published within each format diversifies. Chapter 10 of this manual pays particular attention to the features of mass-market paperback publication, and the advantages and disadvantages of having your book published as a mass-market paperback original. About 5,000 of the books published annually in the U.S. are classified as mass-market paperbacks.

This manual has been written with two presumptions in mind. One is that the publishing process is composed of many small steps, but is inherently easy to understand. The other is that you as a writer are interested in *actively* participating in the process. Some authors think that all they have to do is turn their manuscript in, and then their editor and the other people in the house will take care of everything. But the truth is that if you want your book to be published *well*, you have to participate in the process. Your publisher can and will do only so much. After that, it's up to you. You know the book and the audience for it better than anyone else, and you care more. It is your energy and your commitment that is ultimately going to determine whether the book is published right. The purpose of this manual is to show you all of the ways in which you can make sure that it is.

A final word about pronouns. Like many women (and many men, for that matter), I am sometimes frustrated by the convention of using the male pronoun when referring to a situation that could involve either sex. For this reason, I have frequently used the female pronoun when the male would be more customary. A little consciousness-raising never hurt anyone.

1
How to Find a Publisher

Publication is . . . the auction of the Mind of Man.
—EMILY DICKINSON

Publishing a volume of verse is like dropping a rose petal down the Grand Canyon and waiting for the echo.
—DON MARQUIS

There is no magic formula for finding a publisher. The publishing scene in this country is large and diversified, and there are many houses that are likely to be interested in your book. But finding an editor who actually wants to buy the rights to it—and makes an acceptable offer—is usually a matter of planning, skill, and just plain luck. It's hard to know in advance whether a particular editor is going to respond positively to your book, or has the necessary time and experience to devote to working on it with you. Furthermore, publishing programs often change over time, so that a publisher who is concentrating on commercial fiction one season may shift abruptly to serious nonfiction the next. The best you can do is try to keep up with what's going on, and then approach those publishers that seem most suitable for your work. This chapter discusses the types of publishing options that may be open to you, how you should prepare your material for submission, and how an editor decides to make a publishing offer.

Who Are the Publishers?

Nobody knows for sure exactly how many publishers are in business in this country at any one time. Estimates range from 8,000 to more than 15,000, and the count keeps increasing as new firms go into business each year. The latest *Books in Print* lists over 600,000 books from more than 15,000 publishers, although many of these are self-publishers who have created an imprint for their "press," and others who obviously do not publish trade or mass-market books.

Literary Market Place, a directory to the industry published each year, restricts its list to those U.S. and Canadian publishers that brought out three or more books the previous year; its 1984 edition lists about 2,000 such publishers. Other guides (some of them listed in the Bibliography of this manual) count publishers in other ways. But for the purposes of this discussion, let's say that there are about 2,000 reasonably active publishers in the U.S. and Canada, and another 13,000 or so publishers bringing out books on a somewhat intermittent basis.

The Largest Trade Publishers. One way to start sorting through your publishing possibilities is to identify the largest houses first. This will provide a benchmark for the rest of the discussion, and will enable you to see what most people mean when they talk about the "big" houses.

Figure 1 identifies about 100 publishers that would be considered among the top trade publishers in the U.S. today.* They have been divided into several categories, depending on the size or focus of the list, or the location of the house. I've also included certain subdivisions to indicate ownership arrangements.

Section A, for example, lists those houses that typically publish at least 100 or more trade hardcovers a year, divided into three categories: conglomerate-owned, independent, and independent conglomerate. The *Random House College Dictionary* defines a conglomerate as "a company consisting of a number of subsidiary companies or divisions in a variety

*This list will change over time, but has remained remarkably stable for the last several years.

of unrelated industries, usually as a result of merger or acquisition." Many such conglomerates bought book publishing companies in the sixties and early seventies, when publishing was seen as a strong growth area. This burst of acquisitions has largely subsided, but it's interesting to notice that many of these conglomerates do in fact own other kinds of "communications" businesses.

Holt, Rinehart & Winston, for example, is owned by the Columbia Broadcasting System, which of course is a major radio and television network. Little, Brown is owned by Time-Life, a major book and magazine publisher; Morrow is owned by Hearst, which publishes magazines and newspapers as well as owning Arbor House, a midsized general publisher, and Avon Books, a mass-market house; and Random House is owned by the Newhouse Company, a newspaper publishing company. St. Martin's and Viking are both owned by English book publishing companies, and Putnam's and Simon & Schuster are owned by conglomerates that own major movie studios. (Music Corporation of America owns Universal Studios, and Gulf & Western owns Paramount Pictures.) Thus, of this group, only E. P. Dutton is owned by a conglomerate that is not involved in other publishing enterprises.

Looking to the right of Section A, we can see that four of the major houses are independently owned, although Atheneum and Scribners are in fact associated with a larger entity called the Scribners Book Companies which enables the two publishers to share shipping and billing operations. The other houses listed in Section A of Figure 1 are also independently owned but are so large and diversified themselves that they are essentially mini-conglomerates. Doubleday, for example, not only publishes the largest number of trade books each year (typically between 500 and 600); it also owns its own typesetting and printing facilities, several important book clubs, the Dell publishing complex, and the New York Mets baseball team. The other houses listed in this category all have strong school and college textbook divisions, and McGraw-Hill and Prentice-Hall are particularly well-known for technical books. In actuality, the trade book programs of both McGraw-Hill and Harcourt Brace Jovanovich (HBJ) have shrunk in recent years, but these houses are still re-

Figure 1
LARGE TRADE PUBLISHERS
IN THE UNITED STATES

A. The Large Trade Houses (100+ titles each year)

Conglomerate-owned
E. P. Dutton (Dyson)
Holt, Rinehart & Winston (CBS)
Little, Brown (Time-Life)
William Morrow (Hearst)
G. P. Putnam's Sons (MCA)
Random House (Newhouse)
St. Martin's (Macmillan of London)
Simon & Schuster (Gulf & Western)
Viking (Penguin)

Independent
†Atheneum
Crown Publishers
W. W. Norton
†Scribner's

Independent conglomerate
Doubleday
Harcourt Brace Jovanovich
Harper & Row
Houghton Mifflin
Macmillan
McGraw-Hill
Prentice-Hall

B. Midsized General Publishers (50–100 titles/year)

(Dell)
Delacorte
Dial Press

(Random House)
Alfred A. Knopf
Pantheon Books

Independent
Farrar, Straus & Giroux
Stein & Day

Other
Arbor House (Hearst)
Dodd, Mead (Nelson)
Grosset & Dunlap (Putnam's)

C. Compact General Publishers (20–50 titles/year)

(Crown)
Harmony Books
Clarkson N. Potter

(St. Martin's)
Congdon & Weed
*Richard Marek

(Simon & Schuster)
*Linden Press
*Summit Books

(Putnam's)
Coward, McCann & Geoghegan
Playboy Press
Seaview
Wideview

Other
Acropolis Books
Ashley Books
Beacon Press

Grove Press
New Directions
Rawson (Scribner's)

Beaufort Books
Bobbs-Merrill (ITT)
Georges Braziller
Caroline House
M. Evans
Everest House (Nelson)
David M. Godine

Schocken Books
Lyle Stuart
Ticknor & Fields (H-M)
Times Books (N.Y. Times)
Vanguard
Villard (RH)
Workman

*Editorial imprint
†Combined shipping and billing operation

D. Primarily Nonfiction

Amacom
Arco
Barnes & Noble
Barron's
Chilton
Facts on File
Frederick Fell
Hastings House
Horizon
Keats Publishing
David McKay
Rodale
Stackpole
Sterling
TAB
Taplinger
Universe Books
Walker

E. Behavioral Sciences

Basic Books
Praeger

F. Art/Illustrated

A & W Publishers
Abbeville
Abrams
Dover
New York Graphic Society
Rizzoli
Watson-Guptill

G. Midwest

Contemporary Books
Nelson-Hall
Regnery/Gateway
Van Nostrand Reinhold

H. West

Celestial Arts (Ten Speed)
Chronicle Books
H. P. Books
North Point
Petersen
Price/Stern/Sloan
Tarcher
Ten Speed
Wadsworth
Wilshire

I. Mass-Market Publishers That Publish Trade Hardcovers

Bantam Books
New American Library (NAL)
Pocket Books
Warner Books

garded as major publishers on the basis of their strong back-lists and distribution networks, and for this reason I have included them in the list of major trade houses.

Section B of Figure 1 lists several houses that typically bring out between 50 and 100 trade titles each year. Note that most of them are owned by larger corporations or publishing entities. Both Delacorte and Dial are owned by the Dell Publishing Company, which is a large mass-market publisher that is itself owned by Doubleday. Knopf and Pantheon are two long-established houses owned by Random House (itself owned by Newhouse); Arbor House is owned by Hearst; Dodd, Mead by a large religious publishing company; and Grosset & Dunlap by Putnam's. Only Farrar, Straus & Giroux and Stein & Day are still independently owned—and the latter has tried at least once to find a buyer.

Moving down to the next category, we see that many "compact" houses (a term borrowed from the automotive industry) are owned by others. Crown, one of the large independents, owns two other active trade publishing operations. St. Martin's *distributes* the books of a small house called Congdon & Weed, and also has an editor, Richard Marek, who has his own imprint. (This means that Marek is publishing his own list of books under St. Martin's auspices.) Simon & Schuster also has two editorial imprints, while Putnam's owns several smaller trade book operations (plus Ace and Tempo books—mass-market lines formerly owned by Grosset & Dunlap). But if you look at the column headed "Other," you will see that more than half of these compact publishers are not owned by another company.

The next three sections of Figure 1 list houses on the basis of their subject matter specialty rather than the size of their list, and do not indicate ownership arrangements. Section D lists several houses that publish little or no fiction, and in fact most of these houses concentrate on practical how-to nonfiction. Section E identifies two houses especially well-known for scholarly works in the behavioral sciences, and Section F lists several houses specializing in art and illustrated books.

Since practically all of the houses listed in the preceding sections are located on the East Coast—principally New York and Boston—I've provided separate listings of active trade publishers in the Midwest and West. I've also included one other category in Figure 1, and that is mass-market houses with trade hardcover lines. This calls for a little explanation.

Until a few years ago, the lines of demarcation between mass-market publishers and trade publishers were fairly clear. In contrast to the large number of trade publishers, only about 20 or so houses (identified in Chapter 10 of this book) published small format paperbacks for distribution to nonbookstore outlets. These houses also distributed their paperbacks to the retail bookstore trade, and some of them published books in the "trade paperback" format, but they were still clearly identified as being mass-market publishers.

Since that time, the waters have become somewhat muddied by two factors:

1. Some of the mass-market houses have started publishing books in the trade hardcover format. Section I in Figure 1 identifies the houses that are doing this most actively.

2. Some of the trade houses have started reprinting their own titles in the mass-market format and are distributing them to the mass-market outlets. These houses include St. Martin's Press, Stein & Day, and Penguin at present. Although they are doing this on a limited basis, it still makes them "mass-market publishers" in several important senses of the term.

Thus, it is no longer possible to refer to "mass-market publishers" and "trade book publishers" as though they were two entirely separate beasts. *However*, to keep things from becoming totally confusing, I will continue to use these terms when it is clear that I am referring to the houses *traditionally* engaged in one or the other types of publishing. I will return to this point again a little later in the discussion.

Small Presses, Small Publishers, and Self-publishers. Your publishing opportunities are of course not limited only to these large trade and mass-market houses. As I indicated earlier, there are literally thousands of other publishers in this country, many of whom fall into the category of small publisher or small press.

The distinctions between a small press and small publisher are sometimes difficult to make, and often don't really matter. But the terms are occasionally used in specific ways, and for this reason I will define them here.

A *small press* is traditionally regarded as one that is noncommercial in nature. It exists to provide an alternative for those writers whose work is not likely to be commercially viable, such as poetry, experimental fiction, anti-establishment and countercultural political views, and so on. Many small presses are supported by grants from private corporations or foundations, or from such quasi-governmental institutions as the National Endowment for the Arts (NEA). Press runs tend to be small. Payment for the work (in the form of royalties or an advance against royalties) is usually small or nonexistent; and distribution is generally limited to literary bookstores, ads in "little magazines," or via distribution cooperatives or the services of wholesalers (such as Bookpeople in California) that specialize in the distribution of little magazine and small press publications. Perhaps 3,500–4,000 of the publishers operating in the country today could be classified as small presses. Examples include such operations as the Black Sparrow Press in Santa Barbara, California, and the Feminist Press in Old Westbury, N.Y.

A *small publisher* is simply any publisher that brings out a limited number of books each year but that has a somewhat more commercial orientation than a small press. Such publishers typically specialize in one or more types of books and, like small presses, are often found outside of large urban centers. If they publish books of local interest, they are sometimes referred to as regional presses. Some examples of small publishers are Meadowbrook Press in Deephaven, Minnesota, a well-known and successful publisher of books on infant care, parenting, travel, and health; Yankee Books in Dublin, N.H., which publishes books related to New England; and Howell Book House on Park Avenue in New York City, which publishes hardcover books about dogs, cats, and birds.

A *self-publisher* is a person or persons who publish their own work. This involves getting the book set in type (or perhaps doing it themselves on a word processor), getting it printed and bound, and then trying to distribute it to bookstores and libraries, bookstore chains and wholesalers, or via mail order. It is a strenuous and somewhat expensive undertaking, but has at least one significant advantage: the self-publisher gets to keep all of the money he or she makes from the sale of the book and its "subsidiary rights." This manual does not deal specifically with the joys and hazards of self-publishing; for some excellent books on the subject, see the Bibliography.

However, as you're looking for a publisher, keep in mind that most self-publishers make up an imprint for their "company," and it's almost impossible to tell from an imprint whether this house is a self-publisher or not. (One possibility is to check the *International Directory of Little Magazines and Small Presses* or other guides to see if the publisher is listed there.) A self-publisher usually is not interested in publishing someone else's book, although some do (such as Robert Ringer, who established the Stratford Press after achieving great success with several self-published books). There are also collectives of writers who underwrite the publication of books by their members; probably the most well-known is the Fiction Collective, whose books are distributed by the George Braziller Company.

University Presses. A university press is one that is associated with a college or university and that publishes scholarly materials for the academic community. Technically, such a publisher is not a trade house, but many of them do publish regional books, and an increasing number seem to be publishing books of interest to the retail bookstore trade. Perhaps the most outstanding recent example is the publication of John Kennedy Toole's novel A *Confederacy of Dunces* by the Louisiana State University Press.

There are about 80 such university presses in this country. For a listing, check *Literary Market Place*.

Vanity Presses. A "vanity" press (also sometimes called a "subsidy" press) exists to publish books for those writers who can't get their book published any other way, and are willing to pay a lot of money for the privilege. Fees range from $5,000 to $15,000, depending on the nature and size of the book; in exchange for this, you get an unusually high royalty—typically, 40 percent of the cover price.

The problem with this alternative is that you're not really getting your book *published* in the usual sense of the term. A publisher selects books that he thinks deserve to be published and/or that he thinks he can sell successfully; does whatever editorial work necessary to bring them to their highest possible potential; and then works hard to find the audience for those books.

A vanity press, by contrast, accepts virtually any manuscript submitted to it, no matter how "publishable" it may be. It provides little editorial guidance, nor does it try very hard to sell the books. This is because most booksellers refuse to carry the publications of vanity presses, and few reviewers will review them. The press will therefore probably limit its promotional activities to sending a few hundred free copies to bookstores and reviewers, and running a small ad in the *New York Times*. In many cases, it won't even bother binding the whole press run because it knows that the books won't sell. And to add injury to insult, the press sheets and bound books usually become the property of the vanity press, so that if you want to try selling them on your own, you have to pay for them—again.

Obviously, this is an alternative that I think writers should avoid. However, if you're determined to pursue it, you can check the listings of subsidy publishers in a book called *Writer's Market,* available in most bookstores and libraries. Subsidy publishers also frequently run ads in newspapers and in writers' magazines.

Foreign Publishers. Some writers choose to have their book published first by a house outside of this country—most commonly if they are living in that country for a period of time, or if the book is set there. This is a perfectly OK alternative, although you should be aware that if the book is manufactured abroad, the number of copies that can be imported into the U.S. is limited to 2,000. This is because of the "manufacturing clause" in our copyright law, which was designed to protect our typesetting and printing industries. The clause is due to be phased out on June 30, 1986, but until that time, must be taken into account.

If you're interested in finding the names and addresses of foreign publishers, you can check in your local library for a copy of a directory called *International Literary Market Place.* Also be aware that the American edition of *Literary Market Place* has a list of the most active Canadian publishers, of foreign publishers with offices in the U.S., and of agents representing foreign publishers.

Mass-Market Paperback Publishers. Mass-market paperback publishers have already been briefly discussed in relation to Figure 1. There are about 8 such houses generally acknowledged as being the major houses in the field (with Bantam the largest in terms of sales), and another 8 or so that are smaller or more specialized. Descriptions of these houses are provided in Chapter 10.

The principal differences between trade publishers and mass-market publishers are that mass-market houses:

1. publish books in a "rack-size" format (approximately 4½" x 7") for distribution to nonbookstore outlets;

2. service about 110,000 such outlets via a system of 450 or so independent regional wholesalers (usually called I.D.'s) and through another intermediary organization called a national distributor;

3. publish their books on a monthly rather than a seasonal cycle.

But note again that most of these mass-market publishers bring out books in the trade paperback format, and that some of them also publish trade hardcovers. The advantages and disadvantages of being published in the mass-market paperback format are discussed a little later in this chapter.

House-generated Books and Book Packagers. In addition to the options already mentioned, there are two kinds of operations that may *look* like possibilities for you, but really aren't.

One such operation is a house that generates and produces its own books. These publishers are usually associated with a magazine or mail order business, such as Time-Life, American Heritage, Reader's Digest, or Good Housekeeping (Meredith). What they do is develop books that they think will be of interest to readers of their magazines (or who have gotten onto their mailing lists for some other reason). The editors will think up an idea for a book or series, and develop it to the point where a brochure describing the book (and probably several others) can be sent to their potential audience. If the response is strong, the house will go on to create the book, probably with the help of freelance writers, illustrators, and photographers; if not, the book will never be written. Since all of these books are staff-generated, such a publishing operation is usually not open to submissions from "outside" writers.

A *book packager* is a firm or individual that comes up with ideas for books (or series of books), develops the proposal or manuscript to the point where a publisher is willing to buy the distribution rights, and then delivers either a final manuscript, mechanicals, or bound books. The writing of the book itself is usually done by free-lance writers. Thus, packagers are basically "idea men-or-women" who come up with good projects for publishers and then find the right authors and illustrators to do the work. Packagers are being used much more extensively by publishers than they used to be, and are responsible for many of the series being published by mass-market houses today, such as Bantam's "Sweet Dreams" series or Jove's "Long-arm" series. The series are often written by more than one writer. Packagers also often concentrate on complex illustrated books that might tax the resources of some publishers.

Packagers are usually not looking for manuscripts from writers. However, if you are interested in doing some writing for a packager, or you have a manuscript or idea that you think a packager might be interested in, you can check the listing of "Book Producers" in *Literary Market Place*.

Which Publishing Option Is Best for You?

Deciding which publishing option is likely to be best for you usually involves juggling a number of factors including:

- The type of book you've written;
- The kinds of publishers likely to be interested in it;
- What *you* want to get out of the publishing experience; and
- Who you know—and don't know.

Let's look at these factors a little more carefully.

What Kind of Book Have You Written? This sounds pretty obvious, but you'd be surprised at how many people are not really clear about what kind of book they've written (or are in the process of writing), and what kind of audience they're trying to reach. Yet knowing this has a lot to do with how you go about looking for a publisher.

For example, suppose you're writing a novel. Is it a "genre" western or mystery that you have consciously crafted for publication as a mass-market paperback original? Or have you written it in the hope that it will appeal to a more "upscale" hardcover market? Is it a big "commercial" novel à la Judith Krantz or Mario Puzo, or is it a more "serious" work intended for the *literati*? Is it an "experimental" novel likely to be of most interest to a small press? Being clear about your *intent* in writing the book will not only help you focus on the most likely market for it; it should also help you plot and write it in the first place.

Or suppose you're working on a nonfiction book of some sort. Is this a work intended to help other professionals in your field, or is this a general how-to guide that could be used by the average reader? Does it presume a technical background or general expertise in the area? Is it a historical, social, political, or economic work that ought to have wide appeal, or is it more regional or local in nature? Is it likely to be of interest to a university or scholarly press, or would a large general publisher be best? Having your readership clearly in mind will help you determine the *level* and *scope* of the information you're planning to include, and will also help you determine which publishing possibility has the greatest potential.

What Kinds of Publishers Are Likely to Be Interested in Your Book? The next step is to determine the types of publishers that are most likely to be interested in it. Figure 2 presents, in a very general way, the characteristics of different types of publishers. Studying the chart may help you focus on the best possibilities for your book.

For example, suppose you've written a historical novel that is well-researched but should have relatively broad appeal. Which of these types of publishers is likely to be interested in it?

Scanning down the chart in terms of types of books published, you can see that several types of publishers might be interested in your book. The larger trade houses present excellent possibilities, because they publish a wide variety of books and have the distribution mechanism to get the books out to a wide readership. By contrast, small commercial publishers tend to stay away from fiction unless they have a special reason for publishing the book (such as its regional setting), while small presses would probably find this type of

Figure 2
MAJOR CHARACTERISTICS OF DIFFERENT PUBLISHING OPTIONS

TYPE OF PUBLISHER	TYPE OF BOOKS PUBLISHED	DISTRIBUTION	PAYMENT	STRONG SUITS
Large trade house	Varied.	Bookstores, libraries, etc., and/or commission reps. via own sales force.	Standard royalties; potential for good advance.	Strength in the market place; professional expertise.
Medium-sized trade house	Varied.	Bookstores, libraries, etc., and/or commission reps. via own sales force.	Standard royalties; potential for good advance.	Strength in the market place; professional expertise.
Compact trade publisher	Varied; may specialize somewhat.	Bookstores, etc. May be distributed by larger house, or commission reps.	Standard royalties; potential for good advance.	Good expertise; perhaps more personal attention.
Small commercial house	Probably regional or specialized; little fiction.	General; may also rely heavily on mail order and wholesalers.	Standard royalties; perhaps small advance.	May be just the right house or editor for the book.
Small press	Countercultural, literary, experimental, poetry, etc.	Literary bookstores; ads in little magazines; specialized wholesalers.	May be limited.	Very personal relationship to books & authors; keep books in print a long time.
Specialized house	Only books in certain categories.	Rely heavily on mail order.	Probably slightly lower advance/royalty arrangements than general trade houses.	Expertise in particular subject field.
University press	Scholarly; some regional and general interest.	Mailings to academics; some bookstore distribution.	Probably slightly lower advance/royalty arrangements than general trade houses.	Professional competence; solidity & stability of performance & reputation.
Mass-market paperback	Genre fiction; other fiction & nonfiction of wide appeal.	Bookstores, etc., *and* nonbookstore outlets through ID's.	Standard paperback royalties; advance competitive with trade houses.	Wide distribution; proper audience for book; can be very profitable for author.
Vanity press	Anything.	Limited to nonexistent.	You pay them.	None—except seeing your book "in print."

novel too commercial. A house specializing in nonfiction would not be interested at all; a university press *might* be interested, but this is not very likely; while a mass-market publisher might be *very* interested.

A "literary novel" will have slightly different prospects. Many writers seem to think that the large trade houses are not interested in this type of work. But if you look at these publishers' lists carefully, I think you will see that many literary and "first" novels are published by the large, midsized, and compact trade houses. Small presses and university presses are also pretty good alternatives for this type of work. The mass-market houses traditionally have not published many literary novels, but a few of them have trade paperback lines for this kind of book (Avon's Bard line, Bantam's Windstone books, and Pocket Books' Washington Square Press) and others are expanding their lists in this area.

Poetry and short-story collections present certain problems. Generally speaking, it's hard for a new writer to get this kind of work published by one of the larger trade houses. The reason is that poetry and short fiction by unknown writers sells very slowly, and most big houses with large overheads can't afford to keep a slow-moving book in print very long. For this reason, small presses are usually your best bet until your reputation has become more established.

Nonfiction works involve essentially the same kinds of considerations discussed above. A book of general interest—a cookbook or diet book, say, or a popular biography—would probably appeal to the larger trade houses, perhaps to a regional house (if the recipes in the cookbook are regional in nature, for example), or to one of the mass-market publishers. A more scholarly or technical book should be submitted to university presses, scholarly presses, or technical and scientific publishers, while a book that is highly specialized should go to a house that has a demonstrated expertise in this area. A heavily illustrated art book, for example, should probably be submitted to those houses that have the technical competence to handle the production problems involved. A book on sailing *may* be of interest to several general publishers, but if it is a detailed treatment of only one kind of sailing vessel, you're probably better off looking for a specialized publisher.

Pros and Cons: The Question of Size. Considering the alternatives also means considering the strong and weak points of these alternatives. Figure 2 suggests some possibilities in this regard.

For example, suppose you are thinking about approaching one of the larger trade houses. What are the pros and cons of being published by one of the "giants" of the industry?*

In general, large publishing houses offer various advantages. For one thing, a large house is able to distribute its books widely via its own sales force, and to support that distribution with advertising, promotion, and publicity dollars. It can pay standard royalties and advances to its authors, and if it wants a book very badly, it can usually afford to pay the price that is demanded. Furthermore, a large house will have an experienced and sophisticated staff, with strong editorial skills, and the connections in the industry to get a book "talked about" if it warrants it. (This can be particularly important for large subsidiary rights deals.) On the other hand, a large house has a big overhead that may militate against signing up or keeping in print "marginal" books; it may not be able to give you the kind of personal attention you would like; or it may simply be inappropriate for the kind of book you've written.

A smaller or more specialized publisher can usually offer advantages and disadvantages that are the obverse of those offered by a big house. A small house usually can't distribute its books quite as effectively as a large house with a captive sales force, and has to either use free-lance commission reps, or have its books distributed by another publisher, or perhaps sell them strictly by mail order. Moreover, it may not be able to pay much of an advance or royalties (if any) for the rights to the book, its staff may not be quite as expert as that at a large house, and its books may not be as beautifully printed and bound. On the other hand, a small house often "feels" more personal, and can sometimes find the audience for a book more successfully and keep the book in print longer than a larger house.

Don't make the mistake of thinking that small is always beautiful, however. Small houses can make as many mis-

---

*"Giant" is a very relative term, since the annual earnings of the entire book publishing industry are less than those of one major industrial company like U.S. Steel.

takes as big ones, and they are often less stable. And conversely, big houses are sometimes surprisingly personal, warm, and caring. So the message here is simply to make your decision on the basis of what seems to be best for your book *and* for your temperament, and not on the basis of size alone.

Hardcover Versus Paperback Original. Another alternative has to do with having your book published as a hardcover or a paperback original.

Several years ago, this was a pretty cut-and-dried proposition. There were two basic alternatives. One was to have your book published by a trade house as a trade hardcover, and then hope that a mass-market house would buy the reprint rights. The other alternative was to have the book published as an "original" by a mass-market house, with little expectation of having the book appear in any other format.

Now, however, the possibilities are wider and much more complex. Most of the publishers are now bringing out books in a variety of formats, depending on what they think the audiences for a book is, and how much mileage they think they can get out of each format. And to make this possible, they frequently buy the "volume" rights or make a "hard/soft" deal so that they can control all of these format options. Thus, a house like Bantam, for example, may buy the volume rights to a book so that they can publish it first as a hardcover, and then later (or perhaps simultaneously, as they did with Tom Robbins' *Still Life With Woodpecker*) as a trade paperback and/or a mass-market paperback. Or a house like Villard (a new hardcover imprint owned by Random House) may acquire the rights to a book *jointly* with Ballantine Books so that Villard can do a hardcover edition while (or before) Ballantine does a trade or mass-market paperback edition. Or a book may be published as an original paperback, and then do so well that the mass-market house sells the hardcover rights "backwards" to a trade house.

These varied possibilities make determining the best alternatives for your own book somewhat confusing. If you think it *could* be published successfully in any of these formats, however, you should know the relative advantages and disadvantages of each. Figure 3 summarizes the characteristics of each format. Let's look at trade hardcovers first.

Trade hardcovers. The basic assumption behind different

formats is that they "work" better for certain kinds of books and audiences. Thus, *in general,* the trade hardcover format works best for most kinds of nonfiction books (90% of all trade hardcovers are nonfiction) and for fiction that is seen as either "serious" or "commercial." It is seldom used for the conventionally plotted novels sometimes called genre fiction.

One of the advantages of trade hardcovers is that they are sturdier than paperbacks because the "boards" (heavy grade cardboard) used for covers protect the pages. These boards, and the good quality paper commonly used, contribute to the high cover price of hardcovers—*but they are not the principal reason for the high price.* The real contributing factor is the fact that the audience for *most* of these titles is relatively limited. Although the books of well-known and popular authors can sell hundreds of thousands of copies in hardcover, the *average* hardcover sells less than 10,000 copies—and many sell less than 5,000. And *even if the price were substantially lower,* the number of copies sold would not increase markedly. Thus, this format is typically used for those books that are presumed to have a limited audience *or* for the works of very popular authors who have a strongly established audience.

Hardcover books are distributed primarily to bookstores and libraries, although they are of course sold by mail order as well. The "shelf life" for most hardcovers—that is, the average amount of time that they stay out in the stores—is from 3 to 12 months. Of the three categories of books shown on Figure 3, the amount of review space given to hardcovers is higher than that for the other categories, reflecting historical practice, some reviewers' biases, and the fact that hardcovers have traditionally been used for the most "serious" books being published—those deemed worthy of review attention.

In terms of money possibilities, royalties for hardcovers are usually higher than those for either trade or mass-market paperbacks. Advances tend to be closely related to anticipated royalties, so that if the publisher thinks your royalty earnings in the first six months will be about $10,000, your advance should be close to that level. Promotion dollars spent usually depend on the perceived commercial potential for the book. A book that has the potential for being a bestseller will probably get a hefty promotion budget; a

Figure 3
COMPARISON OF TRADE AND MASS-MARKET FORMATS

FORMAT	TYPE OF BOOK	PHYSICAL CHARAC-TERISTICS	PRICE	MINI-MUM PRESS RUN	DISTRIBU-TION	SHELF LIFE	FRE-QUENCY OF RE-VIEW	PROMO-TION	USUAL ROYALTIES	SUBSID-IARY RIGHTS POTEN-TIAL
Trade hardcover	Nonfiction of all types; serious and commercial fiction	Sturdy; good paper and design	High ($12.95—25.00)	3,000	Bookstores & libraries; some mail order and special sales	3 to 12 months	High	Depends on sales potential, but titles are brought to attention of reviewers	10% to 5,000 or 7,500 copies; 12½% to 10,000; then 15%	Good
Trade paperback	Illustrated books; humor; books for under-30 crowd; literary fiction; reprints of certain trade hardcovers	Flexible design; good paper and typography; soft cover	Medium ($5.95—10.95)	10,000	Bookstores, libraries; some mass outlets	May be longer than hardcover	Moderate	Varies	Usually starts at 6–7½%	Fair
Mass-market paperback	Genre fiction; reprints of popular trade books and classics; reference books; some original fiction and nonfiction	Usually 4½" x 7"; vivid covers; inexpensive paper stock	Low ($1.95—4.95)	30,000	Mass-market outlets; some bookstores and libraries	Relatively short for most titles	Low	Extensive for lead titles only	6-8% common; may go to 10%	Poor

book that will probably not sell widely will be given a small budget, spent mainly on free copies for reviewers. And in terms of subsidiary rights potential, a trade hardcover generally has the best chance of the three formats.

Trade paperbacks. Trade paperbacks play a slightly different role in the book publishing world. They were first developed in the fifties to provide inexpensive supplementary reading for college students—usually, reprints of classics or serious works of fiction and nonfiction. Since that time, the format has expanded widely and is used for many different kinds of books. In fact, it is currently the most popular of the three formats available to publishers. It is being used for illustrated books; for humor books and for books thought to have a relatively young readership (the under-30 crowd); for literary fiction and serious nonfiction; for reprints of serious trade fiction and nonfiction; and more recently, for new books by well-known genre writers such as Louis L'Amour and Janet Dailey. So it is an extremely versatile and popular format. In fact, what often happens is that a publisher will bind the majority of his press run in softcovers, and bind only 1,500 or so for the library trade. (These 1,500 copies will probably have a pretty high cover price, since libraries are less price resistant than book dealers, and the high price helps the publisher earn back some of his expenses in producing the book.)

Trade paperbacks have the enormous advantage that they are not limited by the format restrictions of hardcover binding equipment. They can be virtually any size or shape imaginable and can be printed on practically any kind of paper stock, which means that it's easy to use them for illustrated or "gimmick" books.

Trade paperbacks are moderately priced—usually somewhere between $6 and $10. The minimum press run is higher than that for the average trade hardcover, reflecting the wider potential audience for this type of book; most trade publishers would not utilize this format unless they thought they could sell a minimum of 10,000 copies. Outlets include bookstores, libraries, and some mass-market retailers. And as suggested above, it is the factor of distribution that really dictates the price of the book. The production cost of the average trade paperback is only about 50¢ lower than that for a hardcover, but a paperback can be priced much lower than a hardcover because it is assumed that more copies can be sold. This is an idea that many people have trouble grasping, but is at the heart of the "trade paperback revolution"; if more copies can be sold, the book can be priced lower.

Looking at the other characteristics of trade paperbacks shown on Figure 3, we can see that the shelf life of trade paperbacks tends to be *longer* than that for trade hardcovers. This is because book dealers usually have less money tied up in slow-moving trade paperbacks than in trade hardcovers, and therefore feel less pressure to send them back to the publishers for credit. Besides, trade paperbacks take up less shelf space, can be damaged more easily (and are therefore harder to return), and tend to find their audience more slowly than trade hardcovers.

In terms of review space, trade paperbacks seem to fall midway between trade hardcovers and mass-market paperbacks. They get more reviews than mass-market paper backs, but less than trade hardcovers. Reviewers for the major media are attempting to change this, but the truth is that these books are still seen as slightly less "reviewable" than trade hardcover books.

As for promotion dollars spent on trade paperbacks—that varies depending on the subject matter of the book, whether it's an original or a reprint, and so on. The amount of money being spent to promote trade paperbacks has increased substantially in the last few years, but may still be, *on average,* a little lower than that for trade hardcovers. However, the *kind* of promotion done for trade paperbacks tends to be more imaginative and, well, even flaky at times.

The lower cover price of trade paperbacks is reflected in the usual royalty arrangements for this format. Because the publisher is taking in less money to offset the expenses of publishing the book, authors of trade paperbacks are generally asked to take a lower royalty than those given for trade hardcovers. Royalty rates typically start at somewhere between 6 percent and 7½ percent, and usually do not escalate to a higher rate (if they do at all) until at least 50,000 copies have been sold. Contrast this with rates for trade hardcovers, which normally start at 10 percent, go to 12½ percent after 5,000 or 7,500 copies have been sold, and commonly increase to 15 percent after 10,000 copies of the hardcover book have been sold. Since the cover price of a hardcover is also higher, what this means is that, on a per book basis, royalties for hardcovers are considerably higher than those for trade paperbacks. Here are some examples:

| | COVER PRICE | ROYALTY PERCENTAGE | RATE PER BOOK | ROYALTY ON | |
				5,000 COPIES	10,000 COPIES
Paperback	$ 7.95	6%	.477¢	$ 2,385.00	$ 4,770.00
	7.95	7½%	.59625¢	2,981.25	5,962.25
	7.95	10%	.795¢	3,975.00	7,950.00
Hardcover	$14.95	10%	$1.495	$ 7,475.00	$14,950.00
	14.95	12½%	1.86875	9,343.75	18,687.50
	14.95	15%	2.2425	11,212.50	22,425.00

Thus, a 6% royalty on a cover price of $7.95 means that you earn a little under 48¢ per book sold. If 5,000 copies are sold, you make $2,385.00. A royalty rate of 10 percent on a $14.95 hardcover means that you make about a buck-and-a-half a book. If 5,000 copies are sold, you end up earning $7,475. What this means is that in real life, a publisher has to sell about three times as many trade paperbacks for you to make as much money as you would have if those same copies had been hardcovers. It is to some extent a moot point, because at least one reason that a book sells well is its low price. The publisher may not have been *able* to sell 5,000 copies at $14.95. But I think you get the point in terms of royalty rates and earnings.

What may be even more important is the fact that the subsidiary rights potential for trade paperbacks is generally not very good. There is only one book club (Quality Paperback Book Services) that makes substantial use of trade paperbacks, and few mass-market publishers are eager to reprint a book published originally as a trade paperback. Serial, foreign, and other rights also tend to produce less income than those for trade hardcovers.

Mass-market paperbacks. Coming to mass-market paperbacks, we can see that they fill a somewhat different slot in the book publishing world. Most of these releases are aimed at a so-called "popular" audience, and are widely distributed through bookstores and to various "nonbookstore" outlets, such as drugstores and supermarket chains, newsstands, airport kiosks, and so on. They are priced low—usually somewhere between $1.95 (for a "contemporary romance") and $4.95—and are in the small 4½" x 7" format we're all so familiar with.

As mentioned earlier, the mass-market paperback world is changing somewhat. The format has traditionally been used for genre fiction—mysteries, westerns, romances, sci-fi, etc.—and for reprints of popular trade hardcovers. However, it is now being utilized in different ways. Some publishers have launched ambitious programs for the publication of serious fiction and nonfiction in the mass-market format, and others are doing very little "reprint" publishing at this point. What seems to have happened is that the mass-market houses have become increasingly reluctant to pay large amounts of money to trade houses for the right to reprint popular trade books for short time periods (typically 5 to 7 years). What they've opted to do instead is compete for these authors with the trade houses, buying "volume" rights rather than just reprint rights. This gives them the right to publish the book in the format (or formats) they think best, and to control that book for the term of copyright rather than for a short license period. So that's one element in the brew. The other element is that some trade houses are now beginning to publish mass-market titles as well, so that the distribution networks are becoming increasingly murky. At this point, it's hard to tell how it's all going to turn out, but what *is* clear is that the "mass-market format" can be used in more ways than was thought originally.

However, the term "mass market" does imply fairly wide distribution, and in most cases, a mass-market publisher could not consider printing less than 30,000 copies for his customers. These books are then distributed through a network of regional or "independent" wholesalers as well as through the bookstores. Because these books are on racks in retail outlets, and because mass-market paperbacks are distributed each month, the pressure to keep the books moving is enormous. For this reason, the shelf life for mass-market paperbacks tends to be shorter than that for trade books. For some books that are not moving well, it can be as brief as 9 or 10 days. However, a book that is selling well *does* stay out on the racks so long as it is moving, and mass-market paperbacks that have sold well in the past are frequently reissued—particularly if the author is continuing to produce new books successfully.

Royalties on mass-market paperbacks are usually a little lower than those for the other two categories of books. Most mass-market paperbacks start at 6% and do not escalate until a large number of copies have been sold. A rate of 10%, even after a large number of copies have been sold, is rare, and a rate of 12½% almost unheard of. Since the royalty rate is going to be applied against a low cover price, your per copy earnings are not going to be impressive. However, your *total* earnings may be impressive if the book sells well, and in any case, mass-market publishers tend to pay advances that are a little higher than your per copy earnings might indicate.

As for review attention: most mass-market titles don't get much. This is partially a holdover from the old days when most mass-market titles simply didn't warrant attention, and partially just a built-in prejudice against the format. Matters are improving somewhat, especially for the more serious original titles being brought out by mass-market houses, but the situation still isn't great. Most mass-market publishers try to compensate for this by promoting their titles extensively through point-of-purchase displays, glossy and attractive catalogs, and so on. Subsidiary rights potential is also generally not so hot, although foreign rights sales and movie and television rights sales are occasionally impressive.

Summary. Thus, you can see that the relationships between these three formats is relatively complex. In some cases, the decision is perfectly clear: a trade hardcover format or a mass-market paperback format is simply the best for a particular book. In other cases, each alternative offers advantages, and you may simply arbitrarily choose one or the other. Or it may turn out that your book will eventually be published in two or three formats, depending on the marketing possibilities for the book. The main necessity now is simply to be aware of the differences.

Zeroing in on a Publisher

Now that you have a better idea of the possibilities for your book, the next step is to start actively seeking those publishers who might be interested in it. There are three basic ways of going about this:

1. Finding a literary agent to do the work for you;
2. Looking for a publisher on your own;
3. Being discovered.

Using a Literary Agent. Instead of looking for a publisher on your own, you may elect to use a literary agent. This is a person who represents writers' work to publishers (and certain types of "subsidiary rights" buyers) in exchange for a commission on the sales that she or he makes. The usual commission is 10% or 15% on sales made to buyers in this country, and 20% on sales to buyers outside of this country.

Using an agent has a number of advantages. An experienced literary agent will know the publishing scene better than you will, and should know which houses have money to spend, and which editors might be best for the kind of work you do. An agent will be experienced in negotiating contracts, and will probably be able to extract a higher advance from a publisher than you could on your own. Furthermore, an agent will continue to represent you throughout your relationship with that firm, so that if your editor leaves, or some kind of controversy arises that you find difficult to deal with, you can call on your agent for help. And of course an agent can save you the time and money you might have spent looking for a publisher on your own.

However, using an agent has some disadvantages as well. For one thing, there is the matter of the commission. A ten percent or 15 percent commission is nothing to sneeze at, particularly when you consider that it extends over the life of any contract negotiated by that agent. This means that the agent will continue to collect his/her commission for many years after the deal was negotiated. Furthermore, not all agents are equally effective or available. Good, smart agents are tough to find, and most of them are terribly busy. Many refuse to take on new clients unless they have been referred to them by someone near and dear (such as an important author that they represent), or unless your work has very obvious commercial potential or is already selling so well that you don't really need an agent anyway! And conversely, the agents who are willing to take you on may not be the best one(s) for you. So looking for an agent can be nearly as hazardous and trying as looking for a publisher. If you are interested in this option, however, I recommend that you turn to Chapter 2 of this manual.

Looking for a Publisher on Your Own. Most first-time writers end up looking for a publisher on their own (unless they have friends in New York or elsewhere who can steer them to an agent), and that's not really so bad, because there are plenty of publishers around, and they are all looking for good material to publish. It is not really true that it is impossible for a first-time "unrepresented" (by an agent) writer to get published, but you *do* need a good "product" to sell—something that the publishers really want. More about this a little later.

Looking for a publisher can involve using some reference books or publications, or trying to use your friendship network. The latter is probably easiest, so let's start there first.

Using Your Friendship Network. It's amazing how many people have already had a book published, or know someone who has. One of the best ways to go about finding a publisher is to ask someone who already has. Ask your friends, your neighbors, your family, and your relatives. Ask the local librarian, the local bookseller, or the local celebrity. All of these people are likely to know a published author and/or an author who has an agent, and it is astonishing how many of them will be willing to tell you about their experience, and to recommend their editor or agent to you. Of course, you have to use some intelligence in evaluating the information you're given. You'd better find out if this is the kind of house or editor who's likely to be interested in the kind of book *you're* writing, and not in just your friend's book. Try to get some information about the kinds of books the house publishes, what contract terms are likely to be, and so forth.

A local bookseller can be a really good contact in terms of the kind of information he or she can give you about different publishers' strengths and weaknesses. Since booksellers deal with publishers in the role of a customer, they can tell you the kinds of books a particular house is known for, how well the house supports its books in terms of first printings and in advertising and promotion, how well they handle customer relations, how long they keep their books in print, and so on. If the bookseller likes you, he or she may even be willing to introduce you to the sales rep for the house. If the rep likes you, and is willing to read your work, he or she may then be willing to pass your manuscript or proposal along to an editor in the house.

Another way to make contacts is to attend a writers' conference or seminar, or to take a writing course of some kind. You will not only meet other writers who are facing the kinds of problems you are; you may even meet or get a referral to an agent or editor. There are also writers' clubs and associations in various areas; for suggestions on how to find them, consult Appendix D of this manual.

Doing Some Research. Another way to find a publisher is to do some looking around on your own. You're probably already aware of certain publishers' imprints if you did some research before starting your book, so these are names you should write down and refer to when you start checking directories to publishers. Before you start this research, you might also want to take another look at your own bookshelves, make a trip to a well-stocked bookstore, or consult a library's holdings in your subject area.

Then go to a library and look for the following reference materials:

1. *Literary Market Place (LMP).* This is probably the single best guide to American book publishing available. It is published annually by the R. R. Bowker Company, and lists all U.S. and Canadian publishers that brought out three or more books the previous year. (It characterizes these publishers as the most "active" publishers in these countries.) It also provides a wealth of other listings to the industry, including book clubs, book packagers, literary agents, professional associations of various kinds, and so on. The publishers are listed in *LMP* in several different ways. The first listing is alphabetical and gives the publisher's address and telephone number, the names and titles of department heads and editors, the kinds of book the house publishes, the number of books published the previous year,* and the year the house was founded. There are also several cross-indexes. One lists publishers by geographical location (by state, with a separate listing for New York City), one by subject matter, and one by "fields of activity" (trade book publishers, university presses, scholarly presses, and so on).

Thus, for example, if you want a listing of all the general trade book publishers, you would look under the fields of

*If the house has many divisions, this number may include the publications of all of the divisions.

activity listing. About 600 houses are listed under this category in the 1984 edition of LMP, although if you look at the listing closely you will see that this includes many university presses, religious and children's book publishers, and other more specialized operations. If you want to see which houses publish books in your subject area, check the "Book Publishers—Classified by Subject Matter" listing. And if you want to locate the larger publishers in a particular geographic area, check the "Geographical Region" index.

2. *Writer's Market* (*WM*) is a guide to both magazine and book publishers and can be found in most bookstores and libraries. About 800 book publishers are listed in the most recent edition, so the listing is not as complete as that in *LMP* and some of the publishers listed are very small. However, *WM* has the advantage that the information given for each publisher is quite complete. It usually includes the titles of books published the previous year, the kinds of material the house is currently seeking, the form in which the material should be submitted (query letter, proposal, or complete manuscript), the person to whom it should be submitted, and the usual payment arrangements. *WM* also includes general information for writers, a list of subsidy (vanity) publishers, and a list of author's agents.

3. If you're particularly interested in small presses, check the *International Directory of Little Magazines & Small Presses*, which can be found in most bookstores and libraries. It lists about 3,000 publishers of little magazines and small presses all over the world. Each listing indicates the type of material the press publishes, payment arrangements, usual length of press run, etc. There are cross-indexes by subject and state, and a list of small-press distributors. Other listings of small publishers include the *Book Publishers Directory*, published by Gale Research, and Publishers, Distributors, & Wholesalers of the United States, published by the R. R. Bowker Company.

4. You're probably already familiar with *Books in Print*, which is a multivolume listing of all titles currently available from publishers. The 1983–84 edition lists over 630,000 different titles. To find publishers that are active in a particular subject area, check the volume called *Subject Guide to Books in Print*. Pay particular attention to the books that were published most recently and to those most like your

own; this information will come in handy when you're preparing a proposal for submission to a publisher. In addition, there is a *Subject Guide to Forthcoming Books in Print* (books to be published in the next five-month period), and there are guides to paperbound, children's, religious, business, and scientific and technical books.

5. *Publishers' Trade List Annual* is a collection of the annual catalogs of the 1,800 or so largest publishers. Each catalog lists all of the books the publisher currently has in print, but be aware that this may include books published many years previously; for a better sense of what a publisher is currently bringing out, write to the publisher for the most recent "seasonal" catalog. (For additional reference guides, see the Bibliography of this manual.)

6. Magazines and newspapers are also a good source of information. If you're like most writers, you're already keeping up with the publishing world by reading reviews and book news in publications like *Saturday Review*, the *New York Review of Books*, and so on. And if you're a professional in a particular discipline, you're familiar with the trade magazines for that field.

One of the best sources of book news is *Publishers Weekly* (*PW*), the trade magazine of book publishing. It carries articles about book publishing, a calendar of upcoming events, reviews of forthcoming trade and mass-market books, publishers' advertisements, and so on. The names of editors and agents are often mentioned, particularly in the "People" and "Rights and Permissions" columns.

PW runs special features from time to time on specific types of books, such as children's books and religious books, and the advertisements and reviews in these issues can give you an excellent idea of who the most active publishers are. There are also two issues a year in which publishers announce their lists for the upcoming season. The fall announcements issue usually appears in late August; spring announcements are in an early February issue. The list ads are a simple way of judging the kinds of books the publisher is currently bringing out, and the relative size of the list.

7. Finally, you may want to become acquainted with the various magazines for writers. Two of them, *Writer's Digest* and *The Writer*, are available on newsstands; the *Freelancer's Newsletter* is available by subscription and in some libraries.

All of these magazines have news about potential markets for book manuscripts, plus useful tips on various aspects of writing.

Being Discovered. Another possible way of finding a publisher is to be "discovered" by an editor or literary agent. If you're an expert in a particular field, for example, an editor or agent might approach you to write a book on your own or in conjunction with a collaborator. If you are publishing short fiction or nonfiction articles in magazines or newspapers, you may also be approached by an editor or agent. Or you may be approached if you win a prestigious literary prize.

Sometimes this discovery business can be a bit farfetched. Writer Dennis Smith was discovered when he wrote a letter to the *New York Times Book Review* commenting on a review by Joyce Carol Oates. He signed his letter "Dennis Smith, New York City fireman." He was approached by several editors and agents, and was finally persuaded to write the book that became *Report from Engine Company 82*. While I'm not suggesting that you take up writing letters to the *Times*, I do want you to know that finding a publisher may be easier than you think!

Does It Pay to Advertise? A somewhat less orthodox approach to finding a publisher is to advertise the availability of your manuscript in one of the writers' magazines, or in one of the more important book-review media such as *Saturday Review*. This may not lead to much except invitations from vanity presses to publish with them, but it may be worth a try, particularly if it's a nonfiction book that can be clearly described.

Planning Your Submission Strategy

Once you have found the names of some publishers that you think might be interested in your book, the next step is to prepare your material for submission. This is a very important step because both the content and format of your presentation are crucial to getting an editor's attention and interest, so I recommend that you plan this carefully.

What Type of Material Should You Submit? There are no hard and fast rules about the type of material you should submit to a book publisher. In the case of nonfiction, it's most usual to submit a "proposal" rather than a complete manuscript, and in the case of fiction, it's most usual to submit a complete manuscript or several chapters from the manuscript rather than a synopsis or outline. To find out for sure what a house prefers, you can check *WM* to see whether the house's submission policy is indicated. Another way is simply to call the publishing house and ask.

A Proposal. A proposal is a detailed summary of the material to be included in the book, plus a cover letter providing additional information about the book and your qualifications for writing it. A sample chapter or two may also be included. Trade publishers usually prefer to work with a proposal for a nonfiction book because it allows them to help structure the book at a reasonably early stage. (It also has the obvious advantage for you that you may receive an advance before spending too much time on the book, and gives you the opportunity to develop the book in conjunction with the editor who will be sponsoring it.)

The form of the proposal is usually not crucial. It needs to provide enough information for an editor to make an informed judgment. If this is your first book, it's probably wise to develop the proposal quite extensively since you don't have a track record to rely on. It's not unusual for a proposal to run fifteen or twenty pages; some of them run considerably longer, especially for a complicated book. You can prepare the proposal in outline form, but it's usually best to prepare a synopsis of the material to be included in each chapter of the book instead. It's easier to read and evaluate, and also has the merit of making you really think the book through. One of the most important things is to keep the audience for the book constantly in mind; that is what the editor evaluating the material is going to do.

The cover letter is also an important element in your presentation. This is where you can *sell* the book to an editor, by demonstrating your grasp of the market for the book, the need for such a book, its most important competition, and your qualifications for writing it. You don't have to be a Ph.D., Ll.D., or M.D. to write a nonfiction book (unless these credentials are relevant to the book at hand), but you do have to demonstrate that your background (or your collaborator's) is adequate to handle the material. Acknowledging the competition indicates that you've done your homework and helps the editor "position" the book in relation to other books currently on the market. Be sure to stress how this book differs from similar books on the market. Is it more thorough? Does it present a new viewpoint? Make new information available? Present previously available material in a more attractive form?

Also indicate the projected length of the book, whether it will include illustrations and if so how many and of what type, and when you think you can complete the writing. Keep in mind that the average nonfiction book runs somewhere between 70,000 and 100,000 words—less if the book contains a lot of illustrations scattered throughout the text. It shouldn't run any longer or shorter than this unless you have a very special reason.

What Is a "Query" Letter? A query letter is simply a brief letter describing your book and asking whether the editor wants to see further material. Many publishing houses indicate that they want to be "queried" first, but my feeling is that it's difficult for an editor to evaluate a book without seeing at least some sample material—in fact, what the house may mean is that it wants to see a proposal or sample material rather than a complete manuscript.

In any case, a query letter for fiction usually sounds pretty silly, and you should submit at least two sample chapters (preferably from the beginning of the manuscript) along with a cover letter briefly summarizing the plot, your intended audience, and any other relevant information. If you have a letter of recommendation from a well-regarded teacher or writer, you may want to include this as well.

What's an "Unsolicited" Manuscript? This term generally refers to any manuscript, proposal, or query that comes into a publishing house without the prior knowledge or consent of an editor. In some houses, all unsolicited material is placed in an area called the slush pile, where it may or may not eventually receive careful attention from an editor. A slush pile in a small house is usually less of a dead end than in a big house, because small publishers are more used to dealing directly with authors. (Large houses buy most of their material through agents, packagers, or foreign publishers and generally don't pay too much heed to the slush pile. In any case, large houses tend to be a target for many writers who haven't taken the trouble to carefully research the market for their book, so that a great deal of what's in the slush pile *deserves* to be discarded.)

One way to avoid the slush pile is to address your letter to a specific editor rather than to "The Editors." Many writers are getting wise to this technique, however, and it may not save you from the slush pile if the editor realizes that he doesn't know your name. Some houses refuse to read any kind of unsolicited material and send it back unopened; others indicate that they don't read unsolicited manuscripts but will read proposals and sample material.

What About Multiple Submissions? This is a subject that has been debated for years. I personally feel that submitting to more than one house at a time is perfectly OK—and in fact recommended, since it can take an awfully long time to get a response from a publisher—so long as you indicate that you are doing so in your cover letter. Some editors refuse to consider material that's on submission elsewhere, but this is a risk that's probably worth taking at this point in your career.

Fine-tuning. Here are some things you should do when preparing your material for submission:

1. Type everything. Use a good typewriter and ribbon, and good bond paper. Double-space all of the material except the cover letter. (See Chapter 4 for tips on manuscript preparation.) The cover letter should be an original; the sample material can be photocopied. Check for typos and misspellings after you've typed it; editors notice these things. Address the editor by his full name and title; avoid sending the material addressed only to "The Editors." If you don't have an editor's name, check one of the guides mentioned previously or call the publishing house.

2. If you're sending in a complete manuscript, put it in a typing-paper box or similar container so that it arrives in readable condition. Don't three-hole-punch it and put it in a binder; editors prefer to deal with loose manuscript material. Photocopy the manuscript before you send it out. Avoid

sending original illustrations; if you absolutely have to, make sure they are insured. The publisher is not responsible for loss or damage to materials submitted by authors, particularly if the author is not under contract.

3. Check with the post office for the best way to send the material. First-class mail can be very expensive for a heavy manuscript, and it may be cheaper to use some other method such as United Parcel Service. If you do send it by mail, you might want to register it and ask for a return receipt so that you know the material was received and who signed for it. If you want your sample material back, be sure to include a stamped self-addressed envelope with the correct postage. Small companies in particular can't afford to return material sent in by writers.

4. Keep track of the date you sent the material in. If you haven't heard from the editor to whom you sent the material in four or five weeks, write a brief letter asking about the status of your submission.

What Happens in the Publishing House

The way in which manuscripts and proposals are evaluated varies from house to house, but the scenario below is probably a fair picture of how submissions are evaluated in most trade houses.

1. The mail is sorted. If a piece of mail is addressed simply to "The Editors," it will be placed in the "slush" (unsolicited) pile for eventual review by whoever is assigned to this duty (that person can range from a senior editor to the receptionist); if the house doesn't accept unsolicited submissions, the material will be sent back unopened.

2. Material addressed to a specific editor will be forwarded to his or her office, where it will be logged in by the editor's assistant so that a permanent record of its arrival (and eventual disposition) is created. If the assistant has been given this authority by the editor, she may review everything before giving it to the editor, preparing a reader's report for those submissions that she thinks are particularly promising. Submissions that are obviously inappropriate may be rejected without ever being shown to the editor. But most likely the editor will briefly review everything that is

submitted and will ask for a reader's report from his assistant or an outside reader for those projects that look especially promising. If the submission is from an author the editor has worked with before, or an important agent, the editor will probably elect to read the material himself.

3. Projects that are not of interest to the editor or are clearly not appropriate to the house will be returned with a polite rejection letter. In most cases, this is a form with some vague language to the effect that the project is not "suitable for our list at the present time." This is because a long personal letter from the editor giving a detailed critique of the manuscript often results in a letter of rebuttal from the author. In any case, most editors do not have the time to critique manuscripts they don't intend to publish.

4. If the editor is strongly interested in the material, he may ask one of his colleagues on the staff to read it. This is important both in terms of feedback, and in gathering in-house support for the book. If the sales manager or subsidiary rights manager or another editor on the staff is strongly in favor of the book, the editor is in a much better position to approach his management than if he is working only on his own recommendation. This additional support is not necessary in every case, but is particularly crucial if the author or agent is asking a lot of money for the rights, or the book is slightly unusual for the house.

There are many different elements that an editor takes into account in evaluating a publishing project. Here are some of the most important:

• First, is this book really suitable to our list? Is this the kind of book that we have published successfully in the past? If not, is it something that we have a reasonably good chance of doing well with? Do we know how to reach the appropriate audience for this book?

• Is this a book that I am qualified to edit? Am I comfortable with the subject matter? Will I need the help or advice of an expert in the field? (Most textbook publishers and university presses, for example, have manuscripts evaluated by experts in the field before they sign up a book. This is less common in trade publishing but it does happen.)

• Do I have the time to work on this book? Trade hardcover editors typically sponsor between five and ten original books a list, depending on the complexity of the books, whether they will do the "line" editing or whether this will be done by a manuscript editor, management policies, and so on. If it looks as though your book is going to require a great deal of work, the editor may decide against taking it on even if he is interested in the subject matter and/or your writing.

• Does the author write well? Does it look as though she's done her homework? Does the project seem to be a viable one? These are obviously very subjective judgments, and they may not even be shared by other people in the house. But a good editor will have firm opinions on the matter, and will be willing to stick by his judgments even though his colleagues—and the critical media—may not agree. He may want you to do more work on the manuscript or proposal before he proposes the project to his management, but if he trusts your basic abilities, you are well on your way to getting a contract offer.

• How much competition is there on the subject? Here, the editor will rely to a certain extent on the information that you have provided in your cover letter—and in fact, if you haven't identified any competition, it's grounds for worry. But he may also do some research on his own, by checking *Books in Print,* looking in a bookstore, or talking to people who are expert in the subject of your book. Most trade editors have a wide range of interests and knowledge, but are not expert in every area. He'll want to get a sense of how many other books there are on the subject, how they've sold, and how your book is different from—and better than—the competition.

• How popular is this subject likely to be? This takes into account such things as trends, and how many copies of your book the house is likely to be able to sell. If you've written a book about dogs, for example, and cat books are big this year, you may be barking up the wrong tree—but on the other hand, this may be just the moment when dog books are going to enjoy a surge of popularity. One of an editor's jobs is to be alert to trends and to anticipate what types of books will sell well in the future.

However, it's obviously impossible to estimate exactly how many copies a book is going to sell (unless it is being published on a subscription basis). What the editor will do instead is try to project sales (often with the help of the sales manager) based on the publisher's past experience with similar books, the current state of the marketplace, and other imponderables. Most large trade houses have to sell at least five thousand copies of a hardcover book in order to break even, that is, get back the money paid out in production costs, royalties, and other expenses. The interesting thing is that *many* trade hardcovers sell fewer than five thousand copies, so trade publishers lose money on a lot of the books they publish. (It's estimated that out of every ten trade books published, four lose money, three break even, and three make money.) That's why bestsellers—which help publishers recoup their losses—are so important these days. However, many of the big houses go on publishing "small" books, in the conviction that many of them deserve to be published.

• Can we afford to do this book? Here, the editor weighs the costs to publish the book against the income they hope to derive from it. In some houses, the editor must prepare a formal profit-and-loss estimate before approaching his management for approval to make a contract offer. Appendix A of this manual provides a useful example of how a pre-contract estimate might be done for a trade book. (The forms used for mass-market paperbacks are usually a little different.) The form—and the complexity of the computations—vary somewhat from house to house, but the elements are usually the same. They include:

—the number of copies to be printed in the first (and perhaps only) press run. This will of course depend to some extent on whether it will be published initially as a trade hardcover or trade paperback. In the case of hardcovers, the first printing for a literary first novel is often five thousand copies or less; a book of poetry by an unknown writer, twenty-five hundred copies or less. On the other hand, a hardcover book with the potential of being a bestseller can have a first printing of 50,000 copies or more.

—the number of copies out of that first press run that the company expects to sell during the first publishing season, allowing for returns from booksellers, free copies sent to reviewers, and so on. (About 20 percent of all trade books are returned to the publisher by booksellers for credit. Libraries are not allowed to return books.)

—the probable cover price of the book and the net income after the average discount granted to booksellers is applied.

—costs, including plant and unit costs (see Appendix A for details), royalties paid to the author, advertising and promotion costs, and miscellaneous other costs.

—projected net margin from trade sales after all costs have been taken into account. This *may* be on the negative side of the ledger.

—projected income from subsidiary rights. Not all books have the potential for subsidiary rights income, but this *can* be an important source of income for the house. The usual arrangement is for the publisher to handle the licensing of (and share the income from) book club, mass-market reprint, and various kinds of "second serial" licenses. The split of income is usually 50/50 between the author and the publisher. If the contract with the book publisher is arranged by a literary agent, various other subsidiary rights—such as first serial, foreign, and performance rights—will probably be retained on the author's behalf by the agent; otherwise, they will also be granted to the book publisher, and income will be shared by the author and the publisher.

If the editor is satisfied with these cost projections, he will approach his management and ask for permission to make a contract offer. In a small house, this may simply be a matter of asking the editor-in-chief or publisher for approval. In a large house, this may involve a full-scale editorial meeting and/or evaluation by an editorial board composed of the editor-in-chief, representatives from the marketing departments, the publisher, and perhaps others.

Whatever the situation, the editor will briefly describe the book, indicate the kind of advance he was thinking of offering, and ask for approval. Since this implies a commitment of the house's resources to that project, there may be considerable discussion before the project is approved—if it is approved at all (and many such proposed projects are not). The people involved in the discussion may want more information about the book, may want the author to modify his approach somewhat, or may insist on different terms than those contemplated by the editor. If the editor finally does obtain approval, he will then contact the author and make an offer.

Evaluating a Publishing Offer

The Terms. The editor will either write you a letter expressing the house's desire to publish the book and spelling out the major terms of their offer, or he will call you and make the offer over the telephone. A publishing deal involves many elements besides the proposed advance and royalties, but the other terms are usually not discussed in detail until you receive a copy of the contract. (Chapter 3 spells out typical terms in detail.)

The terms offered will depend on the house and the project. As indicated earlier, the usual royalty rate for a trade hardcover is 10 percent of the cover price for the first 5,000 or 7,500 copies sold, 12½ percent for the next 5,000 copies sold, and 15 percent after that. Trade paperback royalties typically start lower—usually at the 6% to 7½% level—and then "escalate" after a fairly large number of copies (say, 50,000) have been sold. The top of the scale may be at 9% or 10%. (For mass-market paperback royalties, see Chapter 10.) However, terms will vary according to the project and the house's usual royalty arrangements. The advance (if any) will be based on projected sales, although the editor will probably try to hedge his bets. If they're thinking of a first printing of 7,500 hardcover copies, for example, the editor may offer an advance in the range of $5,000, depending on the projected cover price, the number of copies they expect to "net out," and so on. However, the amount of the advance offered usually includes a little room for negotiation.

What Can You Do with a Publishing Offer? If this is exactly the house that you wanted to publish with, and the terms seem reasonable, there's no reason why you can't accept the offer on the spot. Keep in mind, though, that the advance is probably somewhat negotiable and that the editor may be willing to go a little higher if you press him.

Probably the best approach is to find out what the house has in mind for the book. Ask the editor what kind of first printing they are thinking about, and whether it will be a hardcover or trade paperback. Ask him about the royalty rate for the trade (and mass-market) editions, the likely cover prices, and what kind of publicity and promotion plans they have in mind. Then tell him you'd like a day or two to think the offer over. You're not formally committed to the deal until you sign a contract, but it's bad form to accept an offer and then change your mind later. It's also bad form to use an offer as "leverage" with another publisher, although if another publisher has already expressed interest it's certainly fair to mention this to the editor, and to negotiate the most advantageous terms possible.

You may also want to consider getting an agent involved at this point. This is not unusual, and in fact the editor himself may suggest it. The agent will probably not be able to improve the terms of the deal substantially, but can be a help to you in understanding the contract and in subsequent relations with the house, and may also retain certain subsidiary rights on your behalf. For more details, see Chapters 2, 3, and 8. Chapter 3 describes the usual terms of a trade publishing contract in detail. Be sure you read and understand this material before signing any contract with a book publisher. It makes the terms of the relationship very clear and can save you from some nasty surprises later.

2
Working with a Literary Agent

What an agent is supposed to do is ensure there is a competitive spirit when a publisher buys a book.

—THERON RAINES, agent

A literary agent may not be vitally necessary to you at the beginning of your career. In fact, you may never need one—if you are writing scholarly or technical material, or are perfectly happy with your relationship with your present publisher, or just don't want to get involved with an agent for some reason. But if you are producing a lot of work, or are interested in gaining entrée to one of the big commercial houses, or want someone to negotiate the terms of the contract for a book you've received an offer on, an experienced and effective literary agent can be a powerful ally. This chapter tells you how to find an agent, and what an agent can and should do for you.

How Do You Find an Agent?

Finding an experienced agent can sometimes be a problem for a new writer, because the established agents usually prefer to work with writers who are already earning income from their writing (or at least already have an offer for their book). One agent, for example, refuses to take on a new writer unless he is earning at least $10,000 annually from writing. Others are less hard-nosed, however, and you have a good chance of persuading an agent to represent you if you have a good manuscript or proposal in hand *and* you can get a referral to that agent from someone who knows him or her. Like publishers, agents are inundated with submissions and some of them—usually the largest and most well-known— will not accept unsolicited submissions.

Some Listings. If you don't know somebody who can give you a referral to an agent, there are various listings you can check. They include the following:

1. *Literary Market Place* lists about three hundred of the most active author's agents. This includes agencies that specialize in particular types of writers and properties (screenwriters, science fiction and children's book writers, etc.) as well as those that handle a variety of literary properties. Some of these agencies are large and stratified; others are one- or two-person operations. Don't be misled by the size of the agency, however; the small ones are often as effective and well-known as the larger ones. Also note the location of the agency. Most of the firms are located in New York City, but there are several on the West Coast, particularly in Los Angeles, and a few in other cities around the country, such as Boston and Chicago. If you are particularly interested in dealing with the large Eastern publishers, however, it's usually advisable to try to find a New York agent. The listing does not indicate whether an agency will consider unsolicited material or not.

2. *Writer's Market* has a list of author's agents and literary services. Some of the agents are also listed in *LMP*, but many are not. In general, the agents listed in *WM* are more amenable to taking on new clients than those listed in *LMP*. The description will indicate whether you can contact the agency directly or whether they prefer a recommendation from someone they know.

The listing also includes the types of material the agency handles, the form in which the material should be submitted (query letter, proposal, or complete manuscript), whether the agency works on a commission basis or charges a reading fee, and recent sales the agency has made to book publishers. In some cases, the listing will even specify the total number of sales made to publishers the previous year, the number of sales the agency anticipates making in the coming year, and the number of clients handled by the agency.

3. *LMP* and *WM* both have listings that are updated annually. In addition to these listings, there are two guides to agents listed in the Bibliography of this book—and there will probably be more available as time goes along.

4. There are two professional organizations for literary agents: the Society of Author's Representatives (SAR) and the Independent Literary Agents Association (ILAA). Both have brochures describing their business policies and membership. Check the yellow pages at the back of *LMP* for the current addresses of these organizations.

5. There are frequent references to agents in *Publishers Weekly (PW)*, particularly in the "Rights and Permissions" column. *Writer's Digest* carries agents' ads, and both *WD* and *The Writer* occasionally run lists of agents. However, you should be aware that many of the agents who advertise charge fees for reading manuscripts and proposals, and may not be particularly effective at *placing* them with publishers.

What about Using a Friend or an Attorney as an Agent?
Some writers have one of their friends act as their agent. There's nothing intrinsically wrong with this, but you're not gaining much unless your friend knows something about the business. One of the advantages of working with an established agent is that she is known to editors and they are known to her. She knows what particular editors are most likely to be interested in, and how to negotiate a publishing contract effectively.

Many writers are now using attorneys, especially those writers who have been enormously successful and need legal advice in handling their assets. An attorney's fees can be high, however, and you probably won't need one except perhaps to vet your contract with a publisher. To get the name of an attorney experienced in publishing law, you can:

1. Call your local bar association for a referral.

2. Check a publication called *Martindale-Hubbell Law Directory,* which lists attorneys by their specialties.

3. Contact Volunteer Lawyers for the Arts, 1560 Broadway, New York, NY 10036. However, the organization can provide free counsel only to writers whose annual income falls below a certain level; for current guidelines, check with the organization.

What If You're Approached by an Agent? Reputable agents do seek out promising writers. However, if you are approached by an agent I would suggest that you check to see whether she is listed in *LMP* or is a member of one of the agents' associations. Ask her about other writers she represents and about publishing deals she has made. You might also want to talk to one of the writers she represents to get a better sense of what you can expect from the agent.

A Few Other Comments about Finding an Agent. SAR and ILAA are professional associations of agents that espouse certain business practices. SAR is made up primarily of older agents, most of whom charge a 10 percent commission on domestic sales and 15 percent on foreign sales. ILAA is made up mainly of younger agents, some of whom charge a 15 percent commission on domestic sales and 20 percent on foreign sales. Don't be concerned if an agent is not a member of either group, however; she may be relatively new to the business, or just not interested in belonging to an association.

If you are interested in using an agent who charges a reading fee, find out exactly what that fee buys you and whether it will be refunded if the agency agrees to represent you and succeeds in selling the rights to your book. Some of the fees are very high, and a reading report with suggestions for changes is no guarantee that your manuscript will be accepted by a publisher even after you make the changes. The Scott Meredith Agency, for example, charges $200 for reading and evaluating a manuscript running between 10,000 and 100,000 words. Other fees are adjusted accordingly.

Interviewing an Agent

Before you agree to representation by an agent, you should interview him or her first, by telephone if you can't do it in person. This can be an important business arrangement for you, and it's advisable to try to determine in advance if the relationship is likely to be a fruitful one. Some writers interview several agents before making a decision. Here are some things you should find out in advance:

• What other writers does the agent represent and what sales to publishers has he made lately? If you've come to the agent without the benefit of an introduction, you're not going to know much about him and will need to get some sense of his business ability. If the agent is reluctant to answer these questions, it's probably a sign that you should depart quietly.

• How would the agent handle your material? That is, does he see it as a mass-market original, trade paperback, or trade hardcover? Would he approach the large commercial houses, a smaller publisher, or perhaps a university press? Does he think the material is ready for submission now or does he think it requires more work? What does the agent think the book's prospects really are? Can you anticipate a generous advance against royalties, or does he have a more guarded optimism about it? Does he have a particular editor in a particular house in mind, or would the book be submitted to several houses simultaneously?

• What is the rate structure of the agency? Is the commission on domestic sales 10 percent or 15 percent? This commission will extend over the life of any contract obtained for you, so the difference between the two amounts can be substantial if the book remains in print a long time. Also find out if you will be charged for expenses such as telephone calls, photocopying, etc.

A Formal Agreement with an Agency

Some agencies want you to sign a formal agreement of representation but others do not. The advantage of a contract is that it clarifies the terms of the agreement. Even if you don't sign a formal agreement, however, you should be clear about the following points.

The scope of the representation. Will the agency handle all of your work or only one specific project? If you write short fiction, for example, will you have the right to sell this work on your own without having to pay the agent a fee? Furthermore, is the agent to handle *all* of the rights to each particular work? For example, you may already have arranged an option on the manuscript with a film producer. In this case, you may want the right to negotiate a movie sale on your own, or may already be working with an agent on the

West Coast for this purpose. If you sell this or other subsidiary rights on your own, should you pay the agent a commission on this sale? In most instances, the agent will share in all of the income from a particular work, even though she may not have negotiated that particular deal. If this does not seem reasonable in your case, have the agreement modified accordingly.

The right of consultation. Do you wish to be informed of every offer received? If so, this should be stated clearly in the agreement. Also specify whether the agent can make a binding agreement without your consent. Many publishing deals are made over the telephone, and if your agent agrees to terms without clearing them with you first, you may find yourself committed to a deal you dislike intensely. You should have the right of approval of all deals.

Collection and handling of money. The agent's commission for domestic and foreign sales must be specified. If subagents are to be used for foreign or film sales, this arrangement and the commission to be paid the subagent (usually 10 percent) should also be specified. The way in which any money due to you will be handled should be spelled out. On book contracts, the publisher normally pays your advance and royalty earnings to the agent, who will deposit the check in the agency's bank account and then write you a check for the amount due minus the agency commission. This processing usually takes a week to ten days. Money from first-serial, movie, or foreign sales will also be sent to the agency first so that the agency commission (plus the subagent's commission) can be deducted.

Some agencies bill writers for various expenses, such as the cost of duplicating manuscripts for submission to publishers, long-distance telephone calls, and so on. Find out what the agency's policy is and what these charges are likely to run. You should *not* be charged for every phone call made on your behalf, especially if you are paying a 15 percent commission.

Some agreements specify that authors' earnings will be kept separate from the working funds of the agency. This is desirable because if the agency goes out of business, you will want access to your money. You may also want a clause giving you the right to inspect the agency's books after a reasonable period of notice.

The term of the agreement. Most agreements run for a period of one or two years, particularly if the agency is handling only one of your books. If the agreement is for a specified term, it may be set up so that it is automatically renewed at the end of each term until either party gives formal notice that s/he wishes to terminate it. Or it may automatically lapse at the end of a term, at which point it can be renewed by the mutual consent of both parties. If the agreement is not for a specified term, it should expressly stipulate that either you or the agency may terminate the agreement at any time by giving the other party formal written notice. The termination will then take place after a specified period of time, usually thirty days.

If you don't have a formal written agreement with an agency, the relationship can end whenever one of you wants to call it quits. However, if the agent has negotiated any contracts on your behalf, the publisher will continue to send all payments to that agent unless you can negotiate some other arrangement to the contrary.

What happens if you terminate your arrangement with an agent and then find another who sells the rights to your book shortly thereafter? Some agreements specify that if the rights to your book are sold within a certain period of time after termination with the first agent, that agent is entitled to a share of the proceeds. This is an unusual clause, however, and you should resist it. Note also that there may be a clause in the contract stating that this relationship is an "agency coupled with an interest." The meaning of this clause is unclear, although some agencies believe that it means that you cannot terminate your relationship with the agency at will. If there is such a clause, try to have it deleted, or at least find out exactly what the agency means by it.

Modification or assignment of the agreement. There should be a clause stating that the agreement may not be modified or assigned without your consent. In other words, the agency cannot unilaterally change its commission rate or other terms, or sell the agreement of representation to another agency without your consent.

Don't be too concerned about the technicalities of an agency agreement, however. There is little likelihood that any of these points will become an issue, and if one does, you have a mechanism for dealing with it. If your agent doesn't succeed in finding a publisher for your book within a reasonable period of time or you are just not getting along for some reason, it's probably best to terminate the agreement as quickly as possible and go on to something more fruitful.

Planning Your Strategy to Sell Book Rights

Although your agent may elect—with your consent—to try to sell first-serial or film rights before selling the book rights, the usual thing is to negotiate a book contract first.

When you sit down together to discuss your strategy for submission, one of the most important topics should be whether your material is ready to be submitted in its present form or whether it should be reworked. A strong presentation can make a big difference in how a project is perceived by an editor, and it's worth your while to make sure the material is in the best shape possible. Many agents are former editors and can be very helpful in shaping your material. It may also be worthwhile to rework the material if your agent is thinking of submitting it to a particular editor who the agent knows is very responsive to certain kinds of presentations.

Another very important consideration is whether the manuscript will be submitted to one editor at a time, or whether it will go out on a multiple submission. This decision will have to do with the nature of that particular book, the current situation in the marketplace, the agent's preferred way of working, and so on. If the agent knows an editor who she thinks will be particularly interested in the book, she will probably want to submit the project to that editor first. If that editor does not make a satisfactory offer, she may then send it out on a multiple submission. Or she may recommend that it be sent out initially to several editors, or sold at auction. If you have any strong feelings on the matter, now is the time to voice them. But in any case, you should be given the opportunity to discuss the strategy with the agent, and to ask any questions you have about the editors or houses to whom the material is being submitted.

A Single Submission. The agent will probably call the editor first to tell him about the project and to find out whether he's interested in it. If so, she will send the material over (in New York this is often done by messenger) along with a cover letter describing the potential of the book and your virtues as a writer. Money will probably not be discussed at this point, although the agent may indicate that she is "looking for" an advance in the neighborhood of "x-dollars."

The amount of time that you will have to wait until you hear anything varies considerably. Some editors are prompt and respond in a week or less; others habitually take at least a month. If the agent has not heard from the editor in a few weeks, she will call to find out what is going on. If the editor is interested in the book, he will probably want to know more about you: what you are like personally, what your future writing plans are, and so on. If he is satisfied with your agent's answers, they will then start dickering about a price. Typically, the editor will offer a relatively low advance and the agent will ask for a relatively high one; the goal is to arrive at a number that's agreeable to everybody. Royalty rates and other terms will be standard unless this is an unusual deal. The agent will then contact you, explain the terms of the deal, and ask if it is acceptable to you. If it isn't, you have the right to refuse the deal, or ask her to improve any terms you feel you can't live with. If a compromise can't be reached, she will send your material to another editor.

A Multiple Submission. The agent will submit your material to several publishers simultaneously if she feels that several editors are likely to be strongly interested in it and any of them will be satisfactory to you. The material will be sent to each editor at the same time, with the understanding that this is a bidding situation. Sometimes each editor will be allowed to make only one bid; in other cases, the bidding will go on until there is a clear winner.

In the former situation, the bids can be remarkably divergent. NAL, for example, bid $850,000 for the hardcover and paperback rights to Anne Tolstoi Wallach's first novel, *Women's Work*. The second closest bid was $200,000. Don't let these figures mislead you, though; the bids for most trade books seldom get into five figures.

What sometimes happens is that two or three houses want the book, but their offers are quite close and each house or editor offers certain strengths that the others don't. In this case, the agent might try to work out the most favorable deal by asking for such things as a guaranteed advertising and promotion budget for the book, or a "bonus" if the book is used as the basis for a movie or if it appears on the *New York Times Book Review* bestseller list. The bestseller bonuses usually depend on the position of the book on the list (#1 is obviously best) and the number of weeks it spends at that position. Another possibility is to negotiate better-than-usual splits of subsidiary rights income (especially mass-market paperback income) and/or "early pass-through" of your share of rights income (instead of letting the publisher hold on to it until your next royalty statement is due).

An Auction. In an auction, the book is offered to several publishers at the same time but in this case the rules are more formal and stringent. The first bid by each house must be in by a specified date and there may be a "floor" (minimum bid) established by one of the bidders in exchange for the privilege of making the last offer in the auction. Each bid must precede each previous bid by a specified percentage (usually 7 percent or more), and so on. A book will be auctioned only if the agent thinks that several important publishers will be strongly interested in acquiring the rights. For one thing, there is a certain amount of risk involved in putting a book up for auction, because if no one bids (and this does happen), the book acquires a somewhat shopworn aura and it may be difficult to sell the rights at all.

Handling of the Contract. After all of the terms have been agreed on, the publishing house will draw up the contract, including a clause which states that you have empowered the agency to act in your behalf, and that all royalty statements and payments are to go through the agency. Beware of any wording, however, that says you "irrevocably assign and transfer" to the agency a specified commission on this work. This *can* mean that the agency will receive this commission until the copyright runs out, even though you no longer have any dealings with that agency and the publishing rights have reverted to you. Note also that the rights granted the publisher will probably *not* include certain "subsidiary" rights, such as the right to print excerpts from the book in magazines and newspapers ("first-serial rights"), the right to license foreign editions, "performance" rights, and so on. These rights are normally retained on your behalf by your agent so that they can be licensed separately (and so you don't have to share that income with your book publisher).

However, if the book publisher has very good contacts in any of these areas, you and your agent may agree to let the publisher handle them.

The agent will go over the contract carefully, asking for changes where necessary. Many agencies always ask for certain changes on each contract it negotiates with a particular house and these changes will be made before you see the contract. If you disagree with or don't understand any of the terms in the contract, discuss them with your agent *before* you sign the document and return it to the agent. For more details about the terms of a publishing contract, see Chapter 3.

Other Obligations of Your Agent

In addition to negotiating the best possible terms for the publishing rights to your book, your agent will have other responsibilities toward you. One is to try to arrange licenses for those subsidiary rights not granted to your publisher. For more information on which rights may be retained on your behalf by your agent, see Chapter 3; for a detailed discussion of the handling of these rights, see Chapter 8.

Your agent will also continue to be your ally and advocate in your relations with the book publishing house. If you and your editor have a serious disagreement regarding the content of the final manuscript, for example, or if you are not happy with the marketing plans for the book, your agent can act as ombudsman and adjudicator in helping to settle the matter. Furthermore, the agent should be working closely with the publisher's subsidiary rights manager, informing him of any licenses that she has negotiated so that the publisher can use this information in marketing the book (a courtesy that the subsidiary rights manager should extend to the agent as well).

Beyond these services, a literary agent can be an important ally in your ongoing writing career. She may be able to help you plan new projects; you may want her to find writing assignments for you; and she should be your overall business advisor in terms of your writing career. This can be particularly valuable in light of editors' propensity to hopscotch from house to house. It's not unusual to have two or three editors in the course of writing and publishing a book, and having a good relationship with an agent can provide the kind of stability that may be missing in your relationship with publishers.

If your relationship with an agent doesn't seem to be working, it's best to terminate the relationship. If you have a contract with the agency, check to see what the termination procedures are. If you don't have a contract with the agency, you can usually simply agree to disagree. Any contracts that the agent has negotiated on your behalf will remain in force until they can be terminated. In the meantime, you may want to be looking for a new agent—or you may decide to represent yourself.

3

Negotiating a Trade Book Contract

A contract arises only when three elements are present: an offer, its acceptance (but not the proposal of counteroffers) and something called "consideration." Consideration is the *quid pro quo*, the thing given in exchange for the bargain.
— RICHARD WINCOR, *Literary Rights Contracts*

The contract is the document that spells out the *terms* of the agreement between you and your publishing partner—that is, the responsibilities that each of you is obligated to fulfill. Should either party fail to keep his or her part of the bargain, the contract is the basis on which legal action can be brought.

Publishing contracts differ markedly in terms of complexity and comprehensiveness. Some contracts are little more than a letter spelling out the general terms of the agreement; others are many pages of fine print that defy the comprehension of even the most experienced writers and lawyers.

This chapter of *The Writer's Survival Manual* spells out the terms that are likely to be found (although perhaps not stated in the same language) in a contract with one of the large trade houses. Even if these terms are not spelled out explicitly in the contract, however, they are conditions that are implied in *any* agreement between an author and a book publisher, and you should be familiar with them before you sign such an agreement.

Most large houses use a preprinted form that has blanks

for the "variable" terms (such as the advance and royalty rates) to be filled in. Appendix B of this manual provides an example of such a form. Don't be intimidated by the fact that these terms have been set in type; they express the conditions under which the publisher would *like* to do business, but they almost always favor the publisher, and many of them may be open to negotiation.

If the contract was negotiated on your behalf by an agent, it will be sent to the agent first for review (and any changes that the agent deems necessary) before being forwarded to you. If you have no agent, the contract will of course come directly to you.

It is important that you understand and *agree to* every condition that is spelled out in the contract. If you don't, consult your agent, editor, or attorney.

If you don't have an agent, you should probably have the contract examined ("vetted") by a lawyer experienced with literary contracts. Publishing law is not particularly arcane, but it *is* based on accepted ways of doing business and a lawyer inexperienced with these customs and procedures can create a lot of confusion and unnecessary fuss. If you feel that you can't afford such an attorney, try contacting Volunteer Lawyers for the Arts (see Chapter 2).

If you want to make changes in the contract, discuss them with your agent or editor first. They may be violently opposed to them, in which case you have a real problem on your hands. If you can't come to an agreement, the publishing deal will have to be dissolved; however, most such changes can usually be worked out. Ask the editor (or agent) if you can write or type the changes on the form, or whether it should be returned to the house for emendation. If you do make changes on the form, you'll probably have to initial them to indicate that you are aware of and have agreed to this change on the official document.

After the contract has been returned to the publishing house and countersigned by all the necessary parties, you will be issued the check due you (if any) on the signing of the contract. Congratulations! You have a deal.

Identification and Description of Work

The first part of the contract is usually devoted to identifying and describing the work that is the subject of this agreement. At the minimum, it will spell out the date of the contract, the parties to the agreement, the book or books that are the subject of this agreement, and the projected final length of the manuscript. (The contract may be for more than one book, but in the discussion following it is assumed that only one book is involved.)

The Date of the Contract. This is probably the date that the contract was drawn up, rather than the date when the oral agreement to publish the book was made, or the date when the document was signed by the publisher. This date becomes important in the event of a legal dispute, and is usually cited whenever there is any correspondence about the contract to help identify it.

The Parties to the Agreement. The publisher and the author(s) will be clearly identified. Even if you wish the book to be published anonymously or under a pseudonym, your real name will have to be specified in the contract in order for it to be legal.

Note that if the book is published pseudonymously or anonymously, the period of copyright protection* will be seventy-five years from the date of publication or one hundred years from the date that you created the work (i.e., set it down in written form), whichever is earlier. If the book is published under your real name, the term of copyright protection will be your life plus fifty years; if there is more than one author, the term is calculated from the death date of the last surviving author.

Title, Description, and Length of Manuscript. The title of the book may have been settled when the agreement was

---

*These rules apply to books published after January 1, 1978. Prior to that, the period of statutory copyright protection for any work was twenty-eight years plus a renewal policy of twenty-eight years. Books not yet published were protected under the "common law" copyright laws of the various states.

made. If the question is still open, however, the contract may identify the book as an "untitled novel" or "untitled work of nonfiction." Even if a specific title is used, you will probably be allowed to change it later, especially if the word *tentative* or *provisional* appears in the contract.

Titles are often hard to agree on, and there is no industrywide rule about who should have the final say in the matter. Ask your editor how it usually works at this particular firm. If you think the title is going to be a point of controversy, ask to have a clause added stating that the provisional title can be changed only with your consent. This means that the provisional title will be used unless you are otherwise notified.

The contents of the book may also be briefly described in the contract, although this is somewhat unusual.

Length. The projected length of the final manuscript is almost always specified, usually as a total number of words. Since it is difficult to estimate exactly how many words will be in the final manuscript (unless you've already delivered it and it has been accepted), it is usual to express this as a range, such as "between 80,000 and 90,000 words."

Most trade books run between 75,000 and 100,000 words. (If illustrations are going to be used throughout, the text may be shorter.) The expected length should be clearly agreed upon by you and your editor *before* you sign the contract. If you don't meet this length requirement, the publisher has the right to cancel the contract.

Materials to Be Provided, Delivery Date, and the "Satisfactory" Clause

Materials to Be Provided. In addition to specifying the length of the manuscript, most publishing contracts have a clause stating the number of copies to be delivered, and any additional supporting material you are expected to provide. Most publishers only expect you to deliver one copy of the manuscript, which may be the original ribbon copy or a high-quality photocopy. If you prefer *not* to turn in the original, find out from your editor if this is acceptable. Rarely are you required to provide more than the original and one copy.

Additional materials that the author is normally expected to provide include:

Illustrations and charts. This includes such things as black-and-white photographs, color photographs, drawings, reproductions of old maps, charts and graphs, and the like. The publisher expects you to deliver them in "camera-ready" form, *and* to assume all the costs of obtaining them. If these illustrations are going to be expensive but are essential to the book, try to get the publisher to assume at least a portion of the cost.

Copyright permissions. If you are using material from previously published books or other kinds of material protected by copyright, you may be required to obtain formal permission to use the material and to pay a fee for such use. If you are unsure what this is going to involve, ask your editor for guidance and find out whether the publishing house can help you obtain these permissions and perhaps pay part of the cost. (Chapter 4 provides more information on copyright permissions.)

Index. Most nonfiction books include an index. You can prepare the index yourself, or you (or the publisher) can hire a professional indexer to prepare it for you. If you think you are going to want the index prepared by someone else, find out from your editor how much it is likely to cost and whether you will be billed or the cost will be charged against your royalty account. (Chapter 5 provides more information on indexes.)

Delivery Date. The contract will specify a date by which the final manuscript and other supporting materials are to be delivered. If you fail to deliver the manuscript or any of these materials on time, the publisher has grounds for canceling the contract and demanding repayment of any advances you have received.

Some contracts state that if you fail to supply the necessary support materials, the publisher will do so and will charge the cost of these materials to you.

When you agree to a delivery date, be sure it's a date you can make. Remember that this date is for the *final revised manuscript,* not a draft. If you are going to be late, ask your editor for a formal extension of the delivery date and get that extension *in writing.* Some contracts allow a formal "grace period" of up to ninety days, but most do not. (On the other hand, you should also know that most states have a "statute of limitations" which says that after a specified period of time has passed, you cannot be sued for breach of contract. In most states it's six years; in California it's four. This time period runs from the date the manuscript is due.)

The "Satisfactory" Clause. Every publishing contract has a clause stating that the publisher has the right to determine whether the materials you have delivered are satisfactory or not. Sometimes the contract uses the phrase "satisfactory in form and content," sometimes only the word *satisfactory* (or *acceptable*) is used, and sometimes the publisher reserves the right to reject a manuscript not only on the basis of the quality or appropriateness of the material you have delivered but also on the basis of "current market conditions." Thus, if other houses have brought out books on the same topic before you have delivered your final manuscript, for example, the publisher *may* have the right to reject your manuscript even though the quality of the book is satisfactory. (This is based on a law in most states allowing a publisher to reject a manuscript on any "relevant" basis, limited only by its "good faith.")

Since the publishing rights to many book projects are bought on the basis of a proposal rather than a complete manuscript, such a clause protects the publisher from having to accept a manuscript which is not what he expected. On the other hand, such a clause gives the publisher more latitude than may be justifiable, particularly if the house has made no effort to help the author(s) meet the house's standards. In a recent case involving Harcourt Brace Jovanovich and Senator Barry Goldwater, who was working with a collaborator named Stephen Shadegg, a federal judge ruled that "there is an implied obligation . . . for the publisher to engage in appropriate editorial work with the author of a book" and that the publisher does not have "absolutely unfettered license to act or not to act in any way it wishes and to accept or reject a book for any reason whatsoever."

Despite the "Goldwater decision," most publishers will be very resistant to changing this clause. What you might try to get them to do instead is one of the following:

1. Ask the publisher to delete the "market conditions" clause from the contract if it has one.

2. Ask the publisher to change the wording to that suggested by the Authors Guild: "The author shall deliver a manuscript which, in style and content, is professionally competent and fit for publication." This would enable a judge or arbitrator of a dispute between an author and publisher to establish professional competence on the basis of testimony by critics, publishers, and other experts, rather than leaving it entirely up to the publisher.

3. Ask the publisher to add a "first proceeds" clause which stipulates that if the manuscript is rejected as unsatisfactory because of a change in market conditions, you have to return the advance only if you find another publisher for it and receive earnings from it.

4. Ask to have a clause added which requires the publisher to give you a written statement of the defects found in the manuscript and a specified period of time (say, 30 to 60 days) in which to correct the defects.

5. Have your outline, proposal, or sample materials attached to the contract when it is signed, with a clause added to the document saying that the book will be considered satisfactory to the publisher if it is in substantial conformity with these materials.

6. If you are relying on a particular editor in the house, and have cause to believe that the editor may be considering leaving, ask to have a clause added to the contract stipulating that you can terminate the contract if your editor leaves the house.

The Grant of Rights

When you fix a literary work in tangible form, you create a "copyright" in that work. This means that you have sole ownership of that work (unless you created it with someone else and therefore share the copyright), and that no one can duplicate it or make a "derivative" work from it (such as a movie), or quote more than a small portion of it without your consent.

The copyright is composed of many types of exclusive rights. The contract will spell out the various rights that are being transferred to, or "granted," the publisher. This includes the right to publish one or more editions of the book in a specified territory, plus various kinds of "subsidiary" rights. If some of these rights are *not* being granted to the publisher, they will be crossed out on the form. An agent will normally retain first-serial, performance, British, and translation rights on your behalf. She *may* retain commercial and other miscellaneous rights.

The material that follows indicates the rights normally specified in a publishing contract, and the way in which income from subsidiary-rights licenses is usually split between an author and publisher. If any of these rights have not been granted to the publisher, these splits will obviously not apply.

Types of Rights

Book rights. The basic grant is the right to "print, publish, and sell" the work in book form. If you have an agent, this grant will probably be limited to English-language editions sold in the United States and its territories and possessions, and possibly Canada. If you don't have an agent, this grant usually includes the right to sell the publisher's English-language editions throughout the world, plus the right to license foreign-language editions.

Note that "book form" includes such things as a trade paperback edition, a limited edition, a textbook edition, a "cheap" hardcover edition, and so on, although these possibilities are usually not spelled out in the contract.

Periodical publication prior to book publication ("first serial"). The usual split is 90/10 in your favor, so that your publisher is in effect retaining a fee equivalent to that charged by an agent.

Book-club rights, including condensed and abridged versions. The income is usually split 50/50 between author and publisher; few publishers ever deviate from this.

Reprint edition by another publisher. The most usual instance is a mass-market paperback reprint, but there can be other kinds, such as a trade paperback, hardcover reprint, etc. The usual split is 50/50, but you may be able to negotiate a better split after a specified level of income is reached. Some contracts make a reprint license subject to the author's approval. This is unusual, but worth trying for.

Other postpublication uses, such as excerpts in magazines or newspapers ("second serial"), condensations, adaptations, abridgments, selections, anthology, etc. The usual split is 50/50.

Performance rights. This includes such things as movie rights, radio and television rights, and dramatic rights. It *may* include musical rights and recording rights, although the latter would probably be included in the "allied" rights granted a filmmaker. The usual split is 90/10, although if the publisher plans to utilize a subagent to sell these rights, the split may be 80/20.

Commercial or merchandising rights. This is the right to use elements from your book on merchandise such as T-shirts, stationery, etc. Most publishers have little expertise in selling these rights, and you may do better trying to sell them on your own. If you do grant this right to the publisher, make sure that your name cannot be used in any manner without your consent. The usual split is 50/50, but you may be able to negotiate a better split if your book has strong potential in this area.

Miscellaneous other rights, such as filmstrip, printed cartoon versions, microfilm, information storage and retrieval, computer software, and mechanical reproduction. (For more information about these various options, see Chapter 8.) If granted to your publisher, the usual split is 50/50. However, many agents are now insisting on holding onto them for their authors (particularly computer software rights). If you're not certain what to do, you may arrange to grant these rights to the publisher with the stipulation that royalty rates and an advance will be negotiated in good faith at a later date.

British rights. The right to publish an English-language edition outside of the United States is often referred to as "British" rights, because it used to be common for an American publisher to sell these rights to a publisher in England. The territory would then include all of the countries in the British Commonwealth. The U.S. Justice Department felt this was in restraint of trade, however, and American publishers must now negotiate these rights on a country-by-country basis. (In actual fact, however, most such deals are still made with English publishers, and include many if not all of the countries formerly included in the British Commonwealth.)

If you grant British rights to the American publisher, you should receive the lion's share of the proceeds from a British license. The usual split is 75 percent, although it can be as low as two thirds and as high as 80 percent. Note that the subsidiary rights granted the British publisher will include the same kinds of rights held by the American publisher, such as book-club or mass-market reprint.

Some contracts make the rights revocable to the author eighteen months after publication of the American edition. In other words, if you grant British rights to your American publisher and a license is not arranged within eighteen months of American publication, British rights automatically revert to you. This is an unusual but very desirable clause.

Foreign-language rights. This is also sometimes referred to as translation rights, since the rights are usually sold by language without a further breakdown by country. If you grant these rights to your publisher, the split is usually the same as that for British rights. Some contracts make these rights revocable to the author if no license or option has been obtained within three years of publication.

Free rights. There are a number of uses of your work that are customarily granted without charge. One is transcription or publication in Braille or other forms for the physically handicapped; the other is publication or broadcast for publicity purposes, such as an excerpt in a book review or the use of up to 7,500 words for the purpose of advertising and promoting a film based on the work.

The "Pass-Through" Clause. The income from a subsidiary-rights license negotiated by your publisher is normally held by the publisher until the next royalty period, and then is paid to you along with any royalties earned from sales (assuming your advance has been "earned out"). However, you may be able to get the publisher to agree to pay out your share of rights income within two to four weeks after receipt if your account is earned out.

Approval. You may wish to negotiate for the right of approval of any subsidiary-rights license negotiated by your publisher.

The Advance and Royalties

Most publishers work on a royalty basis, although some publishers prefer to pay a flat fee for the copyright to the book. The discussion following relates only to royalty contracts.

The Advance. The advance against royalties will have been negotiated before the contract was drawn up. It is unlikely that you will be able to get the publisher to increase it at this point. However, the schedule of payments may not have been discussed. Arrangements vary from house to house. Many trade publishers pay one half of the advance on signing of the contract and one half on delivery and acceptance of the final manuscript. Others pay one third on signing, one third on delivery and acceptance of the first half of the manuscript, and the rest on delivery and acceptance of the last half; while still others defer payment of the last portion of the advance until publication. The arrangement selected usually depends on how far along you are with the book, how much money is involved (a large advance is usually spread out over several installments), and so on.

The advance is essentially a loan against future earnings, and you will not receive any additional payments until the advance has been paid off. However, after the book is published you will not be expected to repay any portion of the advance, even though your earnings from sales and subsidiary rights may not equal the amount of the advance—that is, the advance is not earned out.

Royalties on Regular Sales. When editors negotiate royalty rates, they are usually referring to royalties on hardcover copies sold to the trade. The usual rate for a hardcover book is 10 percent of the cover price on the first 5,000 or 7,500 copies sold, 12½ percent on the next 2,500 or 5,000 copies sold, and 15 percent on subsequent copies sold. Any other rate scale should be resisted—unless, of course, it's better than this scale, or unless there's a clear reason for a lower rate. Some publishers pay on net income rather than on cover price, but this is usually only for books sold to the institutional market at a low discount. In this case, the base royalty is likely to be 15 percent.

Trade Paperback Royalties. The rates paid for a trade paperback vary quite a bit, depending on the nature of the book, the policies of the house, and so on. The minimum usually starts at somewhere between 6 percent and 7½ percent, perhaps increasing to 9 percent or 10 percent after a certain number of copies have been sold. The intervals between rates are also likely to be wider than for trade hardcover; for example, the publisher may pay 6 percent of the cover price to 20,000 copies, 7½ percent to 75,000 copies, and 10 percent after that.

"Cheap" Hardcover Editions. Another possibility is a lower-priced hardcover edition. Hardcover reprints are less common since the advent of paperbacks, but a few houses continue to publish them, primarily for the remainder book trade. The usual royalty rate is 5 percent of the cheap-edition price, or half the "prevailing" royalty rate (e.g., the royalty rate you are currently receiving). Some contracts stipulate that the price of a cheap hardcover must be one half or less than the current retail price of the regular edition, and that such an edition cannot be published until at least one year after publication of the more expensive edition.

Textbook Editions. Many publishers do not publish textbooks, so this clause would not appear in the contract. Others do, however, and their contract should specify the royalties you would receive if your book were revised for sale as a college or school textbook.

Mass-Market Paperback Editions. In most cases, a trade book publisher does not have its own mass-market line and therefore will be given the right to negotiate a mass-market paperback license only as part of the "subsidiary rights" for the book (as discussed earlier in this chapter). In this case, the advance and royalties from such a license will be *split* between you and the publisher. In other cases, the trade house will arrange to buy the mass-market rights jointly with its own paperback subsidiary, such as Random House might do with Ballantine Books, or will make arrangements to buy the rights jointly with an "outside" paperback house, such as Morrow often does with Avon (they are both, incidentally, owned by Hearst); in this case, it is called a "hard/soft" deal. Or a mass-market house with a trade hardcover line may buy the volume rights to the book, or a mass-market house like Dell may buy the paperback rights on condition that Delacorte will do the hardcover edition.

In any of these permutations, the royalty rate for the mass-market edition will be specified in the original publishing contract, and you will receive the full royalty rather than a split. The normal royalty starts at 6, 7, or 8 percent, possibly increasing to 9 or 10 percent after a certain number of copies have been sold.

Mail-Order Sales. Any copy sold directly to a consumer as the result of a coupon ad run in a newspaper or magazine, or a mailing sent to the customer's home, is called a "mail-order" sale. An order which results from radio or television advertising in which the buyer is instructed to send cash or money order to a particular address is also considered a mail-order sale, however, so it's probably more accurate to call these sales direct-to-consumer sales.

Whatever they are called, though, the royalty paid on such sales is usually 5 percent of what the publisher charges the customer for the book (which may be the full retail price or a slightly discounted price). The rationale for the lower royalty is that the costs of such advertising are high, and it is not feasible for the publisher to try to reach these buyers unless the author is willing to accept a lower royalty. This is probably not a negotiable point with most publishers.

Export Sales. Copies sold to customers outside the United States are called export sales, and generally carry a lower royalty because of the expenses involved in making such sales. The usual royalty is either 10 percent of the amount *received* by the publisher, or one half the rate currently applicable in regular sales. There may be a separate scale for copies sold in Canada, such as two thirds of the prevailing rate.

Premium Sales. Certain customers buy books from publishers in order to offer them as "premiums" for their own customers. For example, an educational television channel may give away books to people who contribute a certain amount of money to the station, or a bank may offer a book on money management to people who open a checking account. The royalty you receive on such premium sales is usually 5 percent of the *amount received* by the publisher, because the books are normally sold to the premium customer at a high discount. The same rate also usually applies to books sold by subscription.

Special Sales. Some contracts lump "special" sales together with premium sales, although they usually mean slightly different things. The Random House contract (see Appendix B) defines special sales as copies sold outside normal wholesale and retail trade channels. For example, a book on tennis might be sold to sporting goods wholesalers and retailers. Since the publisher does not have the costs of maintaining a regular "account" for most of these customers, he will probably sell the copies at a relatively high discount (say, more than 50 percent) but will not allow the buyer to return unsold copies for credit. Since the discount is so high, a lower royalty rate is usually applied on special sales, typically either 10 percent of the net amount received by the publisher or one half the prevailing royalty rate on regular sales.

Other Adjustments on Royalty Payments. There are various situations in which the royalty received on a sale is reduced or withheld entirely:

1. The publisher elects to establish a "reserve for returns." This means he anticipates that some of the copies sold to retailers and wholesalers will not be sold to the public, and will be returned by the dealers to the publisher for credit. To avoid paying you a royalty on sales that ultimately turn out to be credits, he may not show all "sales" to dealers on your royalty statement. This practice is usually *not* stated explicitly in the contract. Ask your editor if the publisher takes reserves on sales, and how high that reserve typically is. The Authors Guild recommends that it be limited to 15 percent of the total sales for that period.

2. The royalty rate on regular sales may be reduced if semiannual sales fall below a certain level, making it more difficult for the publisher to keep the book in print. Some publishers reduce the rate to two thirds of the current rate if semiannual sales are less than four hundred copies *and* these copies are sold from a second or subsequent printing; others reduce it to one half the current rate and have a higher maximum, say, five hundred copies.

3. You will receive *no* royalty on books that you are given free by the publisher, or that are used for the purposes of advertising and promotion, or that are given free to the handicapped. You will also be denied a royalty on books that are

sold to a remainder dealer at less than the "unit cost," or cost of printing and binding the book. For example, if the book cost $1.25 to manufacture and the highest bid the publisher gets from a remainder dealer is 75¢ per copy, you will receive no royalties on these remainder sales. If you want the opportunity to buy some copies at a low price and before they go out of print, ask for a clause giving you the option to purchase copies at either the unit price or the price paid by the remainder dealer.

Royalty Reports and Payments

After your book has been published, you will start receiving a "royalty report" summarizing sales, subsidiary-rights income, and costs associated with the book during a specified period. Most publishers produce these reports semi-annually. However, surprising as it seems in this era of computerization, it usually takes the publisher's accounting department three or four months to gather the data and prepare the reports, so if the royalty period runs from January 1 to June 30, you will get your statement for that period some time in September or October. Similarly, the statement for the period running from July 1 to December 31 is not usually sent out until March or April. The contract should specify the dates when royalty reports are to be mailed; if not, find out when they should be mailed and then note that date on your calendar.

Some contracts stipulate that you will not receive a payment if your earnings during a royalty period are below a certain minimum, say, $10. It's probably not worth fighting about; the money is not going to make much difference in your life.

Here are some other possibilities worth noting:

1. The contract may stipulate that if you receive an *overpayment* of royalties because copies originally credited as sales are returned, the publisher may deduct such overpayments on subsequent royalty statements.

2. The contract may give you the right to inspect the publisher's books insofar as they relate to the sale and licensing of your book. This is a good clause to have, and you may ask to have it inserted if it does not already appear in the con-

tract. However, note that it is often coupled with a clause making royalty statements binding within a year, so that failure to exercise your right to audit in that time will end your right to correct a wrong accounting much sooner than otherwise. Ask your accountant for advice if you're not sure what to do.

3. The contract may have a "limitation of income" clause. This will specifically limit the amount of money that the publisher will pay you in one calendar year, the purpose being to keep your taxable income at a certain level. However, such an arrangement is strictly voluntary, and there are probably better options available to you. See Chapter 9 for more discussion on this point.

Author's Warranties and Guarantees

The publication of a book can involve various legal hazards (discussed in more detail in Chapter 5) that publishers try to protect themselves from in various ways. One way is to have their editors look for potential legal problems in a manuscript, so that if the risk seems grave enough, they can arrange to have the manuscript "vetted" (usually at the publisher's expense) by an experienced libel lawyer. Another form of protection are the "warranty" and "indemnity" clauses in the contract with the author.

The Warranty. The warranty usually includes the following assurances:

1. That you are the bona fide and sole proprietor of the rights to this work, and have the legal right to enter this agreement. If you are under age or if you already have transferred any of the exclusive rights being granted to the publisher to someone else, for example, the present contract is invalid. You will be required to repay any advances you have received from the publisher, and you will be responsible if the publisher is sued.

2. That the work is original, has not been published before, and is not in the "public domain." A work is in the public domain if it has no copyright protection.

3. That you have not used any materials protected by copyright without the formal permission of the copyright

owner, and have not "infringed" on any material protected by someone else's copyright. (To infringe is to make unlawful use of someone else's material.)

4. That the work does not violate certain rights of individuals guaranteed by law, such as the right not to be libeled, the right of confidentiality, and the right of privacy.

5. That any instructions, recipes, or formulas contained in the work will not be injurious to the user.

Some authors have tried to soften this warranty by adding a phrase such as "to the best of my knowledge." However, this does not really constitute any legal protection, and probably should be forgone.

The Indemnity. The indemnity clause spells out what will happen in the event of a claim or lawsuit against the book. Such claims are usually brought against the author, the publisher, *and* any major distributors. The indemnity is likely to include the following provisions:

1. The publisher will notify the author promptly of any "claim, action, or proceeding" and the author will be required to "fully cooperate in the defense thereof." In other words, you must take part in the case. However, what you *can* negotiate is the right to have your own counsel at your own expense in the event of a lawsuit, if you wish to do so.

2. The publishing company has the right to defend against the claim and to use its own lawyers in doing so.

3. The publisher may elect to "settle" the claim out of court; that is, a private agreement will be reached with the person or persons bringing the suit against the book. Probably 90 percent of all such claims are settled out of court, and even if the claim is based on flimsy grounds, the publisher may elect to pay the plaintiff a certain amount of money rather than going through the expense of a trial.

The Random House contract (Appendix B) makes such an out-of-court settlement subject to the author's approval, although such approval cannot be "unreasonably" withheld. Such a consent clause is fairly unusual but is an excellent protection for you, and I recommend that you try to get this if possible. You may also be able to get the publisher to agree that you will be responsible for the costs of such a settlement *only* if the settlement is reached with your consent. You might even be able to get the publisher to agree to split the costs for "nuisance suits" that amount to $10,000 or less.

4. If the case goes to court, the publisher plus anyone else named in the suit will be "held harmless"—that is, only you will be responsible for paying attorney's fees plus "damages."*

Try to have this clause modified so that you will be responsible for these costs only if the judgment is "finally sustained" even after appeal, and that the costs will be *split* if the case is won.

5. If the publisher owes you money, he has the right to withhold payments until the claim is settled. Most contracts allow the publisher to withhold unlimited amounts for unlimited periods of time. The Authors Guild recommends that the amount be limited to the damages claimed by the plaintiff plus the anticipated cost of legal fees, and that the money be held in an interest-bearing account. Other contracts say that the publisher has the right to withhold "reasonable" amounts. Either of these last two alternatives is acceptable.

6. The warranties and indemnities will "survive the termination of the agreement." For example, if the publisher "reverts" the rights to you some time in the future and then a suit is brought, you as the author are still liable. This is also a standard clause, and there's probably not much you can do about it.

Some Comments about Libel Insurance. The Authors Guild and other writers' advocate groups have campaigned vigorously to have warranty and indemnity clauses removed from publishing contracts. Publishers are fiercely resistant to this suggestion, however, because they feel they must have protection from careless authors and litigious readers, particularly when a highly commercial book is involved. It's extremely unlikely that your publisher will consider dropping either of these clauses. If you think there is a high risk of a

---

*There are three classes of damages in libel cases: (1) General or "compensatory" damages for injury to reputation. The victim does not even have to show damages. The amount of the award is decided by the jury, but may be adjusted by the court. (2) "Special" damages which represent actual pecuniary loss suffered because of the libel. The victim must prove damages precisely. (3) "Punitive" damages assigned to punish past libel and discourage any further malice. These are usually only awarded when a high degree of fault is found by the court.

lawsuit, you should consider the possibility of carrying libel insurance. The premiums are high, but it may be worth it.

Another option is to try to find a publisher that provides its authors with free comprehensive liability insurance coverage. Viking Penguin was the first trade publisher to take such a step, and several other publishers have followed its lead, among them Bantam, Warner, and Little, Brown. The terms of the coverage vary, but in most cases, authors, illustrators, and photographers are protected against loss caused by libel, slander, invasion of privacy, plagiarism, copyright infringement, or unfair competition. The coverage will go into effect only when legal action is taken and only when costs exceed the deductible, which is usually at the $25,000 level. In the case of the Viking Penguin policy, the first $2,000 of any loss will be shared equally by the author and Viking Penguin; the next $23,000 will be assumed by Viking Penguin. Costs above $25,000 will be borne by Employers Reinsurance Corporation. The maximum loss covered by the policy in any one year is $3 million.

Copyright Procedures

You hold the copyright to your work (unless you are working as an author-for-hire or are sharing the copyright with someone). What the publisher does is establish your *claim* to that copyright by running a copyright "notice" with your name, the symbol © or the word "Copyright" or abbreviation "Copr.," and the year of publication in the book, and by registering the work with the U.S. Copyright Office in Washington, D.C. However, there are a few situations you should know about:

1. The book should be registered with the Copyright Office within three months of publication, because this gives you better protection in the event that someone uses your material extensively without getting permission from you. In this case, if either you or your publisher brings suit for infringement, and you win, the infringer will be liable for damages as well as for legal fees. If the book is registered more than three months after publication but before five years have passed, damages will be limited to the amount of money the infringer made by selling illegal copies of your work.

Participation in a copyright infringement suit is voluntary. In most contracts, either you or your publisher may bring suit against an infringer and may do so in the other party's name. The party bringing the suit then pays all expenses and retains all monies recovered for itself. If the parties agree to proceed jointly, all expenses and recovery will be shared.

2. The publisher *may* claim copyright to the work in its own name rather than in yours. If the book is published anonymously, for example, you will want the copyright to be registered in the publisher's name. However, there are few instances where such registration in the publisher's name is justifiable, and you should resist the suggestion unless there is a very strong reason for it. If the publisher does register the copyright in its own name, specific provision should be made for the reversion of copyright to you if the book goes out of print or the rights revert to you for some other reason. If the publisher provided illustrations or other material for the book, the copyright to these items should also become part of *your* copyright when the rights are reverted.

3. If a portion of your book appeared in a magazine or newspaper before book publication and is not protected by a copyright notice in your name, you will be required to get a document from the periodical assigning the copyright in that material to you. (This often happens with magazines which run one copyright notice in the name of the magazine for all the material in the magazine.) Your book publisher will then file that copyright assignment with the Copyright Office.

4. Similarly, if your book was published outside of the United States before publication of the American edition, you will be required to furnish the American publisher with one copy of the "foreign" edition, plus the date of publication and information about the place of manufacture so that this material can be included with registration of the U.S. edition.

Editing and Proofreading

After your manuscript has been accepted as satisfactory by your editor, it will be edited and copyedited before being set in type. This editing is usually not mentioned in the contract, but you should be aware that changes may be made in the manuscript without your knowledge. If you are particularly concerned about this, insist that you see the copyedited manuscript *before* it is released for typesetting.

After the manuscript has been set in type, you will be given a set of galley proofs to check. The contract will probably state that you are to read and return these proofs to the publisher "promptly," and that if you fail to do so, the publisher will make any corrections necessary and proceed with the production schedule. Make certain that a clause requiring you to read galley proofs is in the contract; some publishers don't show proofs to the author until much too late in the process.

Many publishers allow an author to make changes in proofs up to 10 or 15 percent of the initial composition cost without charge. This allowance is important because almost every author makes a certain number of changes in proof and resetting can be costly. Obviously, the 15 percent allowance is preferable to the 10 percent one if you have any choice in the matter.

Most publishers deduct the cost of "AA's" (author's alterations) from your royalty earnings. You probably won't see the bills on which these charges are based unless you specifically ask to see them and/or the proofs on which the changes were made. Ask your editor how charges for author's alterations are handled; it's probably not necessary to modify the contract on this point.

Date, Style, and Manner of Publication

When you sign a contract with a publisher, you are "leasing" the use of your "invention" to the publisher, just as an inventor might license a manufacturer to reproduce and sell copies of his invention. Such a leasing arrangement usually stipulates that the manufacturer may produce and market the product in the manner he thinks best—which means that you're not going to have much say in the matter. In the case of a publishing arrangement, the "style and manner" of publication usually involves the following elements:

The publication date. Many contracts indicate that the book will be published "within a reasonable time" after delivery and acceptance of the final manuscript, except for delays caused by "any circumstances beyond its control." (This is called the "force majeur" clause, and applies to such things as fire, flood, union action, and acts of God.) If you want to put a limitation on the length of time until publication, ask for a twelve- or eighteen-month limitation. It is usually not possible to publish a book much faster than a year after delivery and acceptance of the manuscript because of the time required to produce the book, prepare catalogs, and so forth.

The design and format of the book, that is, the typeface used, the paper and binding materials, the trim size, and so on. If you have some expertise in this area or are particularly important to the house, the publisher *may* give you the right to "consult" on jacket art and/or book design.

The cover price. The publisher will select a price that will allow him to recover his costs and compete successfully in the marketplace.

The size of the first printing, and of any subsequent reprints.

The amount of money allocated to advertise and promote the book, and the way in which this money will be spent. Most publishers allocate about 10 percent of the projected net revenues from the book for this purpose, but there is usually no *guarantee* that any particular amount of money will be spent on advertising and promotion, unless you can negotiate a clause to that effect. If you are particularly concerned about "space" advertisements in magazines and newspapers, you might make this part of the guaranteed-advertising clause.

The use of your likeness. There may also be a clause giving the publisher the explicit right to use your "image or likeness" in promoting the book. It's common to use the author's photograph on the jacket flaps and in promoting the book, so if you *don't* want this, you should specifically prohibit it. Note also that it is usually the author's responsibility to provide a photograph. That means you have to pay for it, and get permission from the photographer to use it on the jacket and in advertisements.

Insertion of advertisements. Some contracts permit the publisher to insert advertisements for other books in your book, although this usually happens only with mass-market paperbacks. If you have any reason to worry about this, you might ask to have a clause inserted specifically forbidding it, or at least restricting such advertisements to other books published by that house.

Note, however, that the publisher *does* have the obligation to publish the book in "good faith." In a recent court case, the author of an unflattering book about the du Pont family sued his publisher (Prentice-Hall) and the Du Pont Company on the grounds that pressure from the company had caused P-H to cut back its press run and ad budget for the book. A federal court of appeals upheld the publisher's claim that it had acted "fairly, reasonably, and responsibly in publishing and promoting the book, and that all of its actions were taken for legitimate business reasons," but also asserted that a publisher has to make "a good faith effort to promote the book including a first printing and advertising budget adequate to give the book a reasonable chance of achieving market success in light of the subject matter and likely audience." These are fairly ambiguous terms, but they do indicate that the publisher must have sound business reasons for the marketing decisions made about a book.

Author's Copies

Most publishers give the author a certain number of free copies of his book, usually ten in the case of hardcover and fifteen or twenty in the case of a trade paperback. If yours is a nonfiction book and you expect to ask a lot of people for help in preparing it, you might ask the publisher to increase your allotment.

You should also be allowed to buy additional copies of your book at a discount. The usual discount is 40 percent—the discount normally offered retailers for small orders. You will receive your usual royalty on every copy you buy. It's generally understood that you are buying these copies for your own personal use and not for resale. However, most publishers will not seriously object if you sell copies at lectures or speaking engagements that you have arranged on your own. You may want to ask your editor if there is any specific prohibition against doing this.

Author's Property

The contract may specifically say that the publisher is not responsible for loss or damage to your property unless it is due to the publisher's own negligence. Most contracts do not have this clause, though, so the question of liablility in the event of loss may be difficult to determine. To protect yourself, you should retain good duplicate copies of everything you send to the publisher. Also make sure that you will get your original photographs and other similar materials back *after* publication, particularly if they were not your own property to start with.

The Option Clause

Most publishing contracts have a clause which gives the publisher an "option" to publish your next book, on terms to be mutually agreed on. This is not a very binding requirement, however, since it does not specify the *terms* under which the publisher might acquire the rights. Nonetheless, most publishers continue to have an option clause in their contracts, since it gives them a chance to bid on a book by an author that they have invested in before. You may wish to ask the publisher to narrow the scope of the option clause by specifying the following:

1. The type of work to which the option clause applies. Instead of your "next work," it might be limited to your next work of fiction or nonfiction or of a specific genre. If you are a prolific author using one or more pseudonyms, it might be limited to your next work written under a specific pseudonym.

2. The extent and type of material to be furnished to the publisher. For example, you probably don't want to be obligated to furnish a complete manuscript before the publisher makes his decision, so you might want the contract to stipulate that the publisher will make his decision on the basis of a proposal rather than a complete manuscript.

3. The amount of time the publisher has to consider your submission. This should be no longer than sixty days in most instances, and the beginning of this period should *not* be tied to the publication of the book presently under contract. The Random House contract in Appendix B stipulates that the period should not commence earlier than one month prior to the publication date of the present book. I think this is too

limiting, and should be changed to something like "no earlier than three months after the publisher's acceptance of the present work." Furthermore, negotiations should be limited to thirty days from the date they started.

The publisher *may* stipulate that if you enter into a contract with another publisher, the terms have to be more favorable than those offered for the optioned work by the present publisher. This can be a problem, since you probably wouldn't be looking for another publisher unless you were unhappy with the first, yet you may not be able to find one willing to pay you more. Try to have this clause stricken if possible.

The Conflicting-Work Clause

Many contracts have a clause which prohibits the author from publishing a "similar work" during a specified period of time, ranging from the "life of the agreement" to a much shorter period, such as nine months or a year after publication.

If you do anticipate writing another book on the same general topic for another publisher, you should ask for a short time limit and/or make the language in regard to a "similar" work more explicit. For example, the restriction might be limited to works written from the same point of view, or a work that would *directly* compete with the work presently being contracted for. Thus, if the present book is on the care and feeding of Great Danes, you could agree not to write another book about Great Danes for another publisher, but reserve the right to write about other breeds, such as Schnauzers.

You should be aware, however, that most publishers reserve the right to publish other books on the same subject themselves—although this may not be explicitly stated in the contract. Most publishers try to avoid this, because they are then competing with themselves, but there have been instances where the same publisher has brought out two or three books on a similar topic within a short period of time. This *can* have a depressing effect on the earnings of the authors of these books.

A Revised Edition

Although it is fairly unusual, trade books are occasionally revised and updated for redistribution to the trade, or revised for publication in a different market, such as a textbook for sale to schools or colleges. Most trade contracts make these revisions your responsibility. If you are unwilling or unable to do the work within a "reasonable" period of time, the publisher will probably reserve the right to hire someone else to make the revisions. Furthermore, this revision may be published under your name, as though you had done the work, although some protection is available through laws against misrepresentation of the authorship of a work. The best tactic is to try to get any clauses regarding revisions stricken from the contract. Then if the publisher wants to issue a revised edition, you can negotiate terms at that point.

Discontinuance of Publication and Reversion of Rights

The granting of rights to a publisher implies that the publisher has these rights throughout the term of copyright. However, there are two ways that you can get the rights held by the publisher back *before* the term of copyright expires:

1. If your book was published after the new copyright law went into effect on January 1, 1978, you have the right to demand your rights back either thirty-five years after publication or forty years after the date of the contract, whichever is earlier. (Since this is some time off, I won't give detailed procedures for this now.)

2. The book goes out of print, and your publisher doesn't wish to put it back into print. "In print" may be defined in a variety of ways. Some contracts say that a work is considered in print if *any* edition (including a licensed edition) is in print, or if the book is under *license* to another publisher, or under *option* to another publisher. This obviously gives your publisher a great deal of latitude, and I would recommend that at least the phrase relating to an option be dropped.

The Random House contract (Appendix B) clearly spells out the procedure for reverting rights, and provides a good model for other contracts:

1. It is the author's responsibility to demand that the work be put back into print. Practically all publishers do make this the author's responsibility. Find out from your editor the usual procedure.

2. The publisher has sixty days to notify you that he intends to comply with your request. There should be a limit on how much time the publisher has to consider your request.

3. The book must be reprinted within six months of the date of your request unless there are circumstances beyond the publisher's control. Some contracts give the publisher eighteen months to arrange for a "reprint" edition by another publisher, which is much too long. The publisher should take no longer than one year to get a new edition into the works.

4. If the publisher fails to meet the first two requirements above, the publishing agreement will terminate and all rights held by the publisher will revert to you though the publisher still retains his option on your next book. However, before the reversion "goes through," you will have to pay the publisher any sums you owe him except for an unearned advance against royalties. Furthermore, any subsidiary-rights license continues to be in effect for the length of its term, and the publisher will continue to have the right to receive his share of earnings from such licenses.

5. After termination, you should have the opportunity (for at least thirty days) to purchase the publisher's printing plates or the film used to make the plates, at an agreed-upon and "reasonable" price. Random House sets this price at one quarter of the cost.

Publisher's Bankruptcy

Although it is an unpleasant prospect, you should be aware that publishers can and do go bankrupt. The contract may contain a clause stipulating that if the publisher goes bankrupt or liquidates its assets for some other reason, your rights revert to you and you have the opportunity to buy bound copies or any production materials at their "fair market value," as determined by mutual agreement or as specified in the contract. However, there is a new bankruptcy law that may make such a clause substantially ineffective. You may want to discuss this question with an attorney. A "breach of contract" clause would probably be more effective in terms of getting your rights back from a publisher who is on the verge of bankruptcy. Thus, *any* breach (such as the publisher's inability to pay sums due you) would enable you to get your rights back.

Clauses Relating to the Agreement Itself

Finally, there should be a number of clauses relating to the agreement itself:

Assignment. The contract should state that the agreement will be "binding upon and inure to the benefit of the heirs, executors, administrators, or assigns of the author and the successors or assigns of the publisher." This means that when you die, your heirs will continue to receive the benefits of this contract and also will assume its obligations. Similarly, if the assets of the publisher are sold to someone else, the agreement will remain binding on that purchaser. Furthermore, the contract will probably stipulate that you cannot "assign" any part of this agreement without the prior written approval of the publisher, but that the publisher can assign it without your consent. This is a normal provision in virtually all contracts of any kind.

Modifications. The contract should state that this document constitutes the "whole understanding" of both parties, and cannot be changed except by the written consent of both parties. What this means is that if you and the publisher had any prior agreements in regard to the work, those agreements are invalidated by this new agreement.

State Law. Contracts are interpreted according to the laws of the state specified. This is usually the state where the publisher has his offices, but *may* be where the author resides.

These are all the clauses that should be in your publishing agreement, or at least understood before you sign it. There are many other clauses that can be added to the contract as "riders," of course, and if you have a literary agent, an agency clause will also be part of the contract.

The one thing to remember in all this is that there is an "implied covenant of fair dealing and good faith." The contract spells out the conditions of the agreement, but the good faith has to come from you and your publishing partner. Most publishers are not only honest, they *want* to be fair to their authors. It's important to avoid an adversary attitude on your part, because in the long run all it can do is injure the relationship between you and the publisher. Sign the contract—and then get on to the much more important business of finishing the book and getting it published.

4

Putting the
Final Manuscript
Together

I love being a writer. What I can't stand is the paperwork.
—PETER DE VRIES

Putting your final manuscript together may be more complicated than you had anticipated. Not only do you have to *write* the book, you also have to worry about lawsuits for libel, invasion of privacy, or other infringements of the rights of others; you have to obtain formal permission to use copyrighted material if your use of it is fairly extensive; you may have to round up suitable illustrations; and you have to type the final manuscript in a way that is acceptable to the publisher. *Then* you have to worry whether the "final revised" manuscript will be deemed "satisfactory" by the house.

This chapter gives some practical advice on how to approach these problems and turns the spotlight on an editor's role in helping you solve them.

The Role of Your Editor

The essential function of an editor is to help you write the best book possible *within the guidelines* of the house's expectations for the book and the length and delivery-date requirements. In other words, when you sign a contract with a publisher, you are agreeing to deliver the manuscript the publisher has contracted for. This means that at least part of the control has passed from your hands to those of an editor.

A good editor can be very helpful in shaping the final book and in acting as an intelligent first reader for draft material. You may not agree with every one of his or her suggestions, but it is important to be open to them, both because you'll probably end up writing a better book—and because this is the person you're going to have to satisfy in the long run.

Discussions about changes that the editor would like you to make probably took place before the contract was signed, and may have already been specified in a letter. Once the contract is signed, however, it is essential that you have another talk with the editor to make certain that you understand what she wishes you to do. This is particularly important in the case of nonfiction, where the editor may have specific suggestions to make about the organization, flow, and scope of the material. But even in the case of fiction, the editor may have very specific suggestions about plotting, characterization, voice, and so on that you should pay heed to.

Don't expect the editor to write the book for you, however. Some authors have a vision of working with their editor much as Thomas Wolfe did with the great Maxwell Perkins, poring over and shaping every line. That *may* happen once the manuscript is in, but at this point your responsibility is to get the book *done* and in line with the house's expectations for it.

The editor who acquired the rights to your book may turn the "line editing" over to a junior editor. This may be acceptable—especially if the line editor has more time to work closely with you than the acquiring editor would—but the possibility of such an arrangement should be made clear to you *before* the contract is signed. You may also want the right to veto the arrangement, or at least to be consulted on who the new editor would be.

It may also happen that the editor you've been working with changes jobs, gets fired, or decides to become a clam fisherman before the book is done. There's not much you can do about this *unless* the editor is taking a job in a different publishing house and wants to take your book with her. Your current publisher may or may not be amenable to this. In the event that the original publisher is willing to let the book go, the contract will be "assigned" to the new house and they will pay the original purchaser the amount of money you have already received as an advance. If you don't want to go with your editor, or the current publisher doesn't want to let you go, you will be assigned a new editor.

Be sure to allow yourself enough time to write and revise the manuscript. Many authors overestimate the pace of their work, so if you see that you're running late, let your editor know and ask for a formal extension of the delivery date if possible.

Some Legal Hazards

Writing a book can be very hazardous because under the warranty and indemnity clauses of your contract with your publisher you are responsible for any claims or lawsuits for libel, invasion of privacy, etc., that may arise as a result of the publication of your book. Most writers know very little about this area, and must rely on their editor and their publisher's legal counsel for guidance as to which material might be actionable. In those cases where the legal danger seems high, the publisher will arrange to have the manuscript "vetted" by an experienced libel lawyer to determine whether your backup material is sufficient to support the statements that you make, or whether the manuscript should be modified to reduce the risk of a claim or suit. Most claims are settled out of court, but handling any claim takes time and money, and a prudent publisher will take steps to ensure that the risk associated with your manuscript is within reasonable boundaries.

Libel. The First Amendment to the Constitution of the United States says that "Congress shall make no law . . . abridging the freedom of speech or of the press"—a guarantee echoed by the constitutions of many state and local governments. Yet this guarantee is not intended to permit citizens to say whatever they want. Just as it is illegal to shout "Fire!" in a crowded theater, so is it illegal to make statements that infringe on the rights of other persons.

A libelous statement is one that is *defamatory* in nature; that is, one that injures a person's *reputation*. Each state defines this somewhat differently. The State of New York defines libel as a "malicious publication which exposes any living person . . . to hatred, contempt, ridicule or obloquy, or which has a tendency to injure any person, corporation or association of persons, in his or their business or occupation."

It is sometimes difficult to determine whether a statement is libelous or not, since the *nature* of the person's reputation and the *context* in which the statement is made are both taken into account. However, certain types of statements are usually considered to be libelous *per se,* such as the claim that a woman is "unchaste" or that someone has committed a crime, has a "loathsome" disease, or is incompetent or dishonest in his/her business or profession.

Generally speaking, a successful libel suit must establish that (1) the statement was defamatory, (2) it was false, (3) it was "of and concerning" (that is, *about*) the living person claiming to be libeled, (4) it was "published" and with "fault," and (5) it caused actual injury to the plaintiff. Thus, for example, if you state in your book that Dr. X was responsible for the death of a patient, you had either better be able to prove this allegation (by means of newspaper accounts of his trial and conviction, or the like), or else you had better disguise his identity so that Dr. X cannot claim that this statement was "of and about" him, was libelous, and caused him injury.

In most cases, the person claiming libel must prove not only that the statement was not completely true in every particular, but it was "substantially false in its material elements." However, a person classified as a "public official" must also prove that the statement was made with "actual malice"—that is, with "knowledge that it was false" or with "reckless disregard" of whether it was false or not. The definition of who is a public official is not entirely clear, but seems to include only those who have "substantial responsibility for or control over the conduct of government affairs." This has included a mayor, city commissioner, police chief, etc., but has not (at least in some cases) included a public high school teacher.

The "actual malice" test also applies to those persons deemed to be a "public figure . . . for all purposes and in all contexts" (examples have included Johnny Carson, William F. Buckley, etc.) or a person who "voluntarily injects himself or is drawn into a particular public controversy and thereby becomes a public figure for a limited range of issues." (This latter category is sometimes referred to as a "vortex" public figure.) As in the stipulations regarding public figures, the purpose of such a rule is to allow the free exchange of ideas on matters of public interest that is so necessary to a free society. But it is sometimes difficult to determine if an individual is in fact a public figure in the sense meant by the Supreme Court ruling. In most cases, the final decision is made by the courts in the state where the libel occurred.

Invasion of Privacy. Sometimes it's difficult to tell whether a statement or group of statements about an individual is libelous or an "invasion of privacy." This right has been defined as an individual's "right to be let alone; to live one's life as one chooses, free from assault, intrusion or invasion as they can be justified by the clear needs of community living under a government of law." Invasion of privacy is usually broken down into four main categories:

• The public disclosure of *private and embarrassing facts*. For example, you may comment that someone is seeing a psychiatrist, or is "living with" someone else, or is a former safecracker. Even if all these statements are true, you are opening yourself up to an invasion-of-privacy suit unless that person has given you permission to make such disclosures.

• Placing someone in a *false light* "which would be highly offensive to a reasonable person" by embellishing, fictionalizing, or distorting certain facts. For example, if you report that two people were seen having a conversation "about" something but you were not actually present during that conversation, you can be sued under the false-light concept—even though the conversation may in fact have taken place.

• *Misappropriation* of a well-known person's right to benefit from commercial exploitation of his name. For example, if you make a famous rock-and-roll star a character in your novel, you may be infringing on his "right to publicity."

• Invasion by means of intrusion—that is, obtaining private information through unlawful means or "wrongful conduct," such as wiretapping.

One of the crucial differences between an invasion of privacy "tort" (wrongful act or damage for which a civil suit can be brought) and a libel tort is that *truth is no defense* in a privacy suit. Even if what you say is true, you can still be sued for invasion of privacy, especially under the false-light and embarrassing-facts concepts.

Some Strategies in Writing Nonfiction. It can be difficult to protect against a lawsuit for libel or invasion of privacy because complete accuracy is sometimes impossible, because different people can view the truth differently, and because some individuals will bring a suit not because it is justified but because they wish to gain publicity or harass the writer or publisher. The exact precautions you should take against such lawsuits will depend on the book you are writing. The risks you run in writing an autobiography, for example, are slightly different from those you run when you are writing some sort of exposé. Nonetheless, here are some rules of thumb to keep in mind when you are gathering information for your book.

1. If you are interviewing people for the purpose of gathering information, tell them *ahead* of time what you're doing. Ask them to sign a release form giving you permission to use any information that they have provided in your book. (Ask your editor for such a form.) If you interviewed someone before you had the book contract, ask him to sign a release now to cover the material that you obtained earlier.

A release should be "irrevocable"—meaning that the person can't later withdraw consent for you to use the material. Furthermore, you should avoid agreeing to show the interviewee the material you write, by using the argument that you are gathering information from many sources and must be free to form your own interpretation. Finally, to give the release the status of a contract, you may wish to pay the interviewee a fee, or promise to provide him with a copy of the finished book.

Another possibility is to tape-record the interview, clearly identifying who is speaking, the date of the interview, etc. Then if the person denies later that he made a particular statement, you have the evidence to disprove his claim.

Also evaluate this source of information from the point of view of reliability. If you have some reason to doubt a statement, or feel that it should be buttressed by the statements of others, speak to other people on the subject. If the person being interviewed is saying critical things about someone else, you might want to call that third party and solicit his opinion, being careful not to identify the source of your information, of course.

2. If you are relying on printed material, keep complete records of the places where you have gathered information—books, magazine and newspaper articles, etc. If you are dealing with a topic that is very sensitive, try to gather two or three corroborating sources. Try to make sure they are reputable ones. The *New York Times* is regarded as a much more reliable and reputable source than the *National Enquirer,* for example.

3. Be aware that children present special difficulties. It is very difficult to get legally binding consents from or on behalf of minors, so the best course here is to change identifying details such as name, physical appearance, location, etc., for any children depicted in your book.

4. Keep in mind that the status of a public figure may change over time. Thus, a former bank robber who has led a blameless life for the last 30 years is not likely to be regarded as a public figure at this point.

5. When you have the material in draft form, look at it with an objective eye. Are you portraying any private individual in such a way that you might be accused of invasion of privacy, no matter how innocuous that presentation may appear to be? If you are at all uneasy about it, show the material to that person and get his written permission to use it, or else disguise him so that he is not identifiable.

If any statements appear to be libelous in nature, are you reasonably sure that you can prove the truth of what you are saying? One way to reduce the risk here is to soften the statement by casting it in the form of an opinion. However, even using a phrase like "I believe" or "in my opinion" will not protect you if the statement is held to be one of *fact* rather than opinion. And accusing another person of a crime is particularly risky.

6. Photographs can also be a problem, particularly from the point of view of invasion of privacy. There is probably no problem if you show an individual in a clearly public place, such as a busy street corner. But even this can be hazardous if you are showing children, or clearly recognizable "couples." If the gathering has a certain onus—such as a meeting of the Ku Klux Klan or the American Nazi Party—you may also be at risk. However, the courts have generally held that if a group is *large* and heterogeneous enough, and if the con-

text does not indicate that a particular person is being singled out for denigration, a statement (or photograph) does not refer to each member of that group in such a way as to be "of and concerning him or her." Definite limits on the size of the group have not been set, but most cases in which "recovery" has been allowed involved 25 people or less. If you are showing individuals at a *private* function such as a party, however, you should get a release from everyone shown.

7. Statements about corporations, associations, etc., are generally not libelous unless they affect their financial credit or standing in their own fields, or cast aspersions on their honesty, and cause the organization to suffer specific monetary damages.

Libel and Invasion of Privacy in Fiction. Since fiction is—at least theoretically—purely imaginative, libel and invasion of privacy would not seem to be an issue here. But many fictional "characters" are actually based on real-life people—sometimes on purpose and sometimes by accident—and the degree of risk has to do both with the way the character is depicted and how identifiable that character is.

A well-known example is a novel by Gwen Davis called *Touching*. The book includes a depiction of a psychiatrist running a "nude marathon." Davis based the account on a marathon she had attended herself, although she disguised the psychiatrist by changing his name and his physical characteristics. However, she also included a number of events, statements, etc., that had actually occurred. The psychiatrist, Paul Bindrim, brought suit against Davis and her publishers (Doubleday, NAL, and Book-of-the-Month Club) on the grounds that he was identifiable in the book and that he was libeled by various depictions that were defamatory and untrue. The California court found in his favor, partially because Davis had signed an agreement with the sponsors of the marathon ahead of time agreeing not to write about it. Bindrim was awarded $75,000 in damages.

Many writers and publishers feared this ruling would have a "chilling effect" on the creation of imaginative literature. However, rulings in subsequent cases have not continued this trend—for example, a sheriff who claimed he was libelously depicted in a novel by Jimmy Breslin entitled *Forty-four Caliber* lost the suit—so the situation may not be quite as grave as feared.

There was also a furor after the case had been decided when Doubleday sued Davis under the indemnity clause of her contract for $138,000—the amount of the libel award plus interest due Bindrim ($15,000), plus legal fees and other costs. They felt she had not been candid with them in regard to the confidentiality agreement she had signed, or in revealing how closely her character was based on a real person. Doubleday and Davis finally reached an out-of-court settlement; the amount was not disclosed.

In writing fiction, let your publisher know when you have based a character on a real person, and disguise him or her as completely as possible. Change everything, including the locale, the character's name, his or her physical characteristics, and so on. Some lawyers even suggest that you add some made-up facts to a character based on a real person, and then use the real person (clearly identified) in a "walk-on" role. Also check the telephone directory for the place where the novel is set to make sure you haven't inadvertently used a real name. If you want to use a well-known figure as a character in your novel or story, try to avoid anyone who may bring a suit for libel or misappropriation. The president of the United States is not likely to bring a lawsuit, but a famous rock-and-roll star might.

Negligence. The law also requires authors and publishers to act responsibly in regard to the physical well-being of others. Thus, if you write a book that gives instructions on how to do something—build a boat, bake a cake—you must take care to ensure that someone following those instructions does not expose himself to injury as a result of the instructions or because of your failure to warn about foreseeable hazards.

Books on health and nutrition also present hazards. There have been cases where a reader has followed advice which was inappropriate, and as a result suffered physical injury or death. It's impossible to anticipate all the ways in which health advice might be misinterpreted, however, so most publishers try to protect themselves and their authors by printing a general notice in the book that warns the reader to exercise caution when following the instructions given. For example, a book giving advice for strenuous exercise should have a disclaimer that cautions the reader to see his doctor first before undertaking such an exercise program.

Censorship. In a sense, *all* limitations on what a person can say or write are forms of censorship. However, the term *censorship* is usually applied to cases in which a private individual or group tries to restrict access to a work by having it removed from the shelves of a school library or otherwise banned (usually on the grounds of obscenity), or when an agency of the federal government restricts publication of material related to national security.

It's unlikely that many readers of this book will find themselves in this situation, but such restrictions on the personal freedom of writers and other citizens must be monitored carefully by both government representatives and private citizens. As Jean Karl of the Association of American Publishers Freedom to Read Committee has stated, we must continue to defend "the perimeters of our interests—the pornographic, the seditious and the generally heretical—in order that the censors, the infringers of our freedom to read, will not come near the core of what most of us choose to publish."

Copyright Permissions

Another possible area of hazard is copyright infringement. If you use material that is protected by copyright, you may have to obtain formal permission and pay for its use. In the case of text material (as opposed to illustrations), this depends on how much material you intend to use and whom you are seeking permission from. This section discusses permissions for text material; illustrations are discussed in the next section.

What Is Not Protected by Copyright? There are several classes of material that are *not* protected by copyright. They include:

• Works of very slight creative authorship, such as titles, names of characters, short phrases, etc. If you use a title or name that has become very well-known, however, you run the risk of a claim on the grounds of unfair competition or trademark violation. For example, you couldn't use the title *Gone With the Wind* without inviting the possibility of a claim by Margaret Mitchell's heirs.

• "Common" or "standard" works such as calendars, forms, etc.

• Material published by an officer or employee of the U.S. Government as a part of that person's official duties.

• Works that are in the public domain. These are works for which the period of copyright protection has expired, or ones that have failed to obtain copyright protection because of an error in the copyright notice or some other technical reason. Prior to January 1, 1978, the period of statutory copyright protection was 28 years plus a renewal period of 28 years. Now, the period of copyright protection depends on various factors:

1. If it is published anonymously or pseudonymously or is a work-made-for-hire, the period of protection is 75 years from the year of first publication or 100 years from the year of creation, whichever expires first.

2. For other types of work created after January 1, 1978, or created earlier but not published by then, protection extends 50 years beyond the death of the author. If it is a joint work, this means 50 years after the death of the last surviving author.

3. For works created before January 1, 1978, but still unpublished by then, copyright does not expire until December 31, 2002, even if the author has been dead for 50 years before then; if such works are published on or before December 31, 2002, the copyright will last until December 31, 2027.

4. For works published before January 1, 1978, and still protected by statutory copyright, the second term has been extended to 47 years, making the total duration of copyright protection 75 years.

Unfortunately, it's sometimes difficult to tell whether something is still protected by copyright. The only certainty relates to those works that were published at least seventy-five years ago. Thus, if the present year is 1984, anything published before 1909 is in the public domain. For further information on public domain material, contact the Copyright Office, Library of Congress, Washington, D.C. 20559.

• Ideas. What the copyright law protects is the *way* in

which ideas are expressed—that is, the *order and arrangement of the words, rather than the ideas themselves*. Thus, you can use ideas and research developed by someone else, but you cannot use the exact language in which these ideas are expressed *unless* you use only a very small portion of that language.

Does this mean that you can paraphrase freely without acknowledging the source? That depends. You are certainly free to use several reference sources in your work, and if you are not actually quoting from them, you are probably safe. It is common practice, however, to *acknowledge* those sources that you have relied on most heavily for your material. In fact, if you ever found yourself in court because of a copyright-infringement suit, the defense would depend partially on your "fairness" to your sources. It's generally best not to rely too heavily on one particular source.

What About Unpublished Material? Manuscripts that have not been published yet, or other kinds of original material such as letters or drawings, are also protected by copyright and cannot be reproduced without the copyright holder's permission.

If the author of the document is alive, you will have to obtain permission from him or her in order to quote from it. And if you want to include a photocopy of the document, you will have to obtain permission from whoever has physical possession of it. Under the new copyright law, you will have to obtain such permission for fifty years after the writer's death.

What Is "Fair Use"? If you had to ask permission for every single word or phrase that you quoted from copyrighted material, the clearing of permissions could take forever. The concept of fair use has evolved through the courts, and basically says that you can quote *limited* amounts of material without permission. The amount that can be fairly used without permission is difficult to specify exactly, because it relates to the nature of the copyrighted work, the length of the material you are quoting, the length of your own book, and the amount of profit you might derive from its use. Ask your editor for guidance. In general, you will probably be advised to seek permission for use of:

Even *one line* from a published song or a recording. Music publishers are very strict about such use, particularly of well-known songs.

More than one line from a poem—unless it's a very long poem.

More than three hundred continuous words from one section of a full-length book.

Another rule of thumb is to ask for permission if you quote more than 5 percent of the total original material. However, you can use more if you're quoting for the purposes of literary criticism or commenting on someone else's point of view. Perhaps the best test is to consider how *you* would feel if someone else used your material extensively.

How to Find the Copyright Holder. To locate the copyright holder in order to seek permission to use, try the following:

1. For material that you are taking from a book, the simplest thing is to write the publisher's permissions department. If the publisher does not have authority to grant permission for use, your letter will be passed along to the appropriate person or you will be told whom to contact.

If the material you want to use has been taken from another source, check the copyright page for a credit line. The publisher or person to be contacted should be indicated. If that address isn't readily available, write the publisher of the book you are using and ask them to pass the request along to the copyright holder.

2. If you are taking the material from a magazine or newspaper, check for a copyright or credit line indicating the source of the material, and write that copyright holder or original publisher directly. Otherwise, direct your request to the permissions department of the magazine or newspaper.

3. If you want to use the words to a song and you got them from sheet music or a book, write the publisher and ask permission. (Fees tend to run *very* high so you might reconsider using song lyrics.) If the publisher got permission from someone else, he will refer you to the copyright holder. If you have taken the lyrics from a recording, write the recording company for the name of the company or person from whom you should seek permission.

If you can't decide who owns the rights to a song, check with the index department of either the American Society of

Composers, Authors and Publishers (ASCAP) at 1 Lincoln Plaza, New York, NY 10023 (212-595-3050) or Broadcast Music Incorporated, 320 West 57th St., New York, NY 10019 (212-586-2000). Most recorded or published songs are registered with one of these nonprofit organizations, and they'll be able to direct you to the holders of the copyright to the song.

What about very old songs, such as "Old Folks at Home" or "Camptown Races"? The lyrics and the melody line are probably in the public domain, but a particular arrangement may be copyrighted, and you'll have to try to find the copyright holder if you want to reprint the arrangement.

How to Write a Permissions Letter. Your letter should specify the author and title of the volume from which you wish to use material and the exact material to be used. Give page numbers and the words with which the quote starts and ends. Another technique is to attach a photocopy of the material. If the lines are not consecutive, be sure to specify this; it may result in a lower fee.

Indicate who will be publishing your book and the approximate date of publication. However, the way in which you specify the *editions* in which the material will be used can vary. Some publishers ask you to spell out the different editions in detail, including the publisher's editions, any reprint or book-club editions, independent publication by an English publisher, and foreign-language editions. Others prefer that you leave the wording as vague as possible to reduce the possibility that you (or the licensees) will have to pay separate fees for each different edition. Ask your editor for instructions.

The person granting permission may specify the exact form in which the credit line should appear in your book and a preference for where it might appear, and may also charge a fee. The fee for the use of song lyrics can be high, but other fees are usually modest unless you are using a lot of material from one source, or that particular work is very well-known, or your book is likely to sell a large number of copies. Most times you are allowed to delay payment until the book is published. The person granting permission may ask for one or two copies of your book, which you are obliged to furnish. However, your publisher may be willing to furnish these free copies for you.

The process of tracking down the copyright holder and obtaining permission can be slow. Leave plenty of time for the process. Also keep copies of the letters you send out as well as any that are returned to you undelivered (in their *envelopes*). You may need them as a record of your having made a reasonable effort to obtain permission.

Illustrations

Illustrations can add a great deal to the value and interest of your book. However, acquiring illustrations can cost you both time and money, and the illustrations can be expensive to reproduce. Make sure that the use of illustrations is acceptable to your publisher before you start.

Illustrations are generally obtained in one of three ways:

1. You prepare the illustrations yourself.
2. You hire someone else to prepare them for you.
3. You make use of "ready-made" illustrations that you've obtained from a published book or periodical or from a picture collection.

Preparing Artwork on Your Own. If you are preparing a how-to book, it is usually more convenient to make your own drawings or take photographs of the scenes you want to show rather than trying to find prepared illustrations.

If you are going to prepare your own artwork, check with the publisher's art department for any specific instructions. If you are not a professional artist, it may be better for you to do some rough sketches and have the publisher's art staff prepare the final drawings, or hire a free-lance commercial artist to do the final drawings for you.

Line drawings should be done in India ink, with good strong lines. It's common to do drawings one and a half to two times larger than the desired final size so they can be photographically reduced to make the lines look sharper. If you are making several drawings, try to make them all to the same scale, so that the printer can photoreduce them at the same time. Protect the finished artwork with a tissue overlay.

Taking Photographs. If you are taking black-and-white photographs, make sure that the focus is sharp, the contrast is good, and you are showing what you really want to show. Plan to provide glossy prints 4 x 5-inch or 8 x 10-inch in size. Avoid scratching or marring the emulsion on the surface of the photograph or getting fingerprints on it. Never paperclip a photograph, or write on or near the surface unless you are using a grease pencil. If you write identification on the back of the print, do so *lightly*.

If you are using color, the publisher will probably want a transparency rather than a print. The transparency should be no smaller than 35mm and the focus should be very sharp. Store transparencies in an envelope or small box. *Never* hold a batch of transparencies together with a rubber band; it can deform the film as well as the cardboard frame.

Hiring a Professional. If you plan to hire a professional artist or photographer and don't presently know someone, ask your publisher for a recommendation. Other sources of names include *Literary Market Place,* a local art school or photographer, or the American Society of Magazine Photographers, 60 E. 42nd St., New York, NY 10017.

The fee structure will depend on the proficiency and reputation of the artist or photographer. A simple line drawing in India ink, for example, will probably cost you between $50 and $100. The fee charged by a photographer will depend on how complex the "setup" is, whether you want to see contact sheets or full prints, and so on. When discussing these fees, be sure that you are being explicit about the image you want to end up with.

Also clarify the question of the copyright to the work. When you commission an artist to do a drawing, the usual arrangement is that you retain the copyright as well as the right to use the drawing in any way you wish, particularly if you provided the artist with a rough sketch. If the artist is to retain the copyright, however, you will need a release from him permitting you to use the artwork in the book and in advertising and promotion materials. Figure 4 (page 86) shows an example of a release from an artist. If the release applies only to your publisher's edition, any other publishers (such as a reprinter) will have to get permission to use that illustration from the artist.

The same situation holds true with a photograph you have commissioned. Sometimes the photographer retains ownership of the negative, but you own the copyright and the

Figure 4
ARTIST RELEASE

To Whom It May Concern:

This is to confirm the understanding that I _____ (photographer, illustrator's name) _____ have _____ (taken photographs, provided line drawings, art, etc.) _____ for a project
tentatively titled _____ (title) _____ by _____ (your
name) _____

All rights in and to the photographs or artwork, including the
copyright and renewal and extension of copyright on these
_____ (photographs or drawings) _____ shall belong to the
author or publisher of the work.

The author or publisher shall have the right to use my name in
sales and promotion or advertising of the work.

Sincerely,

_____ (name) _____

_____ (date) _____

photographer must obtain your permission to make dupli-
cates. If you want to buy the negative you may have to pay an
additional fee.

Find out what type of "credit" the artist or photographer
wants, and where they would like it to appear. The preferred
position is next to the illustration, but it may have to be
placed elsewhere, such as at the end of the caption or in a list
of acknowledgments elsewhere in the book, depending on
practical bookmaking considerations.

If a photograph shows people who are recognizable, you
may need a release from each individual giving you the right

to use the photograph in your book. Check with your editor for instructions.

Using an Illustration from a Book or Periodical. If you want to use an illustration from a book or magazine, you will probably have to get permission to use that illustration. Exceptions are if the photograph or drawing was prepared by an agency of the federal government, or if the illustration is in the public domain. (Very old illustrations are usually safe to use; Dover Books publishes many collections of out-of-copyright illustrations.)

The illustration will be accompanied by a credit line indicating its source. If you have the address, you can write the person or company directly; otherwise, write the publisher and ask to be put in touch with the source of the illustration. Unfortunately, illustrators don't always provide publishers with their current addresses, and you may never succeed in finding the individual artist or photographer, in which case you will have to select other material.

Picture Collections. Another possible source of illustrations is a public or private picture collection. Most large public libraries have picture collections, as do many agencies of the U.S. Government. One of the largest public collections is the Library of Congress in Washington. There are also many private collections of various types. To locate a picture collection:

1. Check your local library to see if it has a picture collection. Also check the Yellow Pages of your telephone directory under such headings as "photo agencies," "photographic research services," or "picture libraries."

2. Check the listings of "photo and picture sources" in *Literary Market Place*. This lists about seventy-five companies that provide stock photos, etc.

3. Find the book *Picture Researcher's Handbook* by Hilary and Mary Evans and Andra Nelkin (Scribners, 1974) or *Picture Sources 3*, edited by Ann Novotny and published by the Special Libraries Association. *Picture Researcher's Handbook* is an excellent guide to picture sources in Britain, as well as some American and continental European ones. *Picture Sources 3* is a comprehensive guide to collections of

prints and photographs in the United States and Canada, and also gives a number of helpful hints on how to go about picture research. Its indexes list collections by subject (military history, fine arts, etc.), name of collection, and geographic location.

Note that some of these collections are open only to researchers with special credentials, and some have very limited hours.

Some collections provide a search service. Write or call to find out how many subjects you can have searched, whether the researcher will send you photocopies of illustrations that you can choose from, what the fees will be, and approximately how long the search will take. Certain collections lend original prints, others provide only photocopies. Note also that some of them charge high fees if you *lose* one of their original photographs.

In some cases the agency or library can give you permission to reproduce the illustration in your book, but in most cases you have to go back to the artist or photographer for permission.

Other Sources of "Prepared" Illustrative Material. There are also other sources of illustrative material you can try, depending on the subject matter of your book. Many large businesses and organizations, for example, make material on their particular business or industry available. Embassies, tourist offices, religious groups, and societies and professional associations of various types may also be a possibility. Newspapers sometimes are willing to open their archives, although this can require some elaborate arrangements. There is usually no fee for this use, so long as you provide a credit.

Another source of material is art galleries and museums. The difficulty here is that the art is generally "one-of-a-kind," and reproduction facilities may not be available. Check with the gallery manager or museum curator to see if a reproduction of the piece you are interested in is available. If not, you may arrange to have a photograph taken. Some museums recommend photographers with whom they prefer to work. Find out the requirements, and what the cost is likely to be. Also check the copyright permission situation. You may have to obtain written permission to reproduce the material from both the museum and the copyright holder (probably the artist).

Similarly, if you wish to use a private photograph that has never been published before, you will have to get permission to use it from the individual who owns it, or his heirs and assigns. You may also have to get releases from people shown in the photograph.

Fees. Fees for the use of illustrations vary greatly, depending on the rights you are asking for and the source of the illustration. If you are buying the rights from a photo agency, you will pay about $25 for *one-time* use of a black-and-white photograph of a historical subject on one-half page or less; for a more modern picture, the fee will be between $35 and $75 and may go as high as $100 for a full page. Fees for cartoons are high, often $100 or more. The right to use the illustration in a British edition or throughout the world will cost somewhat more; use on the cover or jacket, or in color, usually costs about twice as much. However, you may be able to negotiate a lower fee if your book is going to be published by a small or academic press, or if you plan to make limited use of the illustration. If you are using many illustrations from the same source, you may be able to negotiate a bulk rate.

Typing the Final Manuscript

The Wonders of Word Processing. Typing and retyping a manuscript can be a pain in the neck, and you are likely to go through several drafts before you arrive at the final version. One way to reduce the physical labor is to invest in a wonderful invention called a word processor, which stores the material that you have typed, makes revisions easier, and then produces a clean copy on a printer attached to the system. Up to now, word processors have been fairly expensive, but the prices are coming down and more and more writers are using them. Some publishers are set up so that they can set type directly from your word processing disk or tape, but since there are so many different kinds of equipment available, compatibility is a problem. This automated "processing" of words is definitely the wave of the future, however, and you should at least be aware of what equipment is available. And remember that the purchase of this type of equipment is tax deductible as part of your business expenses as a writer. In the discussion that follows, however, I am assuming that you are struggling along without a word processor.

Some Dos and Don'ts. Before you begin typing the final manuscript, ask your editor whether there is a particular style manual that you should use in choosing a format for your material, solving grammatical problems, and so on. Some houses have their own style guide; others ask their authors to use the University of Chicago Press's *A Manual of Style*, Prentice-Hall's *Words into Type*, or another style guide.

Most publishers are not too fussy about the format of the final manuscript, so long as it is typed neatly, you use a fresh ribbon so that the words reproduce well for photocopying, and so on. Leave wide enough margins (at least one inch on all sides) so that the editor and copyeditor have room to write comments (see Figures 5 and 6). *Double-space everything*, including bibliographies, footnotes, and block quotations. Type on only one side of the paper. Use good-quality bond so that the manuscript will stand up to handling; don't use the erasable type—it smears—or lightweight paper that will tear easily.

Front Matter. The material preceding the text is called front matter. Any material following the text is called back matter, and can include such things as notes, bibliography, appendixes, and so on.

Much of the front matter will be prepared by your editor, and some of it is optional. Here are all of the elements that might be included in the finished book. Ask your editor how much of this you should provide.

The "half title" or "bastard title" page. This is the first printed page in most books, and carries only the main title of the book. It's a holdover from the days when books didn't have covers.

The "card page" or "ad page." A list of your previous publications (if any). This is often printed on the back of the half title page.

Title page. Gives the full title of the book, the subtitle (if any), and your name. The editor will add the name of the publisher, and/or the publisher's "logo," or trademark.

Copyright page. This page carries various types of identify-

Figure 5
COPYEDITED MANUSCRIPT PAGE

~~Chapter~~ LN 5

FROM FINAL MANUSCRIPT TO BOUND BOOKS

Epi [Of making books there is no end.

1/M Ecclesiastes

A Some final fine tuning

Even after your final manuscript has been accepted, you may have to do some more work on it. Your editor may want you to rewrite a section or perhaps add some new material ~~and so forth~~ In fact, this is usually what happens, and you can probably expect to do at least one more month of work on the manuscript after its acceptance.

(After you have made all of the requested changes and provided a clearly typed manuscript, the editor will give it one more quick review to make sure you have done everything required. At this point, she may also have the manuscript photocopied for distribution to other departments in the company. The photocopies may be accompanied by a brief description of the book, prepared by the editor.)

A Copy editing

The next step is to have the manuscript copy edited. This involves going over the manuscript with a fine toothed comb, looking for grammatical errors, stylistic inconsistencies of infelicities, and factual errors. Most fact checking is done in conjunction with

ing data, including: (1) The name of the copyright holder and the year of publication, plus the symbol © or the word "Copyright" or the abbreviation "Copr." If some of the material has been published in a previous year (e.g., this is a collection of articles and some of them were published previously), the various year dates should appear in the copyright notice. The editor will obtain the information to appear here from your records and the contract. (2) Copyright permissions information, unless these "acknowledgments" are so extensive that they are extended into the back matter as well. The copyeditor of the book will probably prepare the "copy" from the information that you provide. (3) Bibliographic information such as the Library of Congress number, "Cataloging in Publication" (CIP) information, printing codes, and so on. This is normally provided by the publisher.

Dedication. Optional. May be printed on a separate page, or on the copyright page.

Epigraph. Optional. An epigraph is a pertinent quotation that serves as a lead-in to the book (or to each chapter, as in this book). Indicate the source of the epigraph whenever possible.

"List" pages, such as table of contents, list of illustrations, etc. Required only for nonfiction. The list of illustrations will be optional, depending on how they've been handled in the book. Don't include manuscript page numbers when typing up these pages.

Preface. This is usually written by the author and is an explanation of why you wrote the book, how it came to be written, etc. (It may also include acknowledgments, and a list of copyright permissions.)

Foreword. This is usually written by someone other than the author; its function is to position the book in relation to other works in the field. The author of the foreword is usually identified at the end of the foreword. This *may* be copyrighted separately and may require a release to use.

Introduction. This is usually written by the author and is a specific commentary on the contents of the book. If it is lengthy, it should be the first chapter of the book.

Acknowledgments. You will have a separate acknowledgments page only if the acknowledgments are so long they can't be included in the preface, or if you don't have a preface. Extensive acknowledgments (such as those in an anthology) may be extended into the back matter.

Other Matters. Your style manual will give instructions on how to type quoted material ("extracts"), footnotes, and the like. However, here are some brief comments on what a trade book publisher generally prefers:

1. *Everything* should be double-spaced, including quoted material. If you are quoting prose, it can be included as part

of the text if it runs ten typed lines (in your typescript) or less; otherwise, double-space down and indent about five spaces from both margins to set the material off. Use quotation marks only if the material is run in with the text. Poetry should be set off if it runs longer than two lines. Use ellipses (three successive dots—four at the end of a sentence) to indicate deletions. If you have changed the original passage in some way, underline the material you have added so it can be set in italics. Figure 6 (page 107) shows how quoted material should be set off.

2. Avoid footnotes if possible. If you want to include more than a few, check with your editor first. Footnotes in trade books are usually not numbered, to avoid making the book look too academic. Use an asterisk or some other kind of symbol to indicate the relationship between the footnote and the text.

3. If a table is fairly simple and short, it can be included in the text; otherwise, it should be typed on a separate sheet of paper so that it can be dealt with separately. Give each table a number and a caption, and indicate on the typescript in *pencil* where the table should be placed. This is called "keying in."

4. If you are using illustrations, keep them separate from the text; don't insert them into the typescript. Each illustration should be numbered and/or have a caption, but type this information on a *separate* piece of paper, since it will be handled separately from the illustration. "Key" the illustration and caption to each other and to the text lightly in pencil, according to some rational scheme. Make sure each caption is *relevant* to the illustration it is explaining.

5. If you make a mistake while typing the manuscript, *don't* just "x" it out; correct it as neatly as possible. If you want to insert something longer than a line, type it on a separate piece of paper. This manuscript may be duplicated for use by other departments in the publishing house and should be as neat as possible. Furthermore, if the manuscript is too sloppy, your editor probably won't accept it because the typesetter's bill will be too high. Or the editor may arrange to have all or part of the manuscript retyped and have the cost charged to you.

6. Avoid cross-references to other pages; it complicates the typesetting. Refer to other chapters or sections of the book by name instead.

7. The front matter should be numbered consecutively in roman numerals, probably in pencil because other elements may be added by your editor. The text should be numbered consecutively in arabic numbers from beginning to end, including the back matter.

8. If you are curious about how long the manuscript is running, you can get a rough word count by counting the number of words in an average line and multiplying this by the number of lines on the page. (The *average* count on most manuscript pages is about three hundred words.) Multiplying this average-word-count-per-page by the number of manuscript pages will give you a rough idea of your total word count. However, allow for chapter openings and closings, which are shorter, and for illustrations and the like.

Delivery of the Final Manuscript

The contract may require you to provide final illustrations and copyright permissions when you turn in the final manuscript, but you may still be in the process of obtaining them when the final manuscript is due. Ask your editor whether it is acceptable for you to provide preliminary material, such as rough copies of illustrations, or copies of your letters seeking copyright permission.

Do *not* staple or three-hole-punch the manuscript. Put the original (or a good photocopy) in a typing-paper box or other suitable container and secure the box with sturdy rubber bands, tape, or string. Be sure to keep at least one copy for your own reference, and for protection in case the manuscript is lost in the mails.

What If the Manuscript Is Not Accepted for Publication?

This is the nerve-wracking part for many authors, since there is no guarantee that the publisher will find the final manuscript satisfactory. If you have been working closely with your editor, there should be no problem. The editor will be aware of what you have been doing, and in this case acceptance is more or less a formality. If you have not been

Figure 6
EXTRACT IN THE MANUSCRIPT

If you ~~are~~ [are] quoting poetry / and the quotation runs less than
two lines, you can "run it on" [in] the text, with the lines separated
by a slash. For example, if you ~~are~~ [are] quoting the first two lines from
Shakespeare's ~~twenty~~ [twenty-ninth] sonnet, you can type it as follows: "When in
disgrace with fortune and men's eyes / [set slash] I all alone beweep my outcast
state / . / . / . / ." If the quotation runs longer than ~~that~~ [two lines], it should be
typed in this fashion: [#]

> When in disgrace with fortune and men's eyes
> I all alone beweep my outcast state,
> And trouble deaf heaven with my bootless cries,
> And look upon myself, and curse my fate,
> Wishing me like to one more rich in hope,
> Featured like him, like him with friends possessed,
> Desiring this man's art, and that man's scope,
> With what I most enjoy contented least,
> Yet in these thoughts myself almost despising,
> Haply I think on thee, and then my state,
> Like to the lark at break of day arising
> From sullen earth, sings hymns at heaven's gate;
> For thy sweet love remembered such wealth brings
> That when I scorn to change my state with kings.

[Poetry extract]   [styled per Player's Shakespeare]

Notice the indentation of the last two lines of the sonnet.

To quote prose that will run ⑩ [ten] lines or more in your typescript,
double-space down and indent about ⑤ [five] spaces from both margins. For
example: [#]

> The summer evenings were long. It was not dark yet.
> Presently Tom checked his (whistle). A stranger was before

[Prose extract]

[Au: "watch" seems to make more sense here]

working closely with an editor, however, or if the editor who
signed up your book is no longer with this company the process may not be so automatic.

The usual procedure is for the editor to read your manuscript and then indicate to his management that the manuscript meets the contractual requirements and he wants to
accept it formally. In some companies a second person in the
house has to approve the manuscript before it can be ac-

cepted. If the manuscript is deemed satisfactory, you will be informed and the check due on delivery and acceptance will be drawn up. The editor may want some small revisions made, but this is usually not enough to prevent payment of the final portion of the advance due you.

Things will become more complicated if your editor or the management of the publishing house feels that extensive revisions have to be made before the house can accept the manuscript. If revisions are required, a reasonable compromise can usually be worked out. If you feel that you understand what is needed and have the time to make the revisions, this should be no problem. If you feel you cannot do this for some reason, the house may opt to hire a rewriter, perhaps in exchange for a share of your royalties. Obviously, if you have a literary agent, the agent should be involved in these negotiations.

If the manuscript is deemed unacceptable because of a "change in market conditions," you may be allowed to keep your advance and look around for another publisher. If the house feels the manuscript is unacceptable because of the quality of your work, they will probably allow you to seek another publisher and to repay the advance they gave you out of the advance you receive from the other publisher. Probably the only instance in which you will be asked to repay the advance immediately is if you fail to turn in a manuscript at all, or if you refuse to make the majority of the revisions that they asked for.

5
From Final Manuscript to Bound Books

Of making many books there is no end.

—ECCLESIASTES

Some Final Fine-Tuning

Even after your final manuscript has been accepted, your editor may want you to make some final revisions. In fact, this is usually what happens, and you should probably allow some time for this.

After you have made all of the requested changes and provided a cleanly typed manuscript, the editor will give it one more quick review to make sure you've done everything required. Then the manuscript will probably be photocopied for distribution to other departments in the company, perhaps accompanied by a brief description of the book prepared by the editor.

Copyediting

The next step is to have an experienced copyeditor go over the manuscript with a fine-tooth comb, looking for grammatical errors, stylistic inconsistencies or infelicities, and factual errors. Fact checking is usually done in conjunction with copyediting and is not a separate procedure except in the case of a complicated book.

Copyediting may be done by the acquiring editor, if this is a small publishing house, or by a person specializing in this work, as is usually the case in large publishing houses. The copyeditor may be on the publisher's staff or may be a free-lancer; in either case, there may be a "middleman" in the person of a managing editor or chief copyeditor. The acquiring editor will have to inform the copyeditor if there is anything unusual about the book (the deliberate misspelling of certain words for comic effect, for example), whether the manuscript has to be copyedited in a rush, whether he wants a list of all quotations needing formal permission, and so on.

The amount of time required to copyedit the manuscript will depend on how long and complicated it is as well as on the copyeditor's schedule. A copyeditor can usually complete about five or six pages an hour on the average manuscript, and the general practice is to allow between two and four weeks for this process.

The copyeditor makes decisions about capitalization, punctuation, etc., and enters them on a stylesheet for his or her own reference. Elements in the manuscript that are clearly in error (misspelling, etc.) are corrected directly on the manuscript. Items open to question will be indicated on a "query slip" glued to the manuscript page.

The copyedited manuscript will then be returned to the editor, who will check the copyeditor's work and answer the queries. If the copyeditor has indicated only minor changes and few questions, your editor will probably resolve these with you by telephone. Otherwise, the copyedited manuscript should be submitted to you for review. Figures 5 (page 103) and 6 (page 107) show corrections made on a copyedited manuscript page.

As you review the manuscript, check the corrections and answer the queries. The queries should be answered on the slips provided; *don't* tear them off. If you disagree with a change made by the copyeditor, you may restore the original, but do so with caution, indicating the page number on a separate sheet so that your editor can quickly review what you've done. If you disagree strongly with the copyediting, or find yourself rewriting substantial portions of the manuscript, call your editor immediately and explain what is going on. Do *not* make major changes without first discussing them.

Mark changes in a different-color pencil than that used by the copyeditor. You can use proofreading symbols if you know them or if you want to work with a style manual, but this isn't necessary as long as you write cleanly and clearly.

The process can be slow, so allow enough time. The editor will probably allow you a week, plus the time necessary for transmission of the manuscript.

When the editor gets the manuscript back, he will review it quickly to make sure you haven't done anything unexpected, and will then deliver it to the copyeditor (or managing editor) for final processing.

The Design and Production Schedule

While the manuscript is being copyedited, work will begin on the design of the "inside" of the book. A copy of the manuscript is given to a designer, who evaluates its different elements and selects the typefaces to be used. When the copyedited manuscript is ready, the designer marks it with instructions for the typesetter. The typemarked manuscript will then go to the production department, where arrangements with a typesetter (compositor), printer, and binder are made. The companies selected for the job will depend on the desired book schedule, the prices quoted by different vendors, and so on.

The production, or manufacturing, schedule will depend on the complexity of the book, the work load in the house, the need to have books by a given date, and various other factors. The whole process usually takes between six and seven months from the time the completed manuscript is released to the copyeditor until the time that finished books are available. If the book is more complicated, the schedule may stretch to eight or nine months or even longer. Conversely, if the book is to be published more quickly, the house will rush matters and perhaps eliminate certain steps to speed the process. A normal production schedule for a trade hardcover book looks something like the one on page 112.

A brief description of each step in the process *after* the book has been set in type is given in the next several pages. For more detailed information about the production process, see the following pages.

Process	Time (weeks)
Copyediting	4
Checking by author	1
Complete design	2
Circulate design for approval	1
Set manuscript and get galley proofs	3
Proofread galleys	3
Correct galleys and prepare pages	2
Proofread pages	2
Correct pages and make repros	1
Check repros and make blues	3
Check blues	1
Print books	2
Bind, jacket, and deliver books	3
Total	28 weeks

Proofreading Galleys

You should receive one or two sets of galley proofs of your book about six weeks after you return the copyedited manuscript to your editor. (It takes a few weeks after the return of the manuscript to finish designing the book, and then three or four weeks to set the manuscript in type and send proofs to you.)

The way the galleys look will depend on the typesetting process used. If it was set in "hot metal" (probably by Linotype machine), the galleys will come on long sheets carrying about 2½ pages of typeset material, with a heading at the top of each page indicating the galley number, title of the book, and codes indicating type size, line length, and typeface used. (Figure 7 is an example of such a galley sheet, with corrections marked on it.) If the manuscript was set by a computer-controlled "cold-type" process, the galleys will look much like final book pages, although the page numbering and headings may not be in final form. The galleys may or may not have "display" type—a larger-sized type used for title pages, chapter heading, etc.—although "tag lines" indicating the material that is to be set in large type may appear if the display type has not been set as yet.

Your job is to proofread the galleys carefully. Even though other sets of proofs are being checked by other readers, this will probably be your only opportunity to catch mistakes and make the book as accurate as possible. However, this is *not* an opportunity to rewrite the book. Correcting a book in galleys costs money, and it's easy to incur charges beyond the 10 or 15 percent allowed in your contract. Beyond that, you may throw the production schedule off, and may actually damage the book more than help it. If you feel that you must make changes, it's better to delete than add material, since you won't incur additional typesetting charges. If you're only correcting a few words, try to make the change conform to the same amount of space; otherwise, several subsequent lines may have to be reset. The set of galleys you receive may already have corrections indicated and carry queries not resolved in the copyedited manuscript. If the queries are for you, be sure to answer them.

Make your changes in the margins. Don't squeeze them in above or below the line; they are apt to be missed by the proofreader who will go over the set of galleys you return. Write horizontally rather than vertically, and indicate where the change is to go by inserting a caret (∧) in the line. If you're making more than one change on a line, separate the changes by a slash (/). Use ink or pencil different in color from changes already marked on the galleys. If a change is too long or complicated to fit in the margin horizontally, bracket it and put it at the top or bottom of the galley with a guideline indicating where the material is to go in the text, or type it on a separate piece of paper and attach it to the galley with its placement indicated.

You will probably be given a week or two to complete the process. If you received two sets of galleys, and you want to transfer your corrections from one set to the other, leave enough time for this as well. Be sure to get the galleys back in the time allotted; delays can cause the book date to be postponed.

The editor will go over your galleys to see what changes you have made. If he doesn't agree with something you've done, or wishes to overrule you, he should discuss the matter with you first. Any alterations made by your editor which require resetting should be indicated as "EA's" (editor's alterations) on the galleys so that you won't be charged for them.

The editor will then pass the galleys along to the copyeditor, proofreader, or managing editor, who in turn will

Figure 7
LINOTYPE GALLEY PROOF

rg6—Tidewater Dynasty—11 on 13 x 27 Garamond   (on 28)   figs. o.s.   (152)

hundred and sixty thousand additional acres of the Fairfax properties. Marshall contacted his relative through marriage, the Philadelphia financier Robert Morris, who agreed to put up the monies when needed in exchange for a share of the profits. Now the money was due, but Morris was over-extended and in great financial difficulty himself. Harry had not told Ann, but he had agreed to loan Morris forty thousand dollars so that partial payment could be made and Morris supported until he could steady his finances. After all, Morris had been the financial wizard behind the Revolution, hadn't he? If anyone could safely pull through these hard times, Morris could. Harry knew his money was safe and in just a little time would be repaid.

"I say, Colonel Lee, shall we walk in the garden after dinner?" The President had turned the full force of his blue eyes in Harry's direction. "It is too nice an evening to sequester myself in my study with newspapers and letters. I would rather continue our conversations."

Harry quickly accepted the invitation. For Washington to break his usual pattern was a compliment. They had already spent the morning together and talked of many things, most of them practical—the prospect of a threshing machine which Washington, who had a great bent for mechanics, was contemplating; the qualities of a new strain of wheat; improvements the President wanted made to his plantation as he contemplated retirement. And they had touched on the disappointment of the canal project at Great Falls, which gave Harry the opportunity to bring up a financial transaction between them.

In February he had given the President shares in the Bank of Columbia, in partial payment for Washington's holdings in the Great Dismal Swamp Company. He had considered the bank shares to be of par value, and Washington had accepted them with that understanding, but in recent months the shares dropped precipitously in value, and Harry felt himself still in the President's debt. What's more, he realized that Washington felt that way as well. This morning he had explained that he was selling some land to pay off the differential, and Washington had readily agreed.

How fragrant the good earth smelled in the afternoon sun. Harry breathed in its aroma as he followed his host down the neat cultivated rows of currants, strawberries, and gooseberries. Before them lay a shady avenue of towering catalpas and magnolias interspersed with deep-green Scotch pine and pale-green weeping willows.

"Look how well Lee cuttings thrive in Washington soil!" The President took his arm and pointed to a thriving horse chestnut grown from a cutting Harry had once sent from Stratford to Mount Vernon along with an assortment of box plantings. Washington led the way to a wooden bench in the shade of a tulip tree. "Shall we sit? I am in the mood to reminisce."

"About the war?" Harry settled himself and stretched out his booted legs. "I could do that with you for hours, sir." He sighed nostalgically. "I most often now think of Greene and that drama played out in the Carolinas. What a hero! Next to you, he was the strength of the Revolution."

"My southern commander gave a brilliant and indispensable account of himself, yet I am afraid it went largely unappreciated," Washington said gravely. "No one yet realizes that without the bravery of Greene and Morgan and Lee, the south would have fallen to the British." His eyes flickered to his companion. "And with the toppling of Virginia, the rest of the states would soon have been reswallowed." He shook his head. "I think often of Greene, with his set, stubborn jaw! He and his Kitty were settled on their seaside plantation in South Carolina, given to them in gratitude by that state, for such a brief time. I still grieve over his early death." Tears clouded Washington's eyes.

Harry nodded without speaking. Nathaniel Greene, next to Washington, headed his list of heroes.

"I think," the President continued, "of those I have known and loved in my life. My first real friend, George William Fairfax, is now dead and buried in England. His widow, Sally, remains there, never to return. And I think from time to time of George Mason. Bonded we were in securing Virginia's rights and liberties, only to fall apart over the securing of the Federal Constitution. That our rift never healed saddens me to no end."

the

poplar

Georgia,

We were bonded

transfer your changes onto a set of master galleys which were proofread against the copyedited manuscript.

The master galleys will then be checked by the book designer to make sure that the changes have not affected the design. If the changes are extensive, she may ask the typesetter to make up revised galleys; otherwise, she will request pages.

Page Proofs

After corrections have been made, the typesetter, or compositor, will arrange the type into final pages with page numbers ("folios") and "running" heads and feet. Headings usually indicate the title of the book or chapter; footings may include the page number and other kinds of design elements. Display type and illustrations are usually not incorporated into the proofs at this point.

You may be given a set of page proofs to check, but this is not usual unless you are going to provide an index. If you do see the pages, you don't need to proofread every line, only the material that has changed from galleys to pages. The corrected pages will then be sent back to the compositor, who will make corrections and prepare a set of proofs called "repros" that will be photographed (reproduced) to make printing plates.

Making an Index

Most nonfiction books contain an index as an aid to the reader, and while it is not an absolute requirement, libraries regard them as important and reviewers are apt to be critical if a book doesn't have one. Providing an index is the author's responsibility, but since this can be time-consuming and complicated, you may wish to have a professional indexer do the work for you. Check the cost in advance—it can be quite expensive, depending on how complicated the book is and how detailed the intended index will be. A simple name-and-place index is probably adequate for most trade nonfiction books. The index for a more scholarly book will undoubtedly list concepts as well. Some authors combine a glossary of terms with their index, or include several types of indexes listing different kinds of information.

The simplest way to proceed is to locate a book with an index similar to the one you would like your book to have. Then discuss the index with your editor to decide what type of index is most appropriate and how much it's likely to cost if it's to be done by a professional indexer. Fees generally run in the neighborhood of $1 per book page for an average trade book, but can be considerably higher for a more complex book and proportionately lower for a simpler book.

If you decide to make the index yourself, find out approximately how long it should take. Publishers usually allow about three weeks for this process. Ask the designer for specifications on the number of lines you can have in the index (this depends on the number of blank pages available at the back of the book, the type size, etc.), whether entries should be indented or run in, and any other specific requirements. For more detailed instructions, see the Chicago *Manual of Style* or one of the other guides listed in the Bibliography of this manual.

The index should be typed neatly on 8½ x 11-inch paper, double-spaced, *in one column*. Be *consistent* in your indenting, capitalization, and so forth.

Your editor will check the index typescript to make sure that the content is reasonable and that its form is acceptable. The index will then be copyedited and marked for typesetting. You probably will not see proofs; they will be checked against the typescript by the copyeditor or proofreader.

Books with Illustrations

From this point on you're not likely to see any more proofs of your book. There is one exception—a book containing illustrations. You should see proof copies of any line illustrations prepared by a professional illustrator hired by the publisher or on the publisher's staff, and you should see proofs of any illustrations (usually photographs) that are being printed in a separate insert. Both black-and-white and color photographs are commonly printed separately from the text because they require special processing and reproduce better on a coated paper. For more details on how they're processed, see later material in this chapter.

There are some books in which photographs are printed along with the text. In this case, the whole procedure is a little different. The book designer will first make up a "dummy" by cutting up a set of galleys and positioning the text in relation to rough representations of the illustrations. You should have a chance to check the dummy at this point.

After the master galleys have been corrected by the compositor, a new proof copy will be pulled on high-quality paper which produces a strong, clear image for photo reproduction—hence the term *repros*. This time the designer will paste up the book very carefully, using "boards" (cardboard mats with a two-page spread of the final book indicated in nonreproducible blue). Screened photoprints of the illustrations in the correct size will be pasted up along with the repros. The final product incorporating illustrations and text is called a mechanical. If you wish to see the mechanical before it is sent to the printer, you should arrange it with your editor.

From Repro Proofs to Bound Books

The book will go through various stages before it finally comes off the bindery line and is jacketed. After the repros have been approved by the publisher, they will be sent to the printer, who will photograph them and then make contact prints called blues (because the images are usually blue-tinged). It's unlikely that you will see the blues unless your book is very complicated.

After the blues have been approved by the publisher and any necessary corrections made, printing plates will be made. Practically all books these days are printed by the "offset" method (also known as lithography), rather than by metal type. The printing process itself takes about two weeks after blues, and binding and jacketing the book takes another two to three weeks. Each task in itself does not take that long, but allowances are made for scheduling and the movement of materials from one place to another.

The Jacket or Cover

Work on the book's jacket (or cover, in the case of a paperback) is going on while the book is going through the production process. A jacket has the components shown in Figure 8 (below). In most trade houses, the artwork and type used on the jacket are the responsibility of the art director; the "copy" (descriptive material) is usually written by the book's editor or by a professional copywriter.

Design. The design of the jacket or cover is very important because it serves as a poster for the book. It should quickly and effectively communicate what the book is about and should also be easily reproducible so that it can be used in advertising and promoting the book.

The design concept is developed by the art director after reading the manuscript or a description of the book and discussing it with the editor. (In a mass-market house, this discussion usually takes place in a "cover conference" also attended by marketing people.) The overall "look" and whether it should be an all-type jacket or should include an illustration will be decided on. This will depend both on the nature of the book and on the budget available. Obviously the budget for a first novel with an initial printing of 5,000 copies is somewhat less substantial than that for a potential blockbuster with a first printing of 100,000.

The art director may develop the design himself, or may

Figure 8
ELEMENTS OF A BOOK JACKET

Back flap copy   Verso ("back ad")   Spine   Front cover   Front flap copy

use a free-lance artist who specializes in jacket design. The first stage will be pencil sketches showing various designs. The art director will select one of these "thumbnails," and a "comp" showing these elements in more finished form will be prepared and submitted to the editor and others for approval. (Again, you won't see this unless you have a consultation clause in your contract.) The final camera-ready art and type will then be pasted up on a mechanical board.

The Copy. The copy on the back and flaps of the jacket, and on the front and back and perhaps the first few inside pages of a paperback, can play an important role in convincing a potential customer to buy the book. One of the most important elements can be quotations from influential people endorsing the book. You can be of considerable help, by providing the names of well-known people who may be willing to read an early copy of the book and provide a "blurb." You may already have provided this information on your author questionnaire (see Chapter 6), but your editor will probably bring up the matter again at this time. He will also ask you for biographical information if you haven't already provided it.

Your editor should also be able to produce the names of people who might be willing to help publicize the book. Some of these may be writers he has worked with in the past; others are likely to be well-known people whom the editor may not know but who can be presumed to have some interest in the topic.

What's usually sent to these readers is a "bound galley," which is produced by cutting up a set of loose, uncorrected galleys, photocopying them, and binding them like a book with a paper cover. These are also called BOM's because the technique was first developed for submissions to the Book-of-the-Month Club. They usually cost about $10 each, so the publisher will try to keep his order to a minimum.

The bound galleys will be sent with a letter from you or the editor briefly describing the book and asking the reader to provide a comment if he wishes to do so. It's difficult to predict the degree of response; sometimes you get excellent quotes from people you didn't really expect to hear from, while people you were counting on don't respond at all.

The editor or copywriter will probably wait about four to six weeks for responses before preparing jacket or cover copy for the book, including a short biography of you. If enough quotes are not received, the space may be filled by reviews of one of your previous books, excerpts or illustrations from the book, the table of contents (in the case of nonfiction), or perhaps your photograph.

Editors don't normally ask authors to prepare their own copy, though it does happen on occasion. You may, of course, ask for the opportunity of submitting a draft. You should be given the opportunity of checking the final copy for errors, although your editor doesn't *have* to show it to you unless your contract gives you the right of consultation or approval.

If a photograph of you is to be used, it's your responsibility to provide it, as well as permission to use it on the jacket and in advertising and promotion if it was taken by a professional photographer. Try to obtain permission to use it on all editions of the book. Also ask the photographer what credit line should be used.

Final Stages. After the jacket copy has been written and copyedited, the art director will specify type to conform with the typefaces being used on the front and spine of the jacket or cover. After type has been set, a proof will be checked by the editor and art director, and then repro copy will be pasted up on a mechanical board and sent to the printer together with the mechanical of the art.

The jacket printer will prepare a "color key" or blueprint showing all of the elements of the jacket in place, and identifying the colors selected by the art director. If all is well, the jackets are then printed. (If the publisher regards this as a major book, he may elect to have color proofs prepared before the flaps are ready so that the company's sales representative can take samples of the jacket on the road.)

Schedule is important here. It usually takes about two weeks to print jackets after mechanicals have been released to the printer, and it can take even longer if the jacket is being printed on special paper such as foil. Copies of the finished jacket are then sent to the production department for approval. If all is well, the printer is then instructed to ship the jackets to the bindery, where they will probably be put on by machine. (Hand-jacketing is rare and expensive.)

Some Additional Information About Design and Production. The design and production of books is a highly technical process and one you may not be interested in. However, for authors who do want to know more about it, I have included the following material. For additional information, see the books on this subject listed in the Bibliography.

How a Book Is Designed

While the original manuscript is being copyedited, a duplicate manuscript is transmitted (usually by the copyediting department) to the design and production departments for use in preparing a manufacturing estimate and designing the book.

The editor will tell the designer how the book should look in terms of overall length, "trim size" (book-page size), and general appearance. For example, if it's a very short book the editor may ask the designer to "bulk it up" by using a large-sized typeface and generous margins; if it is very long, he may ask the designer to "save" space. The editor will also indicate the overall "look" he wants for the book—airy and informal, or "serious"—and the designer will choose the appropriate typefaces, format, etc., to conform to the look.

The designer will start her work by getting an exact count of the number of characters in the manuscript. Each different type of material has to be counted separately; for example, if the book contains long quotations, this "extract" material will have to be dealt with differently from the rest of the text. In a small publishing house, the designer will probably do this character count herself; in a larger house, a copy of the manuscript will be sent to the "compositor" (the firm that is setting the book), and the compositor will provide the count.

When the character count has been completed, the designer can begin planning how the different elements will go into the book—front matter, illustrations, index, etc.—and what kinds and sizes of typefaces will produce the desired results. She or he also has to consider the typesetting and printing methods to be used. (There are some systems now where the author essentially does the typesetting using a word·processor or minicomputer, but this is still fairly uncommon and I'm assuming here that more traditional methods are being used.) The basic aim is to get the book to fit onto printing and binding equipment of a certain size while preserving the feel and legibility of the book. In most instances the designer will be trying to design the book so that it can be printed on 16-page or 32-page "forms."

Another important consideration is the desired trim size of the book. Trade paperbacks can be virtually any size or trim, but for hardcover books, most publishers try to work with three standard sizes: small, medium, and large. The exact dimensions may vary from publisher to publisher, but usually the small trim for nonillustrated books is approximately 5⅜ x 8 inches, medium is 5½ x 8⅜ inches, and large is 6 x 9 inches. These dimensions have to do with the standard press sizes and the page size that results when the sheet is folded and trimmed. The large size is normally reserved for unusually long or important books, the small for very short books. Size also depends on the limitations of the binding equipment available.

With the character count in hand, the designer will first figure out how many pages will be taken up by material other than straight text, such as illustrations, tables, and front matter. She or he will then tentatively decide the margins she or he wants to leave at the top, bottom, and sides of the page, and will turn to a type table that specifies the average number of characters per line which a particular typeface will yield. Times Roman, for example, yields more characters per 26-pica line than does a Helvetica face in the same point size.

To explain briefly: Typefaces have many characteristics, including how they look, how high they are, and how much space they take up across a horizontal line. Figure 9 (page 124) shows two different faces, Times Roman and Helvetica Roman. Times Roman has "serifs," which are the short lines at an angle to the upper and lower strokes of a letter; Helvetica is a "sans-serif," or nonserif, face. A "point" is 0.01384 inch, and type height is always specified in points, with most books set in 9-, 10-, or 11-point type. But note that comparable point sizes run longer in Helvetica than in Times; that is, you get fewer characters on a line. Lines are usually specified in "picas." A pica contains 12 points and runs 0.166 inch, and 6 picas are slightly shorter than 1 inch. Book pages usually have from 24 to 26 pica lines.

After consulting the type book, the designer will multiply

the average number of characters per line the particular face yields by the number of lines that a full page of type will run (usually about 40), to determine how many characters can be contained on an average page. This usually comes out to something like two thousand characters——roughly four hundred fifty words. The designer can then divide this number into the character count for the book to get a rough count of the number of pages that will be required for the text.

If the book is to include an index, the designer will set aside the number of index pages specified by the editor. A cookbook, for example, will need a long index, while a simple nonfiction book may need a very short one. The number of index pages is then added to the number of estimated text pages and the number of pages to be set aside for front matter, etc., to determine how close the book will come to a multiple of 16 or 32, with a few blank pages at the front or back. If the total leaves too many blanks, the design may be reworked, perhaps using a different typeface or different size of the same face, or perhaps different "leading" (space between the lines). If this doesn't work, it may be decided to use one or two smaller press forms.

Once the design is pretty much as desired, the designer makes pencil sketches of sample pages to show the editor, or may have the compositor make up sample pages showing the text type, placement of folios, running heads, and other special elements (such as extracts, dialogue, lists, etc.), and "display" type (18-point type or larger). The display type contributes importantly to the look of the book; a light romance might have a light, flowing, "feminine" display type, while a serious nonfiction book might have heavier, more "masculine" display type.

Once the final design has been agreed on, the designer will write detailed instructions for the typesetter on the copyedited manuscript.

Typesetting

Typesetting has undergone something of a revolution in recent years. Until fairly recently all typesetting involved an operator in a typesetting house sitting at a keyboard, working from a copyedited manuscript with detailed typesetting instructions. He would type ("keyboard") the entire manu-

Figure 9
SERIF AND SANS-SERIF TYPEFACES

Times Roman

BASIC CHARACTERS IN FONT

ABCDEFGHIJKLMNOPQRSTUVWXYZ
abcdefghijklmnopqrstuvwxyz
$1234567890   .,:;!?'`'()—-

8 pt.   He who first shortened the labor of copyists by devic
e of movable types was disbanding hired armies, and
HE WHO FIRST SHORTENED THE LABOR O

9 pt.   He who first shortened the labor of copyists by
device of movable types was disbanding hired a
HE WHO FIRST SHORTENED THE LAB

10 pt.   He who first shortened the labor of copyist
movable types was disbanding hired armies,
HE WHO FIRST SHORTENED THE L

Helvetica

BASIC CHARACTERS IN FONT

ABCDEFGHIJKLMNOPQRSTUVWXYZ
abcdefghijklmnopqrstuvwxyz
$1234567890   .,:;!?'`'()—-

8 pt.   He who first shortened the labor of copyists by de
vice of movable types was disbanding hired armie
HE WHO FIRST SHORTENED THE LABOR OF CO

9 pt.   He who first shortened the labor of copyists b
y device of movable types was disbanding hir
HE WHO FIRST SHORTENED THE LABOR O

10 pt.   He who first shortened the labor of copyi
f movable types was disbanding hired ar
HE WHO FIRST SHORTENED THE LABO

script into the machine, which would then produce type in one form or another.

The advent of computers and telecommunication lines is rapidly changing all this. Some houses are experimenting with their own in-house typesetting facilities, while in other cases, the keyboarding step can be eliminated by using a cassette tape or other magnetic recording medium prepared by the author himself, which can be fed into a computer-controlled system that will translate the material into type. However, both of these alternatives are still in the developmental stage, and a lot of additional work remains to be done before all the "bugs" have been worked out. In the meantime, a few publishers are still using hot-type systems of various kinds, and the majority are using optical typesetting systems.

Hot Type (the Linotype Machine). Most book work involving hot type is done on a machine called a Linotype. Figure 10 (page 126) shows what a Linotype machine looks like. An operator types in the text held in front of him on a copyboard. As he presses a key, the corresponding character, called a "mat," slides down a channel and joins other characters that have already been set on a rail. When the prescribed number of characters for that line have been set, the operator presses a key that causes the line of type to be "justified"—that is, spaces will be inserted between the words so that this line is exactly the same length as the other lines to be set on that page (except for lines at the end of paragraphs, of course).

When the line of type is properly justified, another key is pressed which causes that line of type to be cast from the mats—hence the name Linotype. The single line of type is called a slug. These slugs of type are placed in a long tray called a galley tray, and the trays themselves are stored in cabinets.

When the entire book has been set—with the possible exception of display type that this particular compositor may not have available—the galley trays are taken to a proof press. The tray of type is laid on the bed of the press, the type is inked, and a long sheet of paper is pressed against the inked type. This is the galley proof that you will eventually read. Note that the type in the tray is actually upside down and backwards, so that the type on the paper will come out

Figure 10
<u>LINOTYPE MACHINE</u>

"right reading." Several sets of galley proofs will be pulled. One of these sets will be proofread by a trained proofreader, and printer's errors (called PE's) will be marked on this master set. Then the manuscript (now "foul copy"), the master set, and other sets of galleys ordered by the publisher will be sent to the publisher.

Cold Type. Cold type, or cold composition, is any form of composition in which characters are not cast in lead or metal. Three systems are common.

In *photocomposition,* the type characters are stenciled on a film disk. The disk is positioned in front of a light source, so that when the proper character is rotated in front of the light source, the image of that character is transferred onto light-sensitive paper. When the entire text has been set, the light-sensitive paper is removed from the machine and developed to produce a proof from which photocopies will be made for checking. Figure 11 (page 128) shows a variation of this system in which the correct characters are obtained by rotating a lens turret mechanism. The image is then reflected from a mirror onto a drum carrying the photosensitive material.

Computer typesetting allows the operator to key in all kinds of typesetting commands. The computer can automatically right-justify the text, change from one type font to another, make decisions about dividing words at the end of a line, and so on. Some of these systems are now set up to take input directly from word processors, often via telephone lines or other remote-transmission equipment.

In *"strike-on" composing,* the final text is typed on a special machine called a Composer. This will be text from which the book will be printed; there will be no further stages of proof, or chances for correction. This is usually used for very complicated technical books that involve a lot of mathematical or chemical formulas, or books that will have very short press runs and therefore do not justify the expense of the usual typesetting techniques.

Printing: Three Basic Methods

Letterpress. In the old days, printing was done by a method called letterpress. In this method, metal type (such as that from the Linotype machine) was placed on the bed of a press, along with engravings of any illustrations to be included with the text; everything was carefully adjusted to make sure it was level and "type high"; the type was inked; and printing was done by passing paper over the inked type. This produced excellent image quality, but had the disadvan-

Figure 11
LENS SYSTEM OF A PHOTOTYPESETTER

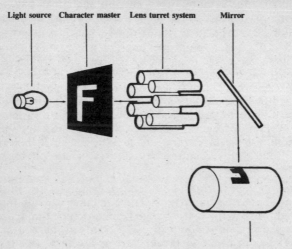

Simplified diagram of a phototypesetter with lens turret system
for character sizing.

tage that it involved a lot of make-ready time, and wore the type out quickly. Eventually, printers began using plastic plates rather than the metal type itself.

Gravure. Other printing methods in which paper was brought into contact with plates bearing ink were also developed. In the method called gravure or intaglio, the plates are etched and then inked, so that when the paper is brought into contact with the plates, the ink is drawn out of the etched surface of the plate and transferred onto the paper. This method is particularly good for high-speed printing, and is still used for printing most newspapers, but is too expensive for most book production.

Offset. The method most commonly used for printing books is called offset. This method capitalizes on the fact that oil and water do not mix. The source of the images is the repro proofs prepared by the typesetter. The repros are photographed by the printer, and the resulting negative brought into contact with a photosensitive printing plate. A strong light shows through the negatives where the images appear and thus the images are transferred onto the plate. When the plate is put on the printing press, the oily ink sticks only to the image areas, while water washes the ink away from the other areas.

Preparation of Plates for Offset Printing. The typesetter and the printer are often different companies, so after the repro proofs have been completely corrected by the typesetter (or pasted up by the publisher's design department), they are sent to the firm that will be printing the book.

The repros have to be carefully arranged so that they "come out" in the right order after the press sheet is folded. This process is called imposition.

To understand what I mean, take a piece of paper and try it yourself. Fold the paper from top to bottom, and then from left to right (see Figure 12, steps 1 and 2). Now number from pages 1 to 8 in the bottom corners (step 3) without cutting the top folds. When you open the sheet of paper up, the numbers will appear as shown in step 4. Printers do the same thing, but the problem becomes more complicated as the number of pages to be printed on one side of a press sheet increases. Most printers work with tables that show them how the negatives have to be arranged for different-sized press sheets.

The negatives are put in the proper position by "stripping" them into proper position on a large yellow sheet usually referred to as goldenrod. (Some machines do this automatically.) Rectangles of goldenrod are cut away from the image areas of the film, leaving "windows" of negatives ready for contacting and exposing to blues and to plates. When all the copy is in exact position, the sheet is called a flat.

Blues are made by putting each flat in contact with a large sheet of photosensitive paper and running it through an ammonia developer. The blues are sent to the publisher for a final review before the book is printed. Editorial changes are prohibitively expensive at this stage, but blues should be carefully checked for position, page sequence, and to be sure that all folios and running heads are intact. The necessary corrections in the film are made but the printer will probably not wait for approval of these corrections since time is of the essence. Instead, he will send the publisher "confirming" blues and proceed to make printing plates as described earlier. The plates are usually made of flexible aluminum with a photosensitive surface; after the plate has been "shot," the nonimage area is washed away in a chemical bath.

Photographs. Photographs have tones which cannot be exactly reproduced in the printing process. So what the printer does is photograph a black-and-white glossy print through a screen that breaks the images on the photograph into little dots of various sizes. The resulting negative is called a halftone, and there will be many large dots where the image is dark, and fewer and smaller dots where the image is light. The simplest way to see how this works is to look at a photograph in a newspaper with a magnifying glass. You will see that what appears to be an image with tones is actually a cluster of dots.

Figure 12
A SIMPLE IMPOSITION AND FOLDING

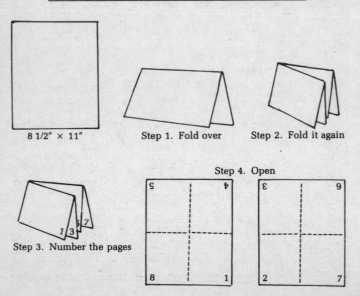

8 1/2" × 11"   Step 1. Fold over   Step 2. Fold it again

Step 3. Number the pages   Step 4. Open

Color Illustrations. Color illustrations present even more problems. The colors that the human eye sees are actually combinations of the three primary colors: red, blue, and yellow. Printing inks cannot reproduce these colors exactly, so what the printer does is separate the colors of the original art into their component primaries for rendering by four ink colors: magenta, cyan, yellow, and black. The illustration is photographed four times: (1) through a green filter which absorbs blue and yellow, yielding film with the magenta (violet-red) portion of the image; (2) through an orange filter which absorbs red and yellow to yield cyan (green-blue); (3) through a violet-blue filter which absorbs red and blue to yield yellow; and (4) through a yellow filter to yield the black film, which is needed for depth and definition.

If the printer is making these separations without the help of an electronic scanner, the film will have to be "color-corrected" (photographically or by hand) to compensate for the impurities of the printing ink. The four separations are then screened to produce dot formations, and the four screened separations are used to make printing plates. If an electronic scanner is used, the film will be color-corrected and screened automatically. Printing can then be done either by running the same sheet of paper through the press four times or by using a large press that can add all four colors in the same pass. Obviously, these processes are time-consuming and expensive, which is why the use of color illustrations has to be kept to a minimum in most cases. (Art books are an obvious exception.)

Paper is also a consideration. The rough, "toothy" paper used for printing text or line illustrations is not satisfactory for color printing because it causes distortions of the colors and is not bright enough to provide a good reflective surface. For this reason, special high-quality paper has to be used for color printing, adding still more to the cost. Black-and-white photographs also print better on high-quality paper, which is why they are usually printed on "glossy" stock and then added to the book as a separate section or "insert."

The Printing Press. Offset printing is done on a press that uses three cylinders (Figure 13). The printing plate is rolled around one cylinder and inked, and the images are then offset onto a rubber "blanket" rolled around a cylinder that is rotating in the opposite direction. The images on the blanket are then transferred onto the paper that is moving across an impression cylinder. The reason for this transferring is that the water being applied to the plate cylinder would make the paper too wet. By transferring it twice, the water problem is negated and the image ends up "right-reading."

Figure 13
OFFSET PRESS

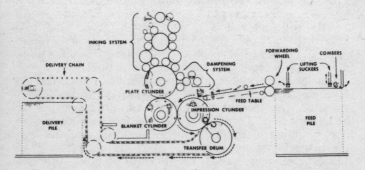

Printing will be done either on large individual sheets of paper or on a continuous roll of paper ("web") which is then cut to proper size. When all of the sheets for the book have been printed, the sheets will be folded into "signatures," "end papers" will be glued to the first and last signature, and the signatures will be "gathered." A few sets of these "F&G's" (folded and gathered sheets) will be sent to the publisher for checking.

Binding. This can be done in a variety of ways. Figure 14 shows some techniques in which the signatures are sewn together. After the signatures are sewn together, the outside edges may be sprayed with colored ink; this is called a top stain. Next, the back of the signatures will be rounded under pressure, glue will be applied, and a strip of gauze extending about one inch on each side (called a crash) is applied. Glue is applied to the back of the crash, "headbands" may be attached, and "lining paper" cut to the exact length and width of the book will be put over the crash.

The "case" usually consists of heavy pasteboard at the front and back of the book, and a strip of paper or paste-

Figure 14
TYPES OF BINDING

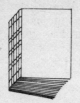

A. Smythe sewing

B. Side sewing

C. Saddle stitching

SEWING THE SIGNATURE

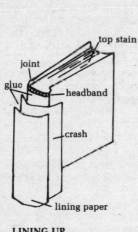

LINING UP

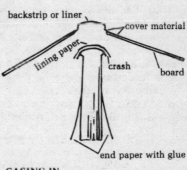

CASING IN

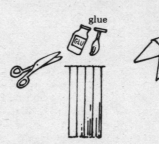

PERFECT BINDING

board along the spine of the book. The boards themselves will be covered by cloth or some other kind of material, and the cloth covering the "spine" will have lettering specified by the designer giving the book title, author name, and publisher's logo. The front of the boards may be stamped or "blind stamped" (impressed with an image but having no color) with some sort of illustration. The signatures approach the cover along a conveyor belt. The end papers are given a coat of paste, the case is dropped into place, and the front and back are tightly clamped so that the cover is firmly affixed to the end papers. Then the books are jacketed by machine or by hand.

A number of other binding techniques have also been developed. In the "adhesive perfect" method, used primarily for trade and mass-market paperbacks, the backs of the signatures (the folded edges) are trimmed off and strong, flexible glue is applied. Each page is held securely, but the back does not lie flat. In the "notch" or "book-lock" method, the backs of the signatures are perforated and cross-hatched and glue is forced into the exposed paper fibers.

A paperback book has many fewer operations. A preprinted cover is dropped onto combined signatures, and the signatures and cover are trimmed together.

6
Marketing: Publicity, Advertising, and Promotion

I am sitting in the smallest room in my house. I have your review in front of me. Soon it will be behind me.
—German composer MAX REGAR, *Lexicon of Musical Invective*

While the production staff is busily turning your manuscript into a handsomely printed and bound book, other people in the publishing company are turning their attention to the problem of letting the world know about your book. There are about 15,000 trade hardcovers and paperbacks and 5,000 mass-market paperbacks published each year, so it can be quite a task to get your book to stand out from the crowd. This is the job of the marketing group, which includes people involved in publicity, advertising and promotion, and sales. (Subsidiary rights may also be included in this group but is usually regarded as being somewhat separate.) In this chapter we will talk about the publicity and advertising/promotion functions; in the next chapter we will tackle sales.

What Is Publicity?

The term *publicity* refers to the efforts of the publishing house to obtain free notice of your book in the media—newspapers, magazines, radio, television. It is "free" only in the sense that the publisher does not directly pay for the cost of the space or time devoted to discussing your book; in fact, these efforts usually cost the publisher quite a bit of money in terms of free books, postage, and staff time.

Publicity is usually the responsibility of a separate department that has close ties with reviewers, feature writers, radio and television show hosts, and other people in the media. Publicists send out books for review, write press releases, set up author tours, help support industry efforts to publicize books, and perform other public relations tasks. Usually these publicists are on the staff of the publishing house, but if the house is small or there is great demand for a book or a complicated author tour has to be set up, the company may hire a free-lance publicist to assist. (This is frequently done if the publisher is on the East Coast and most of the tour will take place in the West, in which case a West Coast publicist will be used.) Authors also occasionally hire a publicity or public relations firm to help publicize their book—a topic I'll return to at the end of this chapter.

How Is the Publication Date for a Book Set?

The publication date for a book depends both on the availability of the finished book and on the needs of the house. The usual practice is to schedule the publication date of a trade book for between four to eight weeks after the books are available. This is to give the publisher enough time (assuming the house is located on the East Coast) to ship books to stores on the West Coast and to get them to reviewers, and to give the reviewers time to read the book and prepare their review. The publication date then becomes the "release" date for reviews of and stories about the book. Sometimes this date seems to be honored more in the breach than in the observance, as some reviews will probably run before the books even reach the stores, while others may run several months—or even years!—after the publication date. This difficulty in observing publication dates has to do with many elements, including the review space available and whether the publishing house ships the books earlier or later than expected. Generally, however, most reviewers (especially those for the larger publications) try to honor the publication date when possible.

The list that your book is scheduled for will depend on both production requirements and marketing considerations. Most trade houses publish two lists a year: one in the fall, taking in books to be published between August or September of one year and January or February of the next (for example, August 1983 to January 1984), and one in the spring. Since it takes approximately six and a half months to produce a finished book—from the time it goes into copyediting— any manuscripts delivered to the publisher between January and June could (at least theoretically) be published on the fall list. Manuscripts delivered between July and December would probably go on the spring list. However, many publishers prefer a longer lead time because of their planning and marketing cycle. Nine months or even a year is not uncommon.

Other elements besides the normal planning or production schedule can determine when the book will be published, however. If it is a particularly important book for the house, it may be put on a crash production schedule to get books faster than usual. If it is an expensive illustrated book, the publisher may deliberately schedule it to come out in October or November, in time for the Christmas gift-buying season. If it is a book with good potential for making the bestseller list (such as a new book by a popular, well-known author), the publisher may also want to put it on the fall list, perhaps for publication in September or October.

If it's a topical book, on the other hand, the publisher will try to schedule a publication date that makes the most sense for the subject matter of the book. A book on skiing would do best in the fall or winter; a book on body-surfing, in the spring. The other books on the house's list, and the books being brought out by other publishers, also have to be taken into account. If the house has two nonfiction books on home repairs, for example, it's usually best to schedule them at least a list apart so that they are not competing with each other for the bookseller's dollar. If the publisher hears that another house is bringing out a very similar book, he may either try to crash the production schedule to get his own book early, or postpone it for a season.

As the author, you generally don't have too much to say about when your book is published, unless there is a clause in your contract which says that the book has to be published within a specified period of time after delivery and acceptance. If there is some reason why this cannot (or should not) happen, the publisher is obliged to tell you about it. In any case, it would be unreasonable for your publisher to postpone publication for too long a period, and you have a right to protest if that seems to be happening.

The Author Questionnaire

One of the most useful tools in the publicizing of your book is a questionnaire that you may be asked to fill out early in the publishing process. This questionnaire provides a great deal of personal information about you and the book which can be used by the marketing staff and by your editor in getting the word out about the book.

Fill out the questionnaire as completely as you can. Information about your hometown, other places you have lived, and your current residence and place of work will signal the publicist to send news about the book to newspapers in these areas. List any honors you have received and professional organizations to which you belong; members of these organizations will be interested in hearing that you are having a book published, and may be willing to buy books in bulk or give quotes for use in advertising and promotion. List other colleagues or "opinion makers" who might give a quote or otherwise help to publicize your book. If you have friends in the media who might be interested in interviewing you or reviewing your book, indicate that as well.

If you've had anything published previously, provide details. This is particularly helpful to the sales and subsidiary-rights departments. If you have done any lecturing or public speaking, let the publicity department know and indicate whether you are planning any appearances or lectures in the future; it may be possible to coordinate these appearances with publicity for your book. (But also indicate if you think you might *not* want to make public appearances on behalf of the book.)

If you are asked to provide a description of your book, make it as useful to the marketing people as possible. What is unique and important about this particular book? How does it compare with others? What is its main competition?

What points would you like to see stressed in the advertising and promotion for the book? Remember, you know your book better than anyone. Also indicate if you are working on a new book.

Overall Publicity Plans

The publicity process begins shortly after you have delivered the final manuscript and it has been added to the publication schedule. Copies of the manuscript are distributed to the marketing staff, and an overall plan for the promotion of the book is formulated.

The amount of money and time devoted to a book usually depends on its first printing. If the publisher is planning a large first printing, that printing will have to be supported by advertising and intensive publicity efforts. The publisher will send out many free copies to reviewers and columnists and will also spend money on ads and a promotion tour. If the book has a small first printing, the money available for promotion will be correspondingly less. Publicity for the book will be mainly in the form of free copies sent to reviewers and others, and possibly a press release. In addition to the plans for specific books on the list, the director of publicity will probably arrange to meet with important reviewers early in the season to go over the entire list, pointing out those books that the house plans to support most strongly, and those books that the particular reviewer is likely to be most interested in.

Reviews

Reviews are important to the publication of a trade book. Without reviews, it is difficult to make a book stand out from the horde of other books being published at the same time, particularly if there is no advertising budget for it. Some people claim that even bad reviews are better than none at all, and others believe that for some books, bad reviews are *better* than good reviews. Whatever the case, the point is that your book needs attention from the media.

There are two levels of reviews: those in the trade press and those in consumer publications.

Trade Reviews. There are a number of trade magazines that are usually sent early copies of the book for review. They include *Publishers Weekly* (*PW*), *Kirkus Reviews, Library Journal* (*LJ*), and *ALA Booklist*. If it's a children's book, a copy will also be sent to *School Library Journal* (*SLJ*); if it's academic in nature, a copy will be sent to *Choice,* which reviews books of interest to universities and high schools.

Both *PW* and *Kirkus* try to run their reviews about six weeks before publication. The *PW* reviews are written by a staff of professional reviewers, plus freelancers. The magazine reviews about one hundred books a week, of which some two thirds are hardcover trade titles; the rest are trade paperbacks, mass-market paperback originals and reprints, and children's books. Thus, *PW* reviews about five thousand books a year—which means that not all of the new trade or mass-market books are reviewed (including some from the biggest and most powerful publishers). About the only thing a publisher can do is make sure that *PW* receives an early copy of the book. The *PW* reviews are heavily relied on by booksellers and librarians in deciding which books to buy, and also can be useful in promoting the book if the review is good and has a few quotable lines or phrases. They also have an impact on the publishing house in the sense that a good review has a tonic effect while a bad one can be somewhat depressing.

Kirkus reviews about forty-five hundred trade adult and children's books a year. Its reviews tend to be longer and somewhat more acerbic than the *PW* reviews; its principal readership is librarians rather than booksellers.

Many librarians will not order a book until it has been reviewed by *LJ* and *Booklist*. The reviews are usually written by librarians or academics, and typically appear much later than the reviews in *PW* or *Kirkus;* it's not unusual for a review to appear several months after a book has been published. Orders from libraries therefore come in to a publisher much later than orders from the bookstore trade, although many librarians order from wholesalers rather than directly from the publisher anyway.

The publisher will probably send bound galleys to these important trade publications so that they have time to write the review and run it six or eight weeks before publication. In addition to being a good source of quotes and providing information to potential buyers, these trade reviews are watched closely by reviewers for other publications to see which books in the upcoming season are likely to be most important.

Consumer Magazines and Newspapers. There are about ten thousand magazines published in this country and approximately the same number of newspapers, so no publisher can afford to send a free copy of the book to every one of them. What the publicity department does instead is pick out those publications that carry the most news about books, or that are most suitable for the book in question.

Certain of the major consumer publications will be sent bound galleys rather than bound books because some periodicals have long lead times and a good review can help a book enormously. Figure 15 (page 142) lists some of the most important publications and syndicates carrying book news. A syndicate provides book reviews and other book news to newspapers that subscribe to this service. Many newspapers use syndicated material exclusively because they do not have their own reviewers.

Publications that do not receive bound galleys will be sent a copy of the bound book if the publicity department thinks a review in the publication will be helpful. Most publicity departments work with prepared lists of publications, broken down on the basis of circulation and/or subject matter. The "A" list, for example, would probably include the publications listed in Figure 15 (and perhaps others). The "B" list might encompass magazines with smaller circulations, and the "C" list, daily or weekly newspapers with smaller circulations plus small literary magazines. In addition, the publicist will consider publications listed on the author questionnaire, magazines that specialize in this subject that you might not have mentioned, and possibly freelance reviewers who have heard about the book and want to write a review "on spec."

The number of free books mailed out will depend on the publisher's budget for the book. The usual number is between 150 and 300 copies. All of these free books cost the publisher money, of course, both in the cost of the books or bound galleys and in postage or messenger costs. Books being sent to important media in New York usually go by messenger, with each delivery costing about $5.

Figure 15
MAJOR CONSUMER PUBLICATIONS
AND SYNDICATES

Newspapers with Sunday book supplements
Chicago Sun-Times Show-Book World
Chicago Tribune Books World
Los Angeles Times Book Review
New York Times Book Review
Washington Post Book World

Daily newspapers in the East
Boston Globe
Christian Science Monitor
New York Daily News
New York Post
New York Times
Philadelphia Inquirer
Wall Street Journal

Other daily newspapers
Chicago Sun-Times
Chicago Tribune
Cleveland Plain Dealer
Dallas Times
Denver Post
Detroit Free Press
Houston Chronicle
Los Angeles Times
Miami Herald
San Francisco Chronicle

Syndicated reviews
Associated Press
John Barkham
King Features
Gene Shalit (Scrooge & Marley)
United Press International

Weekly periodicals
New York
The New Yorker
Newsweek
People
Time
Village Voice

Semimonthly and monthly magazines: general interest
Atlantic Monthly
Commentary
Esquire (bi-monthly)
Harper's Magazine
New Republic
Playboy
Saturday Review

Monthly magazines: women's interest
Cosmopolitan
Harper's Bazaar
Ladies Home Journal
Mademoiselle
Redbook
Vogue

How Reviews Are Assigned. Some of the magazines and newspapers use staff reviewers, but most of them use syndicated material or assign books to outside reviewers. In the latter case, the book review editor is responsible for deciding which books of the hundreds received each week should be reviewed, based on such things as his personal reaction to the book, advice from colleagues and friends, the amount of space available, the amount of attention the book has already received in the media, and the quality of any supplementary material (such as a press kit) provided by the publisher's publicity department. Very often a book that has already received some attention will get more attention because it has been identified as being "worthwhile." However, review editors also often select a previously unreviewed book if it is particularly appropriate to their publication.

Choosing an appropriate reviewer is important. The editor of a major publication like the *New York Times Book Review* is personally acquainted with many excellent writers and reviewers, but will also listen to suggestions from his staff and consider requests from people who ask to review a particular book. These requests are viewed with caution, however, because as Doris Grumbach observed after a stint as the literary editor of the *New Republic,* "There are three dangerous categories of persons who ask to review books: friends of the writer, enemies of the writer, and the academic who has just completed his thesis on the writer and now wants an opportunity to display his erudition. The friend will spoil the review with fulsome praise, the enemy with self-serving destructive spume, and the well-meaning scholar may drown it in academic ambiguity."*

The major publications try to run their reviews within two or three weeks of the book's announced publication date. For a monthly magazine, this means that the review should appear in the issue dated one month before the book's publication date, because the magazine usually arrives on the stands a few weeks before the date printed on its cover. Smaller magazines and newspapers normally run their reviews later (unless they are using syndicated material), because they have to wait to get bound books (usually mailed fourth class from the publisher) and because they may want to wait to see what the bigger publications do.

Incidentally, reviewers for big publications like the *New York Times Book Review* are paid. Freelance reviewers for smaller publications usually work without fee or for a free copy of the book.

*"*An Editor's Report," New York Times Book Review,* August 17, 1975, p. 31.

A Press Release or Press Kit. One thing publicists frequently do to bring a book to the attention of media people and provide additional information for reviewers is prepare a "press release" or a "press kit." A press release is usually a single sheet briefly describing the book and author and pointing up the book's most important features. If your book is being published because you won a literary contest, for example, that fact will be noted. If the book has a "hard news" angle—a new method of treating cancer, say, or the discovery of corrupt practices within some branch of the government—this aspect will be stressed. The top of the release will give the pub date of the book and indicate whether the news can be released immediately or should be held until a later date.

The press release will probably not be prepared until shortly before bound books are due so that the latest publication information and any late-breaking news can be included. The release may then be included with bound books sent to reviewers, columnists, feature writers, talk-show hosts, etc., but will also be sent to other media people who are not getting a free copy of the book. Between 500 and 1,000 releases are usually sent out by a large publishing house.

If the house considers your book to be very important, a press kit containing such things as the press release, a summary of significant rights sales, copies of good quotes and reviews, and a color proof of the jacket will be prepared (probably by the promotion department) for the major reviewers and columnists and for important booksellers. Such a kit is expensive, however, and will be prepared only if the book has a large enough first printing to justify the expense.

Publication Day. For most authors of trade books, publication day comes and goes without much hoopla on the part of the publishing house. For a major book, however, the publicity department may arrange a party or a press conference.

Publication day parties can take many forms, from a tugboat ride around Manhattan Island to a bash in a ballroom attended by hundreds of notables (and not-so-notables). Most times, it's somewhat more subdued: a party in a bookstore, say, or a cocktail party at your editor's apartment, with thirty to forty people in attendance, including some of your personal friends, book reviewers, some paperback and book-club people, your agent, and perhaps even a few key booksellers. It's a chance for people to meet you, rub elbows with other people in the business, and eat and drink for free.

If your book is particularly newsworthy, the publisher might arrange a press breakfast or conference rather than a cocktail party. Press conferences are usually scheduled for the morning, commonly between 10 A.M. and noon so that newspaper and wire-service reporters have time to file stories for the afternoon or next morning's early edition, and television reporters have time to edit their tapes for the evening news show. Holding such a press conference ensures that the story will break in several places at once and that several reporters will be able to interview you at one time.

Taking the Show on the Road: the Author Tour. If your book is likely to interest hosts of radio and TV talk shows and has a large enough first printing to justify the expense, your publisher may ask you to go on a tour to promote it. This happens much less frequently than most writers think, however, and you should *not* expect this as a normal part of the publication process. It's particularly unlikely in the case of a novel, since it is difficult to discuss a work where so much depends on the writing style. It *may* be a possibility if the novel contains a lot of factual information on a subject of general interest.

A tour is a wonderful way to promote a book, and might be enjoyable. But a tour can also take a lot of time and be very demanding physically and emotionally. You should think carefully about how much time and stamina you have before leaping at the chance to be a media star.

The extent of an author tour will depend on the amount of money in the budget and the kinds of bookings the house can arrange. For a book of national interest, the publisher will try to arrange appearances in New York, Washington, Chicago, and Los Angeles, with possible additional appearances in cities like Atlanta, Cleveland, Boston, Minneapolis, Philadelphia, Houston, and Seattle. These are all cities with a number of radio and TV interview programs, good metropolitan newspapers, and a lot of bookstores. Cable television also offers increasing opportunities for author appearances, and in some cases the publisher may elect to prepare a videotape of you rather than actually sending you on tour.

The publicist handling the tour will begin by contacting

the major TV shows a month or two before pub date so that if the show is interested, an appearance can be planned. The first step is a "pitch" letter to the program coordinators telling them why you would be a great guest on the show, accompanied by a copy of the book, the press release, etc. A week or two later the publicist will call the program coordinator to find out if there is interest. This is when the real selling begins, because unless you are well-known or have appeared on the show before, the coordinator may not be eager to book you. It's the publicist's job to convince the coordinator that having you on the show will make for good TV. He will also have to work out any complications, such as the fact that certain major shows want an exclusive on their guests. (For example, if you're booked for the *Today* show you can't be on *Good Morning, America*.)

As each booking is completed, the publicist will prepare a booking sheet with the name of the show, the time and place of your appearance, whether the show is taped or live, and the name of your contact. After the bookings with the major TV shows have been made, the publicist will then try to set up radio talk shows, interviews with newspaper and magazine writers, autographing parties in bookstores, book-and-author luncheons, and so on. Most publicists try to cram in as many appearances in each city as possible because they tend to have a snowball effect—the more often you appear, the greater the cumulative impact. This should be kept to a level you can tolerate, however. Try to get the publicist to leave you some free time for appearances (or disappearances) you might want to make on your own.

Airplane and hotel reservations will be made shortly before you leave. You will probably fly tourist class, and stay overnight at a comfortable hotel. Make sure you know beforehand how you are supposed to get from place to place. The best arrangement is to reserve cabs in advance (unless you rate a driver and/or a limousine). You will probably be on your own most of the time, although the sales representative for that territory may be able to spend some time with you. Also find out if payment arrangements will be made in advance. Most major publishers have charge accounts with the airlines and big hotels, but you may be asked to use your own money in some situations and be reimbursed later.

The publicist will send announcements of the tour to *PW*, to the B. Dalton and Walden bookstore chains' newsletters, and to the *ABA Newswire* which goes to booksellers. These announcements alert booksellers in the cities where you will be appearing to have a stock of your book on hand (although a publicist friend insists that no matter what is done, an author will always manage to find a store that does not have his book). The publisher's sales department will also be notified of the tour. The publicist may stage a rehearsal for you so that you can practice answering questions that interviewers are likely to ask; if not, try to rehearse on your own, with a friend taking the part of the TV or radio host. For TV appearances, find out if you should avoid particular types of clothing.

Many authors have reported that being on the road can be an exhilarating and satisfying experience. It can also be somewhat exhausting and disorienting, and more than one author has folded the roadshow at midpoint and come home. Malcolm Boyd, author of several books and a veteran of the talk-show circuit, advises that the best thing you can do is remember why you wrote the book in the first place, and be willing to explain this over and over again. Be willing to follow the lead of the interviewer; he might not have read the book and may not stick too closely to the topic of the book. Try to stay flexible and good-humored, and remember—you're helping sell the book.

Other Jobs of the Publicity Department

The publicity department usually has other functions besides dealing with reviewers, writing press releases, and planning tours.

Clippings. One job is to keep clippings of reviews and stories about the house's authors that have appeared in magazines and newspapers. Although the magazines and newspapers are supposed to send "tearsheets" of reviews and stories, they don't always do so, so the publicity department will either hire a clipping service or keep an eye on the publications themselves. Copies of the clippings will be passed along to the editors and to the subsidiary-rights, advertising, and sales managers. Your editor should then send copies of clippings concerning your book to you.

Bibliographical Listings. It's also the responsibility of the
publicity department to make sure that the publisher's books
are listed in various bibliographical references. This includes
the Library of Congress in Washington, D.C.; various
Bowker Company listings, such as *Books in Print;* and the
Cumulative Book Index, published by the H. W. Wilson
Company.

Literary Prizes and Book Industry Events. Publicity departments may be responsible for submitting books for literary prizes sponsored by the book industry and others. This
includes such awards as the Pulitzer Prize, Nobel Prize for
Literature, the American Book Awards, and the National
Book Critics Circle award. For other types of prizes, the
nominees are selected by the sponsors of the prize, or the
books or manuscripts are submitted directly by authors.

The book industry also sponsors events that involve participation by publishers' publicity or promotion staffs, such
as the annual "New York Is Book Country" promotion in
which kiosks displaying current books are set up along New
York's Fifth Avenue.

Corporate Public Relations. Finally, publicity departments
usually represent the company in events involving public
statements, and they also prepare releases regarding the
publisher's staff and program for *PW.*

Who Handles Advertising
and Promotion?

Publicity involves efforts made by your publisher to have
someone else draw attention to your book. Advertising and
promotion are those functions that a publisher pays for directly, such as ads in newspapers and magazines, or promotional materials such as catalogs and posters.

The planning and execution of ads and promotional materials is the responsibility of an advertising and promotion
director, who usually works closely with an advertising
agency that prepares the ads and promotional materials and
buys space or time from the media. The agency is reimbursed by the publisher for the cost of preparing the ads, and

makes a 15 percent commission on the "buy" from the publication, network, or station. A few publishers have their own in-house agency, but most publishers work with an outside agency that specializes in publishers' accounts.

The term *promotion*, incidentally, is often used as an overall term for *any* publicity or advertising efforts on behalf of a book, but it is also used to refer specifically to materials such as catalogs or posters that are aimed at book dealers or used for in-store promotion.

Will Your Book Be Advertised? Whether your book will be advertised—and if so, how and to what extent—will depend on a number of factors, including the nature of the book, the budget for the book, your importance to the house (and the clout and negotiating power of your agent), and various other considerations, such as the house's desire to impress reviewers or potential buyers of subsidiary rights.

If your book is a literary first novel, for example, the advertising manager may withhold advertising dollars until he sees how the book fares in reviews, or he may elect to include it in a group ad with a number of other literary books in a publication like the *New York Review of Books*. If it's a nonfiction title, he will probably consider advertising it in special-interest magazines. For a novel with good commercial potential, however, he may plan an extensive advertising and promotion campaign.

Unless there is a specific advertising and promotion budget in your contract with the house, the amount of money spent usually depends on the budget for that particular book *and* for the list as a whole. Most publishers work on a percentage of the projected net income from trade sales of the book—typically 10 percent. Thus if the book is priced at $15 and the publisher expects to sell about 5,000 copies at an average discount of 45 percent, his net income will be about $41,250 ($8.25 per book × 5,000 copies) and his promotion budget for the book will therefore be $4,125. He won't necessarily spend all of the money on this book, however. What he may do instead is calculate the projected net income for all of the books on the list, then reapportion the monies to the books based on what he thinks is most appropriate for each book and the media he plans to use. He will also set aside a certain amount of money to advertise the list as a whole, including backlist titles. All of these figures are subject to change, however, as reviews come in and the sales pattern develops. It's possible that the budget for one book will be reduced and the budget for another increased.

Another element taken into account is the importance of the book to the house. All authors are important to their publisher, of course, but it's undoubtedly true that some authors are more equal than others. A writer whose books already represent an important part of the house's income is obviously going to receive more attention than a first-timer. And if there is a possibility of a big subsidiary-rights sale, the advertising manager may deliberately launch an elaborate advertising campaign designed to impress the big book clubs and mass-market reprinters. The campaign is also intended to help the trade sales of the book, although this may be a secondary goal.

The Seasonal Catalog and Other Catalogs

One of the first things the advertising or promotion manager will work on is the catalog for the books to be published during the upcoming season. The catalog will be used by the sales representatives when they call on accounts, by the publicity department in getting in touch with reviewers and other people in the media, and by the subsidiary-rights department in dealing with potential rights customers.

Work on the catalog usually begins a few months before the sales conference for that season. Each editor will be asked to provide a description of his upcoming books, which the advertising or promotion manager or a professional copywriter will then use (along with any available manuscript material) to prepare catalog copy. The art director will prepare artwork for the jackets and covers, and the production manager will prepare estimates of final book length, dimensions, and prices so that this information can also be included. The subsidiary-rights director may provide news of significant sub-rights sales, the promotion manager will spotlight unusual promotion plans, and bestsellers from the backlist may be highlighted.

There are also other kinds of catalogs in which books from the current list and the backlist may be advertised. Several large bookstore chains and wholesalers publish Christmas catalogs in which publishers can buy space to advertise their wares. Since this space is costly, publishers usually list only their more expensive books or ones that are proven or potential bestsellers. The Ingram (a wholesaler) catalog is particularly well-known, as are the catalogs published by Scribners (both a publisher and a bookstore), Rizzoli, the Kroch & Brentano's chain, and the Walden, Dalton, and Cokesbury chains.The Waldenbooks chain also runs its catalog as an insert in major consumer magazines like *Newsweek* and *The Economist*, and B. Dalton is planning on running their catalog in *People*. There are also various kinds of mail-order operations that publish catalogs in which your publisher might elect to buy space.

Ads in Trade Magazines

Booksellers and wholesalers are among the most important audiences for a publisher's ads, because if the books aren't in the stores, even extensive consumer advertising is not going to do much to sell the book.

Of particular value is the "list ad" which most publishers run in the spring and fall announcements issues of *PW*. In the case of a large publisher this is usually a simple listing of authors, titles, and prices. Smaller houses with fewer books usually include a brief description of each book on the list as well. In addition to the ads, information about the outstanding books on each publisher's list will appear in *PW*'s editorial pages; the copy is supplied by the publisher's publicity department.

The larger trade houses also usually take ads in one or two other issues of *PW* to feature their list, often buying the outside and inside front cover plus several additional pages. The ad typically shows the jacket and includes a brief description, news about important rights sales ("A main selection of the Book-of-the-Month Club"), and first-printing and promotion plans ("50,000-copy first printing! $50,000 ad budget!"). The idea is to let booksellers know what the house considers its most important books, to alert reviewers and subsidiary-rights buyers to books that may be of particular interest, and to keep authors and agents (at least of these books) happy. *PW* also has a number of issues highlighting particular kinds of books—children's books, religious books, etc.—in which the publisher might want to advertise.

In addition to ads in *PW*, the advertising manager may also take space in other trade journals such as *Choice* and *LJ*. Another possibility is magazines published by wholesalers or retailers for their customers. Baker & Taylor, for example, publishes a monthly magazine called *Forecast*, and the Dimondstein wholesaling company (which is owned by Bro-Dart) publishes the *DBE Digest*. These magazines carry lists of new purchases from publishers, news about recently published books that the wholesaler thinks will sell well, and publishers' ads. The Kroch & Brentano bookstore chain publishes a bimonthly magazine called *Book Chat* that carries publishers' ads.

Ads in Consumer Magazines and Newspapers

You may not be particularly aware of or impressed by your publisher's ads in the trade media, but if you are like most authors you *are* going to be very much interested in consumer advertising, and may find it hard to believe that ads don't really sell books—at least, certain types of books.

Why Not Advertise? There's no real way to prove the assertion that ads don't sell books, but most people who have been in the book business for a while eventually come to two conclusions. One is that it's almost impossible to tell exactly what does cause a particular book to sell well. Many books that don't seem particularly meritorious become bestsellers, while others that are very highly regarded by their publisher and the review media don't sell well at all. The most potent factor seems to be that mysterious phenomenon known as word of mouth—something nobody seems able to control.

The other conclusion is that advertising does not do much to *create* demand for a book, but does support and sustain it. There is really only one exception, and that is if the publisher is bringing out a book by a well-known author who has an established audience. In this case what the publisher usually does is run large "announcement" ads letting that author's audience know that a new book by one of their favorite authors is available. But in general, running an ad for someone who is "unknown" does very little. It may sell a few more copies than if the book were not advertised at all, but the cost of the ad almost always far exceeds the additional sales revenue generated.

Planning the Campaign. The decision as to how, when, and where a book should be advertised is made by the advertising manager in close cooperation with the advertising agency. Three factors will be taken into account: (1) the most appropriate medium in which to advertise, (2) the cost of advertising in that medium, and (3) the schedule of the ads.

Obviously, if your book is on a specialized subject, the advertising manager will want to run ads in the magazines and newspapers directed to that audience. If you've written a book about how to raise bees, for example, the ad manager will probably consider an ad in the *Beekeeper's Journal* but not in the *New York Times*. The cost of advertising in specialized journals is also much lower than advertising in high-circulation mass magazines and newspapers. To find these specialized magazines, the advertising manager will check guides to periodicals, the agency's media department, and your author questionnaire for tips on good places to advertise the book.

For a less specialized book (and assuming there's enough money in the budget to justify this), the manager will turn to general-interest magazines and newspapers. The single most popular print medium for trade-book advertising is the *New York Times Book Review*. *TBR* has a circulation of about 1½ million and is distributed to many subscribers outside the New York area. *TBR* is closely followed by the daily *New York Times* and the *Washington Post*. National magazines like *Time* and *Newsweek* are used much less often (although the publisher may elect to run an ad in one of the regional editions), because the rates are too expensive for most trade books. To give you an idea of the relative costs of different media: a half-page ad on the book page of the daily *New York Times* now costs about $13,000; a "standby" ad, which may appear anywhere in the paper at any time, costs approximately $7,000. A half-page ad in *Woman's Day* magazine runs about $32,000. The position of the ad in a publication also affects the cost. Preferred positions in *TBR* are opposite the index, opposite the bestseller list, or near the "Book Ends" column, but these positions cost more and have to be reserved well in advance.

Other considerations are timing and frequency. Most consumer ads are scheduled to run on or shortly after book publication date. However, if the publisher is making some kind of special prepublication offer, he may start running ads earlier. Or he may try to build up curiosity about a book by running a series of "teaser" ads in several issues of one magazine or on several pages of the same issue. If demand for a book develops rapidly, he should be prepared to support it by running follow-up ads as quickly as possible.

Radio and Television Advertising

Neither radio nor TV are used much for advertising trade hardcovers because it is felt that buyers of these books pay more attention to print reviews and ads than to the "boob tube" or the radio. However, TV and radio are occasionally used for particular kinds of books and audiences.

Television will normally be used for a book with wide appeal and a big advertising budget. The cost is tied to the nature of the show, the time slot, the range of broadcast and estimated audience size, and the number of times the ad is run. Some shows are rated as having a higher percentage of potential book buyers than others (*Donahue*, for example, is rated higher than *Dynasty*), and certain geographical regions are also rated higher than others. Depending on all of these factors, a typical TV campaign shown on network television over a period of ten days will probably cost in the neighborhood of $150,000 (not including the cost of preparing the ad, hiring actors, etc.). Local bookstores or chains sometimes advertise on television, however, because the rates at a local station are much cheaper than those for a network or nationally syndicated show. Cable television and late-night nonnetwork shows provide alternative methods of TV advertising. The use of cable television is sometimes referred to as narrowcasting.

Radio advertising is much cheaper than television and is therefore used more frequently by trade book publishers, especially for self-help books, popular novels, or nonfiction books that are easy to describe. The advertising agency will either provide copy to be read by a station announcer or will have the author or a well-known performer prepare a tape.

The elements the advertising manager or agency will consider here are the station's format, the time slot, and the market. Most radio stations have a "tight" format geared to very specific listener interests, such as country and western music, disco, hard rock, "beautiful" music, or all news/talk. The time slots are A.M. drive or prime time (5–10 A.M. Mon.–Fri.), daytime or housewife time (10 A.M.–3 P.M. Mon.–Fri.), P.M. drive or prime time (3 P.M.–7 P.M. Mon.–Fri.), evening (7 P.M.–12 P.M. Mon.–Sun.), overnight (12–5 A.M. Mon.–Sun.), and weekend. Spots usually run 10, 30, or 60 seconds, and there is also a choice of the type of program or feature for the ad's position: sports, weather, newscast, interview, etc. Package plans are available, and some publishers will make a "run of station" buy for a general-audience book.

Cooperative Advertising

One excellent way to extend the advertising budget for a book is through cooperative advertising with bookstores, chains, and wholesalers. In this arrangement, the publisher pays a percentage (usually 75 to 90%) of the cost of an ad run by the dealer, so long as the dealer fulfills certain requirements of the publisher such as buying a minimum number of copies of the book to be advertised or having a minimum dollar volume with the publisher the previous year. This is particularly effective for books that have a strong regional appeal, and for encouraging dealers to buy adequate stock when an author is touring in that area. It is also good for books with bestseller potential. Dealers like coop advertising because it gives them extra money for advertising and because they can advertise their store; publishers like it because local dealers generally have a contract with the local newspaper or radio or TV station that entitles them to lower advertising rates if they do a minimum amount of advertising during the year.

Coop money can be limited to individual titles, to specific lines of books, or to book dealers of the same type in a particular geographical region. The books eligible for coop money will be announced at the publisher's sales conference for that list, and promotional literature will be sent out to the dealers eligible to take advantage of this offer. The publishers are also required to publish their cooperative advertising policy once a year in *PW*.

Promotion

As noted earlier in this chapter, the word *promotion* can apply to *all* of the publisher's efforts to put the title of a book before the public or can be used more narrowly to mean materials and campaigns aimed at dealers or intended for use by them. The term is also sometimes used for sales efforts directed at schools and libraries, but the group that has this responsibility is usually part of the sales department and I have postponed discussion of this to the next chapter.

Dealer promotions can take several forms. One of the most common techniques is to prepare materials for use at the "point of purchase" (in store), such as posters, banners, window streamers, blow-ups of ads or book jackets, counter displays, or "dumps" (free-standing floor display units). Other commonly used promotional materials are catalogs, order forms, statement stuffers (mailers which the retailer can include in his monthly statement to his customers), reprints of good reviews, newsletters, and various kinds of giveaways such as buttons, bookmarks, and tote bags. Or a publisher may sponsor a contest in which the bookseller who creates the best window display for a book wins a handsome prize. Special terms being offered the trade, such as free freight or a "1-free-for-10" offer, also fall under the heading of promotion. All of these are ways for the publisher to sell more books to stores and wholesalers, and to encourage the ultimate consumer to buy them.

What Can You Do to Help Promote Your Book?

Happily, there are a lot of things you can do to help promote your book. Basically, the way is wide open, and you are limited only by the amount of time, energy, and imagination you have available. Here are some suggestions to consider.

1. First, become acquainted with the people in the publicity, advertising and promotion, and sales departments of your publisher. They are not going to be eager to see you if you make a pest of yourself, but if you approach them with professionalism, tact, and quiet determination you will eventually earn their respect. Keep in mind that all of them have a great deal of work to do, and yours is not the only book on the list.

2. Seek out and utilize the sources you know best. Call on bookstores and libraries in your area and let them know you are having a book published. Send them a press release or flyer describing the book if the publisher has made one up, or make one up on your own; the investment will probably be worth it. Send the flyer to civic groups (Rotary, the D.A.R., etc.) and other types of organizations and associations that might be interested. Perhaps you can donate a copy of the book for use as a prize, or send a complimentary copy with some order blanks. Volunteer to be a speaker at one of their meetings, or suggest an autographing party, and keep your eyes open for other speaking opportunities. "Local person makes good" is always news, and also lets the local newspapers and radio and television stations know about your book. They may be interested in interviewing you or having you write an article about the book or a related subject.

3. Check the listings of book-review services, syndicated columnists and commentators in *LMP*, and consider sending a copy of your book or a press release to them if your publisher has not already done so. There are also other guides to publications, several of which are listed in the Bibliography.

4. Consider hiring your own publicist or public relations firm. *LMP* has a list of public relations services, and the Poets & Writers booklet on literary agents (see Bibliography) also mentions publicity and lecture agents. Hiring such a representative can be expensive, however. Most publicists require a retainer fee, and in the case of a well-known publicist, this can run between $2,500 and $4,000 a month, plus expenses of $200 a day or more. Others charge on a per-hour, per-city, or per-tour basis. Ask your publisher if he would be willing to pay part of the cost or to provide cooperative advertising money in cities where you will be making appearances on behalf of the book.

5. You may also want to hire a lecture bureau; again,

check *LMP* for a listing. A lecture bureau sets up formal speaking engagements on college campuses, before civic groups, etc., and the fees can be substantial, although such groups usually prefer speakers who are well-known. (John Kenneth Galbraith reportedly gets $10,000 an appearance.) Sometimes a lecture tour can be set up in conjunction with the publisher's plans for the book, so that other engagements can be arranged while you are in a city giving a lecture. (This is particularly nice when travel expenses and lodging have been paid for by the group you are addressing.) If you are worried about your speaking abilities, you might consider hiring a professional coach to help you.

6. If your book is nonfiction (and even if it isn't), try seeking out groups that might be particularly interested in this subject. You probably already have a number of professional acquaintances and connections you can utilize. You might also check a directory of associations at the library; this may spark new ideas. Check the local college and adult education programs that might be interested in having you as a guest speaker. Always bring copies of your book along to speaking engagements. Most publishers allow you to buy copies of your book at a 40 percent discount, and you can then sell them at the full cover price, thereby making a handsome profit besides earning your full royalty on these sales. However, this may not be allowed if the publisher has booked the appearances for you.

A book-and-author luncheon, for example, is usually set up in cooperation between a department store or major book chain and a publisher's publicity department. The purpose is to raise money for a charitable cause, but it's good exposure for you and your books are usually offered for sale there. There are usually several speakers on the program.

7. You may want to contribute to the cost of the publisher's ads or run some ads on your own. If you run a coupon ad, you can fill the orders yourself. For a direct-mail list, check the references in *LMP*.

8. Check books on self-publishing for other suggestions on how to promote your book. Keep in mind that your book is more important to you emotionally and psychologically than it is to the publisher, who must sell many other books in any particular season. A publisher's commitment to one title is necessarily limited by personnel and financial considera-

tions. The more you can express your commitment through selling and promotion on your own, the more satisfied you are going to be.

7
Sales

If you want to get rich from writing, write the sort of thing that's read by persons who move their lips when they're reading to themselves.

—DON MARQUIS

All of the efforts made by the publicity, advertising, and promotion departments have one aim in common—to sell books. However, the direct responsibility for soliciting orders and making sure they are filled belongs to the publisher's sales department.

The Sales Department

The exact character of the department will of course depend on the nature of the house. A big trade publisher will have a staff of sales representatives calling on bookstores, wholesalers, libraries, and other types of customers throughout the country, plus a customer-service department handling customers' complaints and questions, a computerized order-processing and -fulfillment department, perhaps a telephone-order department, a direct-mail facility, and so forth. A smaller publisher won't have the sales volume to support a staff of sales reps, so it will arrange to have its books distributed by a larger publisher, or use freelance commission reps who work in defined geographic regions and carry the books of several publishers on a commission basis, or perhaps sell its books entirely by mail order. Or a small house might distribute its books through a wholesaler or jobber that specializes in handling small-press books, or by selling directly to individual bookstores and to bookstore chains. This chapter describes different types of customers for books, how publishers reach these customers, and how you might get involved in the selling process.

The Customers: Sales to Bookstores, Wholesalers, and Libraries

The principal outlets for most trade publishers—particularly the large general houses—are bookstores and bookstore chains, book wholesalers, and various types of libraries. Before I describe how a publisher reaches these markets, let's look at the number of outlets involved.

Bookstores and Bookstore Chains. According to the most recent edition of the *American Book Trade Directory*, there are 19,841 bookstores of various types in this country. The breakdown includes the following categories:

1,717	antiquarian (old and rare books sold to collectors and libraries)
2,857	college bookstores (primarily textbooks, some general books)
948	department store book departments
5,757	general bookstores
154	juvenile bookstores
767	paperback bookstores (*not* including paperback departments of larger stores)
3,664	religious bookstores
724	used bookstores
16,588	
3,253	all other (educational, export-import, specialized)
19,841	Total

This represents an increase of nearly 8,000 bookstores in the last ten years, with the greatest growth in the area of bookstore chains—that is, firms owning more than one store. The two largest chains are Waldenbooks and B. Dalton. As of late 1983, Waldenbooks was the country's largest bookstore chain, with about 850 outlets. The next largest is B. Dalton, with over 700 stores plus a chain of bookstores called the Pickwick Book Company. Thus, Walden and Dalton together represent nearly one third of the general bookstores.

There are a number of other good-sized bookstore chains as well. Cole's, a Canadian-based chain, operates about 60 retail bookstores in the United States. Kroch & Brentano's has 17; Doubleday, 27; and the wholesaler Bro-Dart owns a total of 89 retail outlets. Barnes & Noble has about 45 college and discount stores; Crown Books has 115 outlets; and two large religious bookstore chains—Zondervan and Cokesbury—have about 80 stores between them. There are also small local chains of three or four stores, plus a few chains owned by local wholesalers who also distribute mass-market paperbacks. When you add them all up, you discover that about half of all bookstores in the United States are part of a chain of some sort.

This phenomenal growth of bookstore chains has produced considerable concern in the industry, because the "independents" have a difficult time competing against chains that can buy books in bulk and therefore qualify for high discounts from publishers. Many publishers are attempting to ease the situation by giving breaks to smaller bookstores where they can, but the independents are finding it a tough fight. Many are attempting to compete by offering special service to their customers or by specializing in particular subjects.

Wholesalers and Jobbers. A wholesaler is a dealer who buys books from a publisher and then sells them to other customers, such as bookstores and libraries. A "jobber" is usually defined as a dealer who handles only books, while a wholesaler may handle newspapers and magazines as well, but the terms are often used interchangeably.

Wholesalers are an important link in the book distribution chain, because they provide a central source of books for small retailers or libraries that prefer not to deal with a large number of individual publishers and are also a convenient source of books for quick reorders, particularly for bookstores located far away from the big book publishers in the East. Some wholesalers specialize in selling to libraries and provide many special services such as "prebinding" (replacing publishers' bindings with heavy duty library-grade bindings), preprinted Library of Congress cards, checkout cards and pockets, and so on. In addition, publishers typically give low discounts to libraries, so the library can usually get a better discount by dealing with a jobber or wholesaler.

There are about one thousand general book wholesalers in this country, some of which are regional wholesalers and some of which sell books nationally. The largest national wholesalers are Ingram, Baker & Taylor, and Bro-Dart. Ingram is headquartered in Nashville, Tennessee, but also has warehouses in Maryland and Los Angeles. Baker & Taylor has warehouses in New Jersey, Illinois, Georgia, and Nevada. Bro-Dart is headquartered in Williamsport, Pennsylvania. Each of these wholesalers carries hundreds of thousands of books in stock, has its own staff that solicits orders from bookstores and libraries, serves between three and four thousand accounts, and offers a microfiche service to booksellers who want up-to-date information on the wholesaler's stock of individual titles. Ingram concentrates on retail bookstores, Bro-Dart on libraries, while Baker & Taylor's accounts are split about equally between the two.

Libraries and Schools. Schools and libraries are often referred to as the "institutional" market and are usually not called on directly by publisher's representatives because there are so many of them and because they buy most of their books (particularly libraries) through wholesalers and book jobbers. There are over 110,000 libraries in this country, as follows:

70,000	elementary school libraries
20,000	high school libraries
2,000	college and university libraries
9,400	public libraries
9,000	special libraries (collections in particular subject areas)
1,300	libraries at military bases and government installations
111,700	Total

In addition to the elementary school libraries, there are about 20,000 schools without libraries that buy books from publishers. About 90 percent of all children's books are sold to elementary school libraries. For general publishers of adult books, the public library system is the most important.

Probably 50 percent of all books with first printings of 5,000 copies or less go to libraries, and in the case of first novels, the total is closer to 80 to 90 percent. So this is obviously a very important market for trade publishers.

The Sales Conference

The selling cycle for a list of trade books begins at a sales conference held a few months prior to the start of the publishing season. For publishers bringing out two lists a year, this semiannual rite takes place in mid-May for fall books, and in early December for spring books. Depending on the publisher's size and pocketbook, the conference will be held at the publisher's home offices, a nearby hotel, or perhaps a glamorous spa in Florida or the Caribbean.

Presentations. When the sales reps arrive, they are given a copy of the catalog for the upcoming season, order forms, proofs of jackets, and other promotional materials. The first day or two of the conference is usually taken up by presentations of the books on the list, either by the editors or by people from the marketing staff. (Authors are occasionally invited to talk about their books, but this is much more the exception than the rule.) The reps are encouraged to ask questions about the books, and to point out any problems that they see, such as ineffective jacket art or their confusion about the content of a book.

Marketing plans will be presented by the advertising/promotion manager and the publicity manager, with contributions by the subsidiary-rights manager if any significant rights sales have taken place at this point. A particular item of concern will be the "handle" for each book. A handle is a brief description which summarizes the book and positions it in relation to other books on the market. A book about camping, for example, might be described as "the one book you'll need on a camping trip in the mountains." One of an editor's most important jobs is to come up with a memorable and succinct handle for a book, but the sales reps will also refine it for the accounts they're calling on. Since most reps are presenting between 150 and 200 new titles on each sales call, a good handle can be vitally important to the success of a book.

The Sales Advance. After the editorial and marketing presentations have been completed, the sales manager may meet with the sales reps to estimate the number of copies of each title that they will be able to "advance" in their territories. These are not really quotas because it's impossible to *make* a dealer take a given number of copies; instead, they represent the house's (and reps') expectations for each account. The hope is that this advance will be about three fourths of the planned first printing. This should leave enough stock to cover additional demand and reorders, and for use in advertising and promoting the book. If demand develops more rapidly than expected, the house will have to order a second printing—*unless* they expect the wave of demand to drop off sharply or unless they expect a lot of unsold copies to be returned from bookstores and wholesalers.* The problem is that trying to guess the demand in advance can be a kind of self-fulfilling prophesy. If there are not enough copies in the stores, it can be hard for demand to build. On the other hand, if too many copies are forced out, the publisher may end up with a lot of returns—a dilemma no one has been able to resolve.

Deals and Discounts. The discounts offered to booksellers, wholesalers, and libraries are based on the number of copies purchased of each title, or of books of similar types (all hardcovers, all trade paperbacks, etc.). Each publisher has his own discount schedule (partially because of a Federal Trade Commission ruling which forbids "collusion") so this produces a welter of different plans, but a typical schedule for trade hardcovers might look something like this:

Number of Copies	Discount
1–5	40%
6–50	41%
51–150	42%
151–300	43%
301–500	44%
501–1000	46%

This type of schedule inevitably favors the larger dealers, chains, and wholesalers, since they are buying in much

---

*Most publishers allow dealers to return unsold copies for credit, but some assess some type of penalty, and others sell certain types of books on a nonreturnable basis.

larger quantities than single "mom-and-pop" stores. In an effort to make life easier for the "independents," and to get substantial quantities of selected titles out, publishers offer various special deals, many of them centering around the problems of freight costs and returns. Dealers have traditionally paid the cost of having books shipped to them as well as the freight for books they are returning for credit. Now a number of publishers are paying the outward freight on certain titles, or are adding a specified percentage (such as 3 or 4 percent) or amount (such as fifty cents) to the invoice price before establishing the jacket price of a book. This is called "freight pass-through" (F.P.T. appears on the jacket or cover next to the price) and means that the cost of the freight is essentially paid by the final customer. (The author's royalty, however, is computed on the *invoice* price rather than on the cover price.) Other publishers offer high discounts in exchange for selling the books on a no-return basis; still others discourage returns by charging some sort of percentage penalty or issuing credits to booksellers whose returns are below a specified average. New deals and discounts, and special offers, are frequently revealed and explained to the sales reps at the seasonal sales conference.

Calling on the Customers

A Typical Cycle. After the sales conference is over, the reps will return to their homes to plan their itineraries for the upcoming season. Figure 16 shows a typical calendar for a trade-book sales representative.

Most trade publishers hold the sales conference for the fall list in mid-May, shortly before the American Booksellers Association (ABA) convention, which is usually held over the Memorial Day weekend. This is the biggest trade show of the year and is attended by publishers, booksellers, librarians, and members of the public. Authors are occasionally asked to appear by their publisher if their book is being published on the fall list.

After the ABA. After the ABA is over, the sales reps will spend the next week or ten days making appointments with their accounts, and will then set off on a sales trip. All of the other publishers' reps are trying to make appointments at the same time, so this is an intensely competitive period.

Figure 16
A SALES REPRESENTATIVE'S CALENDAR

May 12–15	Sales conference for fall list (Sept.–Feb. pubs)
May 16–29	Go over materials; plan tentative itinerary
May 30–June 2	Attend American Booksellers Association convention
June 3–15	Schedule calls on accounts
June 16–Aug. 30	Sell fall list, concentrating on Sept.–Dec. pubs
Sept.–Thanksgiving	Swing through territory again, checking sales for Sept.–Dec. pubs and selling Jan.–Feb. titles
Thanksgiving–Dec. 14	Keep jobbers stocked
Dec. 15–18	Attend sales conference for spring list (Mar.–Aug. pubs)
Dec. 19–25	Plan itinerary
Dec. 26–Jan. 15	Handle Christmas exchange business
Jan. 16–Mar. 30	Sell spring list
Apr. 1–May 11	Swing through territory again, checking sales for Mar.–Aug. pubs and calling on accounts missed previously

Most sales reps call on about two hundred accounts of varying sizes. The usual procedure is for the rep to travel through his or her territory once during the summer, calling on the larger accounts and concentrating on the books to be published between September and December. From September to Thanksgiving the rep may travel through the territory again, picking up small accounts missed on the first trip and presenting the books to be published in January and February. Most booksellers are very busy from Thanksgiving to Christmas and don't have time to see sales reps, so during this period the rep will concentrate on making sure that his accounts have adequate stock.

The sales conference for the spring list will be held in mid-December. The rep will travel through his/her territory from January through March selling the spring and summer books, then will swing through again in April and May seeking backlist stock orders and picking up accounts missed on the earlier trip. The sales conference for the fall list will be in mid-May, and the cycle will start all over again.

Selling to a Bookstore. Most reps start the first sales trip of the season by calling on a few small accounts to smooth out their presentation of the list. The procedure is pretty much the same in each case. The rep sits down with the buyer and goes through the catalog. Some buyers like to stop and discuss practically every title; others ask the rep to discuss only the "top of the line" (the books with the largest first printings) or only the books that particular store will be interested in. Most reps know their accounts well and are able to judge the books most likely to be of interest. An experienced rep will let the buyer specify the quantity she wants of each title, although he will tell the buyer if he thinks she's buying too many or too few of a particular title (based on what the rep has heard at the sales conference or has decided after reading the galleys of the book). If the house is pushing a book strongly, he may ask the bookseller to take a higher quantity than she would ordinarily. As the rep works his way through the catalog, he will show any additional sample materials he has and will explain any special offers applying to a particular book or to the list.

After the "front list" buy is completed, the rep will then take orders for back stock. Sometimes this involves an actual check of the bookstore shelves by the rep. If the rep thinks the demand for a particular title will increase because of a related title being published, he will point this out, and will also tell the buyer about any books that are about to go out of stock or out of print. They will discuss any complaints the bookseller might have about slow deliveries, the publisher's order-filling procedures, credit problems, and so on.

The average sales call takes one and a half to two hours—which means that if the rep is selling two hundred titles, he can spend about thirty seconds on each. A rep can call on about three accounts a day if they are close together and the buyers can accommodate his schedule. When he's not busy calling on accounts, the rep does his paperwork, travels from place to place, and stays in touch with the home office.

Selling to a Bookstore Chain. The biggest chains are usually the responsibility of the sales manager, but a rep may have smaller chains to call on. Some of these chains allow individual stores to buy independently; in other cases, all buying is done by the home office and books are then "drop-shipped" to the stores.

The Walden and B. Dalton operations are so big that each chain has several buyers who specialize in different subject areas. Furthermore, the inventory in these chains is computerized, so that manual checking of sales figures and backstock status is not necessary. Each book has a code number that is punched in whenever a sale is rung up on the cash register. The sale goes into the computerized inventory-control system which analyzes the rate of sale and automatically generates an order if more stock is needed.

Selling to Wholesalers. The major wholesaler accounts are normally handled by the publisher's sales manager, but the sales reps will probably have a few smaller wholesalers to call on. A sales call is much like that on a bookstore or small chain; the difference is that the quantities can be considerably larger. A large wholesaler will normally buy enough copies in its initial order (an order for 5,000 copies of a fairly popular title is not unusual) to qualify for the maximum discount (generally around 50 percent), and will resell the books to its customers at discounts averaging from 35 to 40 percent.

School and Library Sales. As noted earlier in this chapter, there are about 110,000 libraries in this country, plus another 20,000 or so schools that do not have libraries but buy books (usually children's books) from trade publishers. Most publishers do not try to sell directly to these accounts, but instead work through the wholesalers or through an "institutional sales" group.

Institutional sales managers are often former librarians or teachers who speak the language of their customers. They reach their markets primarily through reviews and ads in the trade journals (*LJ*, etc.) and through special catalogs and mailings. Conventions are also popular, particularly the mid-winter meeting of the American Library Association and the International Reading Association, National Council of Teachers of English, and Modern Language Association conventions. Free copies are often provided to teachers in the hope that the book will be "adopted" by the school.

One of the peculiarities and frustrations of dealing with

the institutional market is that much of the buying is done by committees rather than by individuals. School committees and library boards wait until a book has been extensively reviewed or until they have received a "review" copy of the book itself before deciding whether to buy it or not, which means that the success or failure of a particular title may not be evident until a year or two after publication. School library purchases are clustered near the end of the fiscal year (June and July), while purchases for classroom use are made mainly in July and August.

Export Sales

Books sold to buyers in countries outside of the United States are called export sales. The royalty that you will receive on such sales is usually lower than that for trade sales, because of the middlemen and handling costs involved.

The countries in which your publisher will be able to sell his editions depends on the territory granted him in the contract. If an agent negotiated the contract on your behalf, you probably retained all foreign rights; if not, the publisher has the right to license other English-language editions or to try to sell his own editions abroad. The usual procedure is to try to arrange a license first, then export the American edition if a license cannot be arranged. Any territory that is not specifically reserved to a publisher is called the open market.

Canada. This can be an important market for trade books, especially if the author is well-known in Canada. However, the books have to be sold through a Canadian firm, either an agency which resells the books to Canadian booksellers or wholesalers, or the publisher's own subsidiary. One problem is that Canadian prices are higher than American prices (primarily because of the exchange rate) so that Canadian booksellers and wholesalers sometimes try to "buy around" by ordering books directly from an American publisher or wholesaler—a practice strongly disapproved of by Canadian trade organizations.

Other Countries. Export sales can be complicated by currency differences, customs problems, and the like. The larger American publishers usually have an international division to handle these sales. Smaller companies work through an export firm that buys books from the publisher, then has its representatives in different parts of the world solicit orders and handle the details of collecting payment and transmitting the orders to the American publisher. There is also another type of middleman called a stockist, who works on a commission basis rather than buying the books outright.

About sixty countries buy books from American publishers. Some of the larger European countries such as Germany, France, Italy, and Spain do not buy large quantities because they prefer to buy the translation rights rather than importing an American edition. The Scandinavian and Latin American countries are good markets, although they are also increasingly buying translation rights. Japan and the Middle East are both becoming strong markets.

China has no copyright law; the present arrangement is for American publishers to deal with one large import agency there. Piracy is widespread in other Far Eastern countries. Publishers in Korea and Taiwan make reprint arrangements with American publishers; so do Indian publishers, but they then export their editions all over the world. In the Philippines, any book with a cover price higher than 29 pesos (about $5) is reprinted without permission.

Direct Mail

Any book sold directly to a customer by means of a mailing, coupon ad, or radio or television ad to which a customer responds by sending money to a specified box number is classified as a direct-mail sale. The royalty payable on such sales is usually one half of the prevailing royalty rate.

A book sold by direct mail usually has to have a relatively high cover price to cover the costs of the sale, and also has to be easily describable, such as a self-help or how-to book. It does not have to be a new book, however, and a book that lends itself to direct-mail selling can have its life extended by several years.

A coupon ad should obviously be run in a publication read by the intended customers for the book. The *New York*

Times Book Review is also frequently used by publishers for running coupon ads. These are usually single-book ads with a lot of descriptive copy about the book.

The success of a mailing is very dependent on the accuracy of the lists. Large mail-order publishers like Time-Life and Meredith are divisions of companies that publish magazines, and have access to subscriber lists computerized by customer "profile." University presses and other publishers selling heavily by mail accumulate lists of people who have bought similar books in the past. And there are mail-order houses and brokers of mailing lists that can be purchased for a fee. Publishers using their own lists have to be careful to keep them up to date, because as the lists "age," the percentage of return from a mailing goes down below the generally accepted 2 percent level. Since the cost of preparing a brochure and mailing it is so high, a publisher will usually combine several books in the same mailing.

Special Sales

Books sold to customers outside of the normal book-trade channels are called special sales. This can take in a wide variety of possibilities, including sales to organizations and associations, catalog sales, books used as "premiums," and certain kinds of sales to government agencies and the educational market. Books sold by direct mail are also sometimes classified as special sales by their publishers. The royalty rate here is usually either 10 percent of the amount received by the publisher or half the prevailing royalty rate that you are receiving on regular trade sales.

Many people in the industry feel that special sales are the wave of the future, at least for certain special-interest nonfiction books. Some large trade and mass-market publishers have a special department or individual handling these types of sales, and some of the more specialized publishers rely heavily on this source of income for their business. Like mail-order sales, special sales can extend the life of the book and also find readers who are not bookstore browsers.

How Book Orders Are Filled

Selling books is only one part of the sales department's job. Another very important job is making sure that orders are filled quickly and accurately.

Filling an order usually involves a number of steps. In a large house, a certain amount of the process will be computerized; in a smaller one, it will all be done by hand. Here are the steps an order will normally go through in a large publishing house:

1. The order is reviewed by an "order editor" to make sure that all necessary information has been provided and is accurate. The correct discount will be computed, and the account checked for possible credit problems. A bookseller who is behind on his payments may not be allowed to buy more books until the bill has been settled (which may be why your book is not in stock at that store).

2. The order is keypunched and input to the computer. If stock is not presently available for shipment, a "back order" will be generated so that the order can be filled when the stock comes in. Another possibility is that the book is out of print and the publisher does not plan to reprint it, or it is temporarily out of print (TOP), which means that the publisher plans to reprint it but stock is not available yet. (Sometimes publishers use a TOP code as a device for holding onto the rights for a book without having to reprint it.)

3. If stock is available, the computer will reduce the inventory by the quantity ordered, credit the author's royalty account with the sale, calculate the total weight of the order and the cost of postage or freight, and generate an invoice. If the computer system is very sophisticated, it may also generate "pick and pack" orders and shipping labels for use by the warehouse. If drop shipments to branch stores are to be made, an invoice will be generated for each separate shipment.

4. The invoices and other documents will be sent to the warehouse, where the order will be "picked," checked, packed in a suitable carton, and shipped by mail, UPS, or truck.

How Does a Book Get on the "Bestseller" List?

Many magazines and newspapers run bestseller lists (*PW,* B. Dalton's *"Hooked on Books,"* etc.), but the list most publishing people refer to is the *New York Times Book Review* bestseller list, and it is to this list that most bestseller bonus clauses in author contracts are tied.

TBR actually has several bestseller lists: one each for hardcover fiction, nonfiction, and "Advice, How-to and Miscellaneous" titles, and the same for paperbacks. The hardcover lists indicate the number of weeks a title has been on the list and its position the previous week (the fiction and nonfiction lists have 15 positions, the "Advice and How-to" list has five); it also has a section called "And Bear in Mind" which briefly describes the editors' choices of other recent books of particular interest. A footnote below the lists indicates that the listings are based on computer-processed sales figures from about 2,000 bookstores in every region of the United States, and that only five titles are included in the "Advice and How-to" categories because beyond that point, sales in that category are generally not large enough to make a longer list statistically reliable. The paperback list includes both trade and mass-market titles, with 15 fiction, 10 nonfiction, and five "Advice, How-to and Miscellaneous" positions. A footnote below the lists states that the listings are based on "computer-processed sales figures from 2,000 bookstores and from representative wholesalers with more than 40,000 retail outlets, including newsstands, variety stores, supermarkets and bookstores. These figures are statistically adjusted to represent sales in all such outlets across the United States. The number of titles within the two subdivisions of nonfiction can change from week to week, reflecting changes in book buying."

What neither of these lists indicates is that what is being measured is the *rate* of sale, not total volume. There are many million-copy sellers that do not appear on the list because (1) they are sold primarily by mail order or through outlets such as religious bookstores that are not polled by the *Times,* or (2) the book is an old standby, like the Bible or

The Joy of Cooking, or (3) the rate of sale of that book is not quite fast enough relative to that of other books currently being sold.

In order to get on the *TBR* bestseller list, a hardcover trade book normally has to sell at least 70,000 copies in a reasonably short time. This number is of course relative, depending on the sales volume of other books at the time. Many of the bestsellers are by well-known authors with an established audience that moves quickly to buy the new book, so it's sometimes difficult for a new author to break onto the list—but it's certainly not impossible, and there are many examples to prove it. There are also occasional rumors of a movie company buying a large number of copies in order to move a particular book onto the list, or of a bookseller reporting an artificially high rate of sale in order to move some of his stock, but these are probably rare occurrences. In any case, these attempts to force a book onto the list are probably washed out by the large number of outlets sampled.

Reprint or Remainder?

The rate of sale is also going to affect whether a book is reprinted or not. The first printing was set to accommodate the surge of demand around publication time plus reorders for the next several months. If a book seems to be selling faster than expected, however, the sales manager will have to decide whether to go back to press or wait until he's sure that the demand is real so that he doesn't end up with a lot of returns three months later. If the sales manager waits too long to order a reprint (which usually takes four to six weeks), he may end up losing a lot of orders. If he orders too soon, the demand may drop just when he's getting new stock and returns are starting to come back—a sure way of losing money on a book, especially one with a small first printing.

Most trade houses keep a hardcover or trade paperback title in print for at least two years to give the book a decent chance at life and to give book dealers time to return unsold stock. (Dealers are usually allowed to return copies from three to eighteen months after publication.) The time span may be shorter, however, if a mass-market edition comes out a year after hardcover publication or if sales are unexpectedly poor. In this case, the publisher may elect to run a stock-reduction sale or even "remainder" the book.

In a stock-reduction sale, the publisher sets aside a certain amount of stock to fill demand for the next year or so and then offers the rest of the stock to retailers at a reduced price for a limited period of time, after which time the book will go back to the regular retail price. In a remainder sale, the publisher puts all of the stock up for sale to remainder dealers. The highest bidder takes all of the stock, then re-sells it to retailers, discount book chains, or other outlets. Any stock that is not sold will probably go to the shredder. Nobody makes much money on a remainder sale; the bids usually run between 49¢ and $1 for the average trade hard-cover, although it can drop as low as 10¢ for some titles. If the bid is below the most recent unit cost of the book, you won't receive any royalties on the sale. One thing you can do to ease the pain is arrange to buy copies at the remainder or unit-cost price, in the hope of eventually reselling them. Some publishers notify you when your book is being remain-dered; in other cases, you have to keep track of the in-print status of the book on your own.

Why Isn't My Book in the Stores?

Few things are more frustrating to an author than going into a bookstore and discovering that his book isn't there. But before you accuse your publisher of criminal neglect, consider the following possibilities:

1. The publisher's sales rep did call on this store and offer your book to the dealer, but the dealer did not buy it because he didn't think he could sell it or because he'd used up all of his "open to buy" money. Even if a rep did not call on the store, the bookseller probably got the publisher's catalog in the mail and could have bought from that.

2. The bookstore ran out of stock and either did not re-order or is awaiting a new shipment from the publisher. In this case, you might find out whether the dealer could get at least a few copies from a local wholesaler. You might also ask your editor whether your book is out of print or out of stock, and what the reprint plans are.

3. The store is on "credit hold," and will not be shipped any books until the publisher's bill is paid.

4. The clerk did not really look for the book on the shelves, and has just assumed that the store doesn't have it.

5. The copies the store had on hand did not sell, and were returned to the publisher for credit.

What Can You Do to Help Sell Your Book?

Chapter 6 suggested several ways that you can help promote your book, efforts that it is hoped will result in improved sales. But there are several other things you can do, either in cooperation with the sales department or on your own.

You can call on bookstores and wholesalers in your area to let them know that you appreciate their carrying your book and that you will do as much as you can to promote and support sales. (For a list of bookstores and wholesalers, check the *American Book Trade Directory* at your local library.) This should be done with great diplomacy, and it's probably a good idea to let the sales representative for that particular area know what you're doing. It also doesn't hurt to become friendly with that rep; he can use your support too. Be willing to autograph copies whenever you are asked, and to participate in any book-industry functions that help promote the sale of books. And *always* bring along any promotional materials that you have been provided by your publisher or prepared on your own.

You may also want to investigate the possibility of special sales if your publisher is not set up for them or does not have any objections to your becoming involved in them. There are various directories of associations that you may want to check for ideas, and you might try approaching suitable wholesalers or retailers in other types of businesses to see whether they would be interested in carrying your book. There are also conventions, book fairs, trade fairs, and other types of gatherings where you might be able to sell your book. Suggest your book as a possibility for a premium by a suitable organization or business. Also investigate the possibility of catalog sales, or a "per inquiry" sale to a magazine (the magazine gives you coupon ad space free in exchange for a percentage of the proceeds).

But probably the best idea is to go home and write another book. Nothing keeps a book alive quite so well as another book by the same author!

8
Subsidiary Rights

The single best exercise for writers is endorsing checks.
        —ELAINE FANTLE SHIMBERG, *The Writer's Digest Diary*

To many writers, subsidiary rights is the most glamorous part of the business. It's wonderful to have your book published and sell well in bookstores, but for some lucky authors, the income from the sale of subsidiary rights can far exceed the royalties they earn from book sales. This chapter describes the different kinds of rights that can be sold and what you can expect from such a sale. Not all trade books are good candidates for subsidiary-rights sales. On the other hand, there is probably no trade book that does not have at least some potential for additional income from the sale of rights, and you may be able to play some part in that sale.

Who Sells Subsidiary Rights?

Most large publishing houses have a separate department that specializes in the licensing of subsidiary rights. In a smaller house, these negotiations may be handled by the editors, by the publisher, or possibly by an outside firm that handles such sales on a commission basis. And certain of these rights will probably be handled by your literary agent if you have one—specifically, first-serial, movie, and foreign rights.

First-Serial Rights

First serial is the right of a periodical (serial) to publish an excerpt from or condensation of material from a book before the book is published. Second serial is the right to publish such material after book publication. Many magazines and some newspapers are interested in buying first-serial rights to book manuscripts because they are a relatively easy source of material for the publication (an original article doesn't have to be written) and because a well-known or popular author can appeal strongly to their readership.

Why Sell First-Serial Rights? A first-serial sale has definite advantages for you and your publisher. The most obvious benefit for you of course is the money. The income from a first-serial sale to a large-circulation magazine can be substantial, and even if your publisher holds these rights, your share of the income is likely to be 85 or 90 percent, depending on your contract with the publisher.

The book publisher will not derive much income from such a sale, but he gains other benefits. For one thing, it's essentially free advertising for the book. Readers who enjoy the excerpt or condensation may go out and buy the book, or at least mention it to a friend. If the book is mentioned on the cover of the magazine, it's even more potent advertising for the book.

Secondly, a first-serial sale tends to have a positive effect on the attitude of other rights buyers. A book club or reprinter is likely to pay more attention to the book if the publisher or agent sells an excerpt before publication, since it demonstrates that someone else has enough faith in the book to put his money down. The only hazard is that a large first-serial sale may discourage an important buyer of second-serial rights.

Finally, a first-serial sale can help your publisher assess the true market value of the book. The book publisher obviously had confidence in it or you would not have been offered a contract in the first place. But until the manuscript has been exposed to readers outside of the publishing house, no one is sure exactly how the book will be received by the public. The sale of an excerpt to a major magazine can have a very bracing effect on your publisher, while a lukewarm response or a rejection can sometimes dampen the house's enthusiasm for the book. Whatever the case, the magazines rejecting the material will usually let your agent or publisher know why they are rejecting it, and this can be helpful in planning the marketing strategy for the book.

How Are First-Serial Rights Sold? First-serial rights are generally bought by the larger magazines and newspapers. Figure 17 (page 182) is a list of major magazines that frequently buy first-serial rights. Most of them have large circulations and pay substantial fees for the right to use an excerpt from a book.

Deciding which magazines to submit material to will depend on the nature of your manuscript, the nature of the magazine, and—to a certain extent—your reputation as a writer. The big magazines are usually most interested in well-known writers. If your book is seen as being particularly attractive to the big magazines, it may be submitted simultaneously to several magazines and then sold at auction to the highest bidder. At any rate, the submission will be made many months before the projected book publication date, to give the magazine editors time to consider it and—assuming they buy the rights—time to edit or excerpt or condense it, set the material in type, and get it approved by your editor (or you). Most magazines close an issue at least three months before its on-stand date, and the on-stand date is three to four weeks before the issue date. If your agent is handling the submission, he may submit the material to magazines at the same time that he is submitting it to book publishers.

The Terms of the Deal. Three important elements are taken into account in negotiating the deal: (1) the circulation of the magazine (and therefore how much they can afford to pay), (2) the amount of material they want to use, and (3) how badly they want the rights. *Playboy* magazine usually pays about $10,000 for first-serial rights, but reportedly paid $100,000 to use 60,000 words from Norman Mailer's *The Executioner's Song* in three separate issues of the magazine. This is an unusually large amount of material; the more customary arrangement is to use one or two chapters from a book, or perhaps only a part of a chapter. If the material is

Figure 17
TOP MAGAZINE MARKETS

TYPE	MAGAZINE	CIRCULATION
Women's	*Ladies Home Journal*	5,000,000
	Redbook	4,300,000
	McCall's	6,500,000
	Women's Day	8,100,000
	Family Circle	8,400,000
Shelter	*Good Housekeeping*	5,000,000
	Better Homes & Gardens	8,000,000
	House Beautiful	850,000
Fashion	*Vogue*	1,000,000
	Mademoiselle	1,000,000
	Glamour	2,000,000
New woman	*Cosmopolitan*	2,700,000
	Playgirl	800,000
	Ms.	500,000
Male interest	*Esquire*	700,000
	Playboy	5,300,000
	Oui	900,000
	Penthouse	4,500,000
	Sports Illustrated	2,300,000
	Sports Afield	500,000
General interest	*Omni*	1,000,000
	Science Digest	155,000
	Atlantic Monthly	325,000
	Harper's Magazine	300,000
	The New Yorker	500,000
	New York	400,000
	New West	306,000
	Commentary	65,000
	New Republic	80,000
	Saturday Review	525,000
	Book Digest	1,000,000
	Reader's Digest	18,000,000
	Saturday Evening Post	535,000
	Life	1,400,000
	TV Guide	20,000,000

used as a feature or lead or given cover mention, the fee will be higher. First serial is usually exclusive, so that if a magazine buys rights to one chapter of your book, other magazines may not use that material until the first magazine is off the stands, athough they may be able to use material from a different section of the book.

An excerpt implies that the material is taken from the book as is, or has certain material deleted. A condensation implies a certain amount of rewriting and bridging material (and is usually necessary in the case of fiction). Whatever the case, an "advance cut" should be sent to your agent or editor for approval before the piece is run, especially if a lead-in has been added or the material has been condensed.

Since the material will be published before the book is, it must be protected by a copyright notice. Some magazines run a copyright notice on the first page of the excerpt; others run a general notice at the front of the magazine that covers all of the material in the magazine. In this case, the copyright to the material will then have to be transferred back to you by means of a copyright assignment. Incidentally, if the material being used includes previously copyrighted material (say, a quote from a poem by Robert Lowell), the magazine and you are equally responsible for obtaining permission to use that material from the copyright holder.

Second Serial

Magazines that buy second-serial rights are usually smaller and more specialized than those that buy first serial, because second-serial rights are usually cheaper and because these magazines may not know about your book until it has been publicized in the trade and elsewhere (although a few big magazines like *Cosmopolitan* actively buy second-serial rights).

The rates paid for such use vary quite a bit, depending on the circulation of the magazine and the amount of material used. A magazine with a circulation of 1 million or more will probably pay at least $1,500–$2,000 while a magazine with a circulation of fifty thousand to sixty thousand copies may only be able to pay a few hundred dollars for the right to use material from your book. The magazine cover price also affects how much it can afford to pay; a high-priced magazine can usually afford to pay more than a less expensive one.

Newspapers also buy second-serial rights, particularly big papers like the *Chicago Tribune* and *New York Post*. A smaller newspaper might buy second-serial rights if the book deals with a subject of interest to the geographic area it serves. Payment runs in the neighborhood of $200 to $500 and will be a flat one-time fee. The newspaper may elect to run short cuts in several issues, so the term of the license can be as long as six months to give the newspaper time to schedule the material.

Syndication

Syndication occurs when one of the newspaper syndicates buys the rights to portions of your book, then offers the material to newspapers that subscribe to its service. A number of syndicates buy these rights to trade books. United Features, for example, serves about seven hundred newspapers that pay a fee for the use of specific material, plus a "spotlight" list of thirty larger newspapers that pay an annual fee for the right to use any material they wish.

The amount of money paid for the rights depends on the amount of material to be used, an estimate of the number of newspapers that will pick up the material, and how badly the syndicate wants the rights. The usual arrangement is to pay an advance against 50 percent of the gross receipts from subsequent licensing; that is, the syndicate will pay 50 percent of the money that it expects to receive from the subscribing newspapers to your publisher who will in turn split it with you. United Features might estimate gross receipts of $4,000, for example, while a smaller syndicate might pay only $750 to $1,000 for the same material.

What Can You Do About Serial Sales?

You may know the market for your book better than anyone else, especially if it is on a specialized subject. Let your agent or publisher know about magazines, newspapers, and associations with newsletters that might be interested in buying serial rights. (You may also want to check some guides to publications.) Try to think up imaginative ways in which a magazine or newspaper might be able to use the material. Can it be condensed or slightly rewritten in some way to make it more attractive to a serial buyer? Also find out if you can make such sales on your own.

Book-Club Rights

A book club is an organization that offers selected books to its members. It may require each member to buy a minimum number of books within a specified time period. *LMP* lists about three hundred different book clubs that can be broken down into several different types:

General-interest clubs. These clubs offer a wide range of fiction and nonfiction to their members. The largest, longest-established, and best-known are the Literary Guild (LG) and the Book-of-the-Month Club (BOMC). BOMC has about 1½ million members and LG has nearly 2 million. There are also some smaller general-interest clubs, such as the Preferred Choice Book Plan Club, Playboy Book Club, The Readers' Subscription Book Club, and Quality Paperback Bookclub.

"Professional" book clubs. These offer books of interest to people in professions such as law, medicine, accounting, and business.

Religious book clubs. There are clubs for Catholics, Jews, Protestants, and others with more ecumenical interests.

Special-interest book clubs. A number of clubs appeal to people with particular interests or hobbies, such as poetry, movies, aviation, cooking, or history. Some of these clubs are independently operated, others are owned by larger clubs.

Children's book clubs. These operate primarily through the elementary school system. A classroom teacher can have every child in her class join a club so that the books can be used as classroom texts, or make club membership optional. Scholastic Book Club and Xerox Education Publications are active in this field.

Condensed-book clubs. Books from different publishers are edited so that several condensed books can be published in one volume. Reader's Digest Condensed Books is the undisputed leader in this field.

Subscription book clubs. Instead of offering its members a number of unrelated books, a subscription club offers a series of related books. For example, one of the offerings of The Franklin Library is a fifty-volume series called Great American Fiction, with the books chosen and introduced by James Michener.

Why Were Book Clubs Invented? BOMC and LG were started to make a broad range of books available to people who did not live close to a well-stocked bookstore, or who wanted help in selecting the most worthwhile books to read. Most of the club selections were discounted from the publisher's list price, as an added inducement for people who wanted to build up their libraries as inexpensively as possible. Bookstore operators were initially very antagonistic toward the clubs because they felt they were taking away business. Gradually, however, most of the bookstore owners came to feel that book clubs serve a different audience from people who buy books directly from bookstores, and that the advertising that clubs do to attract members helps bookstore sales as well. There are still people in bookselling who do not agree, but in any case, clubs seem to be here to stay. Most book publishers like them because they provide an additional outlet for their books, bring in additional income, and enhance the value of a book in the eyes of bookstore customers and other rights buyers.

How Does a Book Club Get Members? Most book clubs solicit members by running ads in magazines and newspapers or by mailing brochures to selected lists. As an inducement to join, the club may offer a number of books at a low price; this is called a premium offer. Once the member has joined, some or all of the selections will be available at a discount from the publisher's cover price. Some clubs also offer "dividends"—a credit toward obtaining other books offered by the club either free or at a very low price.

The conditions of membership vary from club to club. Some clubs allow their members to buy no fewer than four books a year; some have no minimum purchase requirements at all. Discounting policies also vary. Not every book is offered at a discount, and the percentage of the discount may depend on the retail price of the book, with the more expensive books given higher discounts.

After a new member joins the club, he will begin receiving

a brochure that describes the books being offered during that cycle, plus other books available for purchase through the club. Most clubs mail catalogs thirteen to fifteen times a year. The types of selections usually include:

A *"main selection."* This is the lead book for the month. If the club uses the so-called negative option, the member will automatically receive the selection unless she returns a postcard refusing the selection. Sometimes a club will offer two books as a main selection; this is known as a dual main.

"Alternate" selections. There are usually several alternates offered each month. Each alternate is given a full description in the catalog, and each alternate purchased will earn the member at least one book dividend, depending on the club's rules.

A *"featured alternate."* This falls somewhere between a main selection and a regular alternate. It will have a better position and more space in the catalog than an alternate.

How Does a Club Select Books? Clubs usually want to offer a book to their members at the same time that it is being published in the trade, so negotiations for a license start about the time that galleys on the book are available. The publisher's subsidiary-rights director either will submit bound galleys to clubs or will use copies of the manuscript if the book is on a rush production schedule. A cover letter describing the book and giving other important sales information, such as a movie sale or a large first printing or promotion budget, will accompany the bound galleys or manuscript. If good quotes or reviews have been received, they will be included in the package.

Each club has its own selection process. Most small clubs are run by a manager who makes all of the selections for the club. BOMC and LG have more complicated procedures because they deal with so many books.

BOMC receives about one hundred submissions each week in its New York offices. The editorial director and several senior editors go over the submissions and assign them to outside readers who are experts in particular fields. If the author of the book is particularly important, the book may be assigned to an in-house reader. The reader's report is reviewed by BOMC's editorial director, who decides whether the book should be rejected or given an additional reading. If the report is very positive, the director may immediately classify it as an "A" book for consideration as a main selection. If the book is assigned for a second reading and that reading is also positive, the book will be given a "B" classification and sent to a judge on BOMC's editorial committee (which in 1984 was made up of five judges). If the judge thinks another judge should read the book, it then becomes an "A" book for consideration as a main selection.

The Literary Guild has a somewhat simpler system. There are a number of in-house readers and editors, and everyone on staff reads and recommends books. Second readings are done by senior editors and the final decision for books above a certain monetary level are made by the editor-in-chief with the assistance of the managing editor and the editor of the Doubleday Book Club. Practically all of the Guild's selections are dual mains; a single main selection has become a rarity.

Advance Against Royalties. The size of the advance against royalties offered for the book-club rights will depend on the number of copies the club thinks it can sell to its members. If the Dolphin Book Club thinks that between 750 and 1,000 members will want a book about whales, for example, it will probably arrange to buy 1,000 copies from the publisher. The standard royalty is 10 percent of the price charged the members. If the publisher's list price is $16.95, Dolphin may elect to charge its members $14.95. The royalty payable to the publisher is therefore $1.495 per copy (which will be split with you). Dolphin will probably pay a "guarantee" (advance against royalties) of $750 or so, in case members take fewer copies than expected. If the members buy more copies, the club will pay the publisher additional royalties.

BOMC and LG can afford to pay substantially larger advances than the small clubs because their memberships are so much larger. The advance for a BOMC main selection is usually in the $80,000 to $120,000 range. An LG advance for a main selection is usually a little lower, say $65,000 to $100,000. However, if these two clubs start competing against each other for the rights to a book, the advance may go higher. If either takes a book as a featured alternate, the advance will be $25,000 or so. An alternate should fetch an advance in the $4,000 to $10,000 range from either of these clubs.

One of the larger clubs might also elect to use your book

as an "all-club enclosure." The advance for this is usually slightly higher than that for an alternate. If a club wants to use your book as a dividend, they will again pay an advance against royalties, but in this case the royalty rate is one half that of the other types of club selections.

The club is *not* required to state specifically in the agreement how it will eventually use the book. For example, BOMC may plan to use your book as an alternate, and then decide to make it a featured alternate. The advance against royalties will be adjusted accordingly.

Other Terms of a Book-Club License

Grant of rights. The usual grant is for hardcover book-club rights in English for distribution to members in the United States and Canada. BOMC and LG are granted exclusive rights; that is, only one of these clubs can offer the book, and any smaller clubs must obtain permission to use it from whichever "biggie" has the rights. BOMC or LG usually agrees to such use, on condition that the smaller club wait a certain period before offering the book to its members, and not use the book to solicit new members.

A BOMC license also usually stipulates that the book not be distributed in condensed or paperback form for at least one year from the date that BOMC first distributes the book or the date that the publisher publishes the book, whichever is later, without BOMC's written consent. Obviously the club would prefer to delay this competition for a period of time—especially if it has paid a large advance for book-club rights.

Term and first distribution. A book-club license starts from the club's first scheduled distribution of the book to its members. This date will be stated in the contract as a "no earlier than and no later than" date. The term for BOMC and LG is usually five years; for smaller clubs it is usually three years. If the club wants to continue to offer the book to its members when the term of its license is up, it will have to negotiate a new license with the publisher.

Manufacture of books. Since it is owned by Doubleday, which has its own printing plant, LG sets new type and prints its own edition of most books it licenses, in a standard format and normally using less expensive paper and binding material than the publisher's edition. BOMC also usually prints its own edition, but uses the same paper and binding material as the publisher's edition. The smaller book clubs usually arrange to join the publisher's press run, or buy books from the publisher's stock.

Copyright. Every agreement involving a literary property will contain language concerning the copyright of that work. The book-club agreement states that the club will run the copyright notice used in the publisher's edition of the book and that the publisher indemnifies the club from any legal actions affecting the book.

Once again, it is the author's responsibility to have cleared permissions for any illustrations or previously copyrighted material to appear in the book-club edition as well as the publisher's edition.

Remaindering, termination, and sell-off. The club may want to remainder excess copies of a book after the members' demand for it has ceased. It will probably be required to wait eighteen months after its first distribution, or obtain the approval of the publisher, or wait until the publisher has remaindered its own edition. The license may also require the club to offer excess stock to the publisher first, which is useful if the publisher's stock is low and he doesn't want to go back to press. Once the club is out of stock, the license can be terminated. If the end of the license term is reached and the club does not want to renew but still has stock, the agreement will probably allow the club to sell off this stock, although the club may be required to first offer the stock to the publisher or to other clubs under license to the publisher.

The publisher may be required to serve the club with written notice of termination six months before the license is due to expire. If the club wants to renew the license, new terms will be negotiated and a new agreement will be drawn.

What Can You Do About Book-Club Rights? If you are dealing with a large trade house accustomed to handling book-club rights, there is not a lot you can do. Most of these transactions are pretty routine, without much room for negotiation. However, if you are aware of a specialized club your publisher might not know about, be sure to let your editor know. The other thing you can do is give the house as much ammunition as possible in placing these rights by helping to get good quotes for the book, etc.

Mass-Market Paperback Reprint Rights

"Paperback rights to *Princess Daisy* sell for $3.2 million!" "Puzo rakes in $2.25 million for *Fools Die*!" "Marilyn French's *The Bleeding Heart* goes to Ballantine for a little under $2 million!" The numbers in such announcements are enough to make any normal writer giddy with envy. But before you succumb to runaway greed, there are a couple of things you should know.

One is that the number of books capable of generating an auction for this kind of money are few and far between. Most of them are obvious bestsellers that have already sold very well in the trade and have the imprimatur of impressive first-serial, book-club, movie, and foreign-rights sales. They have to be a safe bet, or the paperback house is going to have a hard time selling the several million copies it must in order to get its money back. But just to let you know exactly what I'm talking about, I've made up a list of the top paperback reprint sales in the last several years (Figure 18, page 192).

Paperback houses do not have unlimited amounts of money, however. If a house spends a lot of money to acquire the reprint rights to a trade book, it may have less money to spend for the rights to other books. Some paperback houses are solving this problem by publishing more paperback originals, which opens up new opportunities for some writers, but also means that the reprint rights for certain "midlist" and "smaller" trade books may go begging. This is a situation that has many trade houses seriously concerned, because they depend on this subsidiary income to maintain a healthy cash position, or even just break even—which may be why some of them are beginning to publish their own mass-market paperbacks. It also presents some problems for those writers who had been hoping for additional income from paperback reprint rights.

How Does a House Go About Licensing Mass-Market Reprint Rights? The person in charge of licensing mass-market rights has to take several crucial elements into account. One is the matter of timing. If the house tries to sell the rights too soon, they run the risk of making less money than if they had waited for reviews—and the reviews turned out to be good.

Figure 18
MASS-MARKET REPRINT RIGHT SALES
FOR $1 MILLION OR MORE SINCE 1972

YEAR	BUYER	SELLER	AMOUNT	AUTHOR AND TITLE
1972	Avon	Harper & Row	$ 1,000,000	T. Harris, *I'm OK—You're OK*
1972	Avon	Macmillan	$ 1,000,000	R. Bach, *Jonathan L. Seagull*
1973	NAL	Bobbs-Merrill	$ 1,500,000	I. Rombauer, *The Joy of Cooking*
1974	Warner	Simon & Schuster	$ 2,000,000	Woodward/Bernstein, *All the President's Men*
1975	Bantam	Random House	$ 1,850,000	E. Doctorow, *Ragtime*
1976	Avon	Harper & Row	$ 1,900,000	C. McCullough, *The Thorn Birds*
1976	Avon	Simon & Schuster	$ 1,550,000	Woodward/Bernstein, *The Final Days*
1977	Warner	Warner bought all rights	$ 2,000,000	R. Nixon, *RN: Memoirs*
1978	Fawcett	Harper & Row	$ 2,250,000	Goodman, *Love Signs*
1978	NAL	Putnam's	$ 2,550,000	Puzo, *Fool's Die* (plus $300,000 for *The Godfather*)
1979	Ballantine	Summit Books	$ 1,910,000	M. French, *The Bleeding Heart*
1979	Bantam	Crown	$ 3,208,875	J. Krantz, *Princess Daisy*
1979	Bantam	Random House	$ 1,500,000	W. Styron, *Sophie's Choice*
1979	Dell	Doubleday	$ 1,000,000	T. Thompson, *Serpentine*
1979	NAL	Putnam's	$ 2,600,000	R. Cook, *Sphinx* and *Brain*
1980	Avon	Simon & Schuster	$ 1,500,000	Collins/LaPierre, *The Fifth Horseman*
1980	Ballantine	Harper & Row	$ 1,000,000 +	E. Segal, *Man, Woman and Child*
1980	Bantam	Linden Press	$ 1,500,000	A. Corman, *The Old Neighborhood*

Figure 18—*Continued*
MASS-MARKET REPRINT RIGHT SALES
FOR $1 MILLION OR MORE SINCE 1972

YEAR	BUYER	SELLER	AMOUNT	AUTHOR AND TITLE
1980	Fawcett	Simon & Schuster	$ 1,045,000	J. Archer, *Kane and Abel*
1981	Avon	Harper & Row	$ 1,000,000	C. McCullough, *An Indecent Obsession*
1981	Avon	Knopf	$ 1,350,000	M. Crichton, *Congo*
1981	Avon	McGraw-Hill	$ 1,000,000	A. Goldman, *Elvis*
1981	Bantam	Arbor House	$ 1,860,000	C. Freeman, *No Time For Tears*
1981	Bantam	Putnam's	$ 1,663,750	T. Harris, *Red Dragon*
1981	Bantam	St. Martin's	$ 3,000,000	J. Herriott, *The Lord God Made Them All* (inc. three renewals)
1981	Bantam	Simon & Schuster	$ 2,500,000	M. Puzo, "Prequel" to *The Godfather*
1981	Bantam	Morrow	$ 1,000,000	M. West, *The Clowns of God*
1981	NAL	Putnam's	$ 3,200,000	R. Cook, *Fever* and Untitled
1981	Pocket Books	Dutton	$ 2,300,000	J. Irving, *Hotel New Hampshire*
1981	Warner	Simon & Schuster	$ 1,150,000	T. Thompson, *Celebrity*
1982	Bantam	Crown	"seven figures"	J. Auel, *The Valley of Horses*
1982	Bantam	Doubleday	"multimillion-dollar layout"	B. T. Bradford, *Voices of the Heart* plus two other books
1982	Berkley (joint purchase)	Putnam	$ 2,250,000+	F. Herbert, Three never-before-published novels
1982	Del-Ray (hard/soft)	Del-Ray	$ 1,000,000	A. Clarke, *2010: Odyssey Two*
1982	Del-Ray/ Ballantine	Doubleday	$ 1,000,000	I. Asimov, *Foundation's Edge* (plus three preceding books in series)
1982	NAL	Little, Brown	$ 1,000,000	J. Carroll, *The Family Trade*

Figure 18—*Continued*
MASS-MARKET REPRINT RIGHT SALES
FOR $1 MILLION OR MORE SINCE 1972

YEAR	BUYER	SELLER	AMOUNT	AUTHOR AND TITLE
1982	NAL	Viking	"seven figures"	J. Guest, *Second Heaven*
1982	NAL	Bobbs-Merrill	"sizable increase over $1,500,000 paid by NAL for original license"	I. S. Rombauer & M. R. Becker, *The Joy of Cooking*
1982	Pocket Books (joint purchase)	Simon & Schuster	"seven figures"	W. P. Blatty, *Legion*
1982	Pocket Books (joint purchase)	Simon & Schuster	"seven figures"	J. Collins, *Hollywood Wives*
1983	Bantam	Weidenfeld & Nicolson	$ 1,500,000 for all U.S. rights	Mick Jagger autobiography
1983	Dell	McGraw-Hill	"seven figures"	E. Bombeck, *Motherhood*
1983	Pocket Books	Putnam's	$ 1,600,000	J. Blume, *Smart Women* plus renewed license on *Wifey*
1983	Pocket Books (joint purchase)	Simon & Schuster	$ 1,000,000 +	Two novels by Clive Cussler
1983	Bantam	Knopf	"close to $1,000,000"	J. Le Carré, *The Little Drummer Girl*
1983	Warner	Houghton Mifflin	$ 1,165,000	J. Rossner, *August*
1983	Warner	Morrow (hard/soft)	$10,000,000?!	Sidney Sheldon's next three novels

If they wait too long, on the other hand, a book tends to "age"; reviews and ads stop running, and the reprinters turn their attention to other books. The usual strategy therefore is to offer the rights shortly after trade publication, when the publicity is likely to be at its peak. If the publicity director thinks that the reviews are going to be bad, the rights director may try to license the paperback rights earlier; conversely, if the consensus is that the writer is going to get a lot of media attention but it may take some time to build up, the rights director may delay a bit longer before submitting the book to reprint houses.

Another consideration is whether the house should reprint the book itself or offer it to outside publishers. Some of the trade houses have mass-market subsidiaries (Simon & Schuster/Pocket Books, Random House/Ballantine Books, Putnam's/Berkley & Jove, etc.) and may have the right by contract to reprint the book in their own line. The decision here has to do with how well this particular book fits into the house's mass-market line, the desirability of cash income from the outside, and so on.

Another possibility is to try to sell the trade paperback reprint rights instead of, or in conjunction with, the mass-market paperback rights. Some books do not work particularly well as trade paperbacks, but this option seems to be increasingly exercised for a wider range of books.

Finally, the question is whether the book should be submitted to one mass-market paperback house at a time, sent out on a multiple submission, or auctioned. The book may be offered to only one paperback house (at least at first) if it seems to fit in particularly well with that house's line of books, or if the house has published this author before and has an option on the new book, or if the author has a very strong preference for a particular reprint house. It is generally a good idea to keep all of an author's books with the same reprint house because the books tend to strengthen one another, but if the reprinter does not come up with the kind of money that the trade house thinks it should, it makes sense to sell the reprint rights elsewhere.

Unless you have the right of consultation, incidentally, your opinion will probably not be solicited on this matter, but you should be kept informed of what is going on by your editor or the rights director, and if you have an agent, he will probably be observing closely as well.

Multiple Submission. Most trade books are sent out to reprinters on a multiple-submission basis. In this situation, several reprinters who have indicated interest will be sent copies of the book plus supporting materials such as reviews, details of hardcover promotion plans, and so on. They are usually given a few weeks to look over the material before being required to respond, although there may not be a formal "closing date." At the end of that time, the rights director will call those reprinters he has not heard from to see whether they will be bidding on the book. Occasionally nobody bids, and in this case there is not much the rights director can do, except perhaps reoffer the book at a later date. If there is a very low bid, the publisher may reject it in favor of resubmitting the book later, or perhaps reprinting the book in its own mass-market or trade paperback line. If there are a couple of bidders, the rights director will try to get the money up by negotiating with both of them until they finally decide they have gone as far as they can go. Besides an advance against paperback royalties, the reprinter may offer an unusually high royalty (say, starting at 10 percent rather than at 6 or 8 percent), a bestseller bonus, or some other enticement for the rights to the book.

Paperback Auction. If several reprinters are strongly interested in acquiring the rights, an auction will be held. This situation can sometimes resemble a high-stakes poker game, except in this case bidding is usually done by telephone instead of around a table, and the bidders do not usually know whom they are playing with. But the pace is fast, the stakes can be enormous, and the whole transaction is hard on everyone's nerves.

Since large sums of money can be involved, the rules of the auction will be spelled out clearly in advance. A closing date will be established and the percentage by which each bid must exceed the previous one may be spelled out. The trade publisher may not allow the game to begin until one of the players has made a minimum opening bid, called a floor, usually in exchange for "last out" privileges. Bantam established a floor of $1 million plus $300,000 in bonuses in the auction for *Princess Daisy*.

On the closing date, the subsidiary-rights director will start calling the reprinters or waiting for their calls. The first round will be blind bidding, but after that, the rights director may set up the bidding order so that the houses with the most money to spend or the keenest desire to get the rights (so far as the rights director can tell, in any case) are positioned near the front and end of the bidding order. The hope is that the first bidders will start each round at a healthy level, while the last bidders will be able to keep up with the escalating prices. The weaker paperback houses will be near the middle of the bidding order, so that the bidding will continue to move upward but the smaller houses can still compete.

It is understood that a verbal bid is a binding one, and that the rights director will not falsify the amount bid by a house. (There is no direct way of controlling this, but reprinters often compare their numbers after an auction is over.) The rights director does not have to tell the bidders who the other players are or what their exact bids were but will reveal the approximate level of the bidding. The bidder must then determine for himself how much higher he should bid to stay in the game, although the rights director will tell him if his bid is too low to allow him to stay in. The game is over when every bidder but one has folded.

It occasionally happens that the first bidder offers such a large amount of money that the trade house agrees not to auction the book. This is called a preemptive bid and is usually not very popular with other houses that were interested in bidding for the rights to the book.

It also occasionally happens that nobody wants to play. This is an unhappy situation because it makes it hard to sell the rights later.

Advance Against Royalties. The money being offered by the reprint house is an advance against royalties. Every house does its figures differently. One mass-market publisher that I know of sometimes goes up to a figure that has about a 4-to-1 relationship to its planned first printing. For example, if the reprinter is thinking about a first printing of 100,000 copies, the advance may be in the neighborhood of $25,000. Other houses, however, do not use such a formula and instead base their advance on such factors as anticipated net sales, production costs, and so on.

The royalty rate is usually between 6 and 10 percent of the cover price, although it will probably be on a sliding scale, say, 6 percent on the first 150,000 copies sold and 8 percent thereafter. These figures are strictly a matter of negotiation, however, and you should not assume that any of them will apply in your particular case.

The schedule of payments can also be an issue. The paperback houses typically pay the advance in thirds with the first third due when the contract with the trade house is signed, the second third when the paperback edition is published, and the last portion six months later; but if a very large amount of money is involved, the payments will probably be broken down into fourths, fifths, or sixths. The money will be split between you and the hardcover publisher according to the terms of your contract.

Other Terms

1. The territory granted the paperback house will be the same as that granted the hardcover house by the author. Any countries not specifically reserved for the American publisher or other English-language publisher are called the open market, and all of the publishers are free to compete there.

2. The usual term of a paperback license is five to seven years, although if the paperback house has paid a lot of money for the reprint rights, it may be granted a term as long as ten or even fifteen years. At the end of the term, the paperback house will either have to negotiate a new license or return the mass-market rights to your trade publisher. (One reason paperback houses like to publish paperback originals is that they can retain the rights for the whole term of copyright, rather than being limited to a specific and relatively short span of time—provided, of course, that they keep the book in print.)

3. The paperback house usually has to wait at least one year after hardcover publication before issuing its edition, to give the hardcover edition a decent life span. A "no later than" date will also be stipulated in the contract, to prevent the mass-market house from postponing publication for so long that the market value of the book is substantially impaired. These dates may be adjusted if there is some special problem. For example, if the English paperback publisher is about to flood the open market with its edition, the American paperback publisher may ask the trade house for permission to release its edition in that market early, so that it has a fighting chance alongside the English edition.

4. The trade house will provide twenty or so free copies of

the book to the paperback house for its use in acquainting its sales staff with the book, putting the book into production, etc. The paperback house will in turn be required to provide a certain number of free copies of its edition (usually twenty) to the trade house. You as the author should receive the lion's share of these copies.

5. It is usually the author's responsibility to clear copyright permissions for the mass-market edition as well as trade editions.

6. The reprinter is usually forbidden to change or add to the text of your work without the approval of the trade publisher. There may also be an additional clause specifically prohibiting the insertion of advertising in the paperback edition, although a reprint house is usually allowed to list other books that it publishes at the back of the paperback edition of your book.

7. The hardcover house may ask for the right of approval of the art used on the paperback cover, but this is rarely granted by a paperback house.

8. The hardcover house will warrant and indemnify the paperback house for possible legal problems resulting from suits for libel, invasion of privacy, etc.

9. To protect the rights being granted the paperback house, the hardcover house may be prohibited from publishing all or a substantial portion of the book (such as a condensation) in softcovers (e.g., a trade paperback) in the territory licensed to the mass-market house. The hardcover house may also be prohibited from remaindering copies of the hardcover edition before a specified time.

10. If the paperback house has unsold copies of the book in its warehouse when this license terminates, it will be given one year to sell off that stock without penalty.

11. The reprinter will probably be given an option on the author's next full-length work.

What Can You Do About Mass-Market Paperback Rights?
You will not have much direct influence over the licensing of these rights, unless you or your agent negotiated the right of consultation or approval as part of your contract with your trade publisher. However, you can certainly be involved in the procedure in the sense of being informed of what is going on, and providing as much ammunition as you can to the rights director. One author, for example, supplied the rights

director with statements of recommendation from book-sellers who had done well with the book. Another helped prepare a "kit" of all the reviews that had been received (sometimes authors collect more clippings than the publisher because friends send them in). If you have a strong preference for a paperback house, you should let the rights director or your editor know. If they are keen to have your next book, they will do their best to accommodate you.

Other Reprint Rights

Trade Paperback. I've already mentioned the possibility of licensing trade-paperback rights. The beginning royalty rate for a trade paperback is usually 6 percent to 7½ percent with an eventual escalation to 9 percent or even 10 percent. The term of the license is usually five or seven years. All other terms are similar to those in a mass-market license.

Hardcover Reprint. There are various possibilities. One is an edition intended for sale to libraries. This type of license is usually arranged several years after publication, when the regular hardcover edition is out of print. The press run will be a few hundred copies and the cover price will be high; $30 or more is not unusual for a book originally priced much lower. The royalty is usually 10 percent of list, with a small advance.

Another possibility is a "cheap" edition for sale to the remainder-book trade. The best bet here is a heavily illustrated book originally published at a high cover price that will sell well in a secondary market at a lower price. The reprinter will probably negotiate to buy the film used to make plates, then reprint the book on cheaper paper and with inexpensive binding, at a cover price of one half or less than that of the original edition.

Some specialty publishers reset books in large type for the visually handicapped, for sale through the retail bookstore trade or through book clubs for such readers. These editions are typically priced a few dollars higher than the trade edition to cover the cost of resetting, but are not as expensive as library reprint editions. The royalty is 10 percent of the large-print edition's cover price, and the first printing will probably be a few thousand copies.

If your publisher does not seem interested in pursuing any of these possibilities, you might check the listings of hard-cover reprinters and large-print publishers in *LMP*, and either suggest that the publisher contact them or approach them yourself.

Abridgment, Condensation, and Digest Rights. Your book can be reprinted in other forms as well. The terms discussed in this section are similar to those used in regard to serializations, but can also apply to publication in book form. Here are some formal definitions:

• An "abridged" version is one where portions of the book have been deleted, without changing the rest of the text.

• A "condensed" version is one where deletions have been made and other material has been rewritten or added to supply needed continuity.

• A "digest" version is one where the content of your book has been summarized or paraphrased; that is, none of your original language is retained. For example, there are companies that prepare digests of business books for publication in a newsletter for subscribers; the usual fee for this use runs around $100. The term *digest* is also sometimes used when what is being published is really an abridgment or condensation, such as the material printed in *Book Digest*.

Terms for a Book-Condensation Deal. Since a condensation involves use of your material in a book rather than a periodical, the payment arrangement is the familiar advance against royalties. However, the royalty rate cannot be determined until all of the condensations to be used in the book have been completed and the publisher knows how long each condensation is going to be. The royalty usually ends up being about 4 percent of the invoice price of the book. There will also be an advance. For a large organization like Reader's Digest Condensed Books, an advance of $50,000 is not unreasonable. Furthermore, an agreement with Reader's Digest (which has branches all over the world) might lead to the sale of translation rights in different languages, worth a few thousand dollars more. A contract with the club will specify that the copyright notice for the trade edition will be reproduced in the condensation, that the condensation itself will be copyrighted, and that (in the case of Reader's Digest) no other reprint rights to the book can be sold for six months from the date of the club's first distribution without the express consent of the club.

Selection, Anthology, Etc. The term *selection* usually means that a limited portion of the book is being reprinted either in another book (such as an anthology) or in a magazine. An anthology is a collection of writings by one author or by several writers (but usually on the same subject or in the same literary form). If material from your book is being reprinted as a selection in a book, it is usual to limit this use to a given number of words, such as ten thousand words in the case of a work of prose, or one story from a selection of stories, etc.

Permissions. In most large publishing houses, second-serial sales to magazines and newspapers are handled by the subsidiary-rights department, while requests for use of the material in books are handled by the permissions department. The fee charged the user depends on the amount of material being used, how popular your work is, whether the request comes from a private individual or a large and presumably well-heeled organization, and the editions and territory in which the material will be used; in other words, it's the reverse of what happens when you write a publisher and ask for permission to use material in *your* book. The minimum charge for poetry, for example, is usually $25, but can go considerably higher if the work being quoted is famous and the anthology will be widely distributed. Income from permissions is split 50/50 between you and your publisher. If you get to be a famous writer (particularly a poet or essayist), this income can be substantial.

What Can You Do About These Reprints Rights? The use of abridgments, condensations, etc., is normally not something you would be involved in. Such uses are usually requested by other publishers who want to make use of your work and such requests are hard to anticipate, as are all types of permission requests. However, if there are some types of uses that you object to, be sure to let your editor know in advance.

Foreign Rights

An increasingly important area of income for publishers and writers is foreign rights, which means any licenses granted to publishers outside of the United States. This includes licenses granted to other English-language publishers and licenses to translate the work into another language.

These rights are sold in various ways. One of the most important ways is through trade fairs, particularly the Frankfurt Book Fair held in Frankfurt, Germany, in October each year. All of the major publishers in the world gather here to sell the foreign rights to their books. Other important trade fairs are held in London, in Bologna (for children's books), and in the United States where the ABA convention is increasingly becoming a place where foreign-rights sales take place.

Another important mechanism is the use of "subagents" in foreign countries. Established agents in the major countries buying foreign rights are constantly on the lookout for books of interest to publishers in their country. This simplifies things for American publishers and agents because it relieves them of the difficulty of trying to deal with a foreign language and because the subagent is on the scene there and knows what the publishing houses in that country are looking for. Some of the larger foreign publishers also have "scouts" in the United States who seek to buy the rights to American books, and a few of them have established offices and even publishing operations here.

A certain amount of selling also goes on by mail and telephone directly with the foreign publishers. This is especially true in the case of English publishers trying to buy "British" rights. There is also travel back and forth, as American publishers and packagers go to England and other countries to peddle their wares, and their counterparts in other countries come here to buy rights or sell American rights.

The books that sell best to foreign countries are the established bestsellers, especially those that have sold for a large amount of money to a paperback reprinter here. A bestseller here is frequently a bestseller in another country. But there are also certain kinds of books that do particularly well in different countries. Westerns seem particularly popular in

Germany, for example, and romances tend to sell well in France.

The increasing international exchange is also very helpful in the case of lavishly illustrated books with high production costs. Publishers and agents try to arrange "coproductions" where publishers in several different countries share the printing and binding expenses. This means that the "plant" cost (typesetting, platemaking, etc.) can be spread out over several editions, and economies of scale can be achieved in paper and binding materials and press time to produce a lower unit cost for each publisher. These productions are often organized by packagers who put together a book project and then call on publishers in different countries to sell the rights.

British Rights. Most American publishers and agents deal directly with English publishers rather than working through a subagent, since there is only a small language barrier. What they generally do is make up a "rights list" showing books for which they hold British rights, and then send this list to publishers in Great Britain and to important English-language publishers in other countries. If the publisher is interested in buying the rights, he will call or write the U.S. publisher or agent to negotiate the terms of a deal. He will usually try to do this before the American publisher has gone to press in order to join the press run (the American publisher will make various kinds of "imprint" changes for the British publisher). If the run is missed, the alternatives are to join a later printing, to buy "duplicate film," or purchase the right to offset from the American edition. The usual offset fee is about $2.50 per page; costs for duplicate film are slightly higher. The American publisher may also add other fees for arranging to get books to the British publisher, such as handling charges and insurance and shipping fees.

The terms of the deal for British rights are as follows:

Advance and royalties. The royalty rates paid by a British publisher usually escalate faster than those of American publishers. A typical rate is 10 percent of the cover price of the British hardcover edition to 3,000 copies, 12½ percent to 5,000 copies, and 15 percent thereafter. The cover price is likely to be about £9 (roughly $15 at the current exchange rate) for a novel; the price for a nonfiction work can be considerably higher.

British publishers usually anticipate selling 3,000 to 4,000 copies of an "average" trade book, so the advance paid for the rights in this case is in the neighborhood of £2,000 ($4,000), although it can go higher if the book is of exceptional interest to the British public. The schedule of payments is usually one half on signing and one half on publication of the British edition. Your share of the income (if it was arranged by your publisher) is usually from two thirds to 75 percent of the income, as per your contract with the American publisher.

Territory and other rights. Prior to 1976, the license granted to a British publisher typically included all of the countries in the British Commonwealth as it was constituted in 1948. Now, American publishers are required to negotiate rights for each of these countries separately. What usually happens is that the American publisher grants a certain number of these countries to the British publisher and "reserves" various countries for sale of the American edition or for licensing to another publisher. British publishers are generally most interested in Scotland, Ireland, Israel, Australia, New Zealand, and South Africa.

Subsidiary rights. The British publisher will also be granted subsidiary rights in the territories granted. This usually includes book club, mass-market reprint, and so on, but may not include first serial if these rights were sold to a British magazine or newspaper before the book rights were sold. The splits of income are usually the same as those in your contract with your American publisher, although in this case the income goes to the British publisher, who retains his share and then forwards the remaining sum to your American publisher or agent. If your publisher arranged this deal, he will retain the portion specified in your contract with him (one third, 25 percent, or whatever). Thus, if the William Collins company holds British rights, and sells the British paperback rights for £10,000, Collins will retain £5,000 (if the split in the contract with the American publisher is 50/50) and send £5,000 to your American publisher, which will then deduct its share of the income before paying you.

Permissions and artwork. If your book contains previously copyrighted material and you did not clear permissions for foreign editions, the British publisher will have to clear these permissions with the copyright holders. Similarly, if the British publisher wants to use the artwork from the cover of the American edition, the jacket designer is paid an additional fee. Note that if the American edition contains a lot of photo inserts, the British publisher may elect not to use them in its edition of the book.

Copyright. The British publisher will agree to take all necessary steps to protect the copyright and to reproduce the copyright notice that appears in the American edition in their book. The agreement will probably also stipulate that neither the title nor the text may be changed without the express written consent of the proprietor (e.g., your publisher or you).

Time of publication. The British publisher will be required to bring out its edition(s) of the work within a certain period of time after the date of the agreement—usually eighteen months—so that the rights are not tied up too long without publication and the British publisher can capitalize on U.S. publication publicity. Otherwise, the agreement will automatically terminate, the rights will revert to the proprietor, and the proprietor retains the advance paid by the British publisher.

Term of license. The license is for the term of copyright. However, if the British edition goes out of print the proprietor can request that it be reprinted. If the British publisher does not comply with the request, all rights will revert to the proprietor.

Foreign-Language/Translation Rights. Foreign-language rights are usually sold by language group rather than by country; that is, a publisher in one country will buy the right to arrange for a translation and then publish and sell that translation throughout the world. Occasionally, however, this right will be broken down by territories; for example, a Spanish-language publisher may be limited to Spain and Central America so that South American rights can be sold separately. Portuguese rights are sometimes split between Spain and Portugal, and French-Canadian publishers frequently buy North American French-language rights only. The most important foreign-language groups currently are Japanese, German, French, Dutch, Italian, Spanish, and the Scandinavian tongues. These licenses are almost always arranged through a subagent.

The terms of foreign-language rights vary, but can be summarized as follows:

Translation costs and arrangements. The buyer normally has to pay for the cost of the translation. Costs vary, but the usual fee is $50 per 1,000 words, so that if your book runs 100,000 words, the translation cost will be $5,000. It is usually left up to the foreign publisher to find a translator and negotiate the fee, although your representative (publisher or agent) may specify a particular translator if desired. In either case, the contract should specify a date by which the translation is to be completed and published. This is usually eighteen months, but may be longer if the book is long and complicated. The agreement should also state that no changes may be made in the text without your consent, although this can be difficult to check unless you or your representative reads that language.

Advance against royalties. The advance depends on the number of copies the foreign publisher thinks he can sell. The Japanese, for example, typically pay advances in the range of $3,000 to $5,000 for an average trade book, as do most Spanish, French, and Scandinavian publishers. The advance for Italian rights can be as low as $500, while the German rights can be much higher because the deutschemark is strong and the audience for German-language books is large. If the book is very popular, however, the foreign-language rights can fetch a great deal more.

If the advance is paid in the currency of the foreign country, the subagent will deduct his commission (usually 10 percent) and deposit the payment in a local bank. The bank will transfer the equivalent in American dollars to its U.S. affiliate, which will in turn issue a check in American dollars to your representative. Some deals are made in dollars to begin with, in which case the foreign agent will forward a check for the correct dollar amount. If the deal was made by your publisher, the house will retain its share of the income and remit the rest to you at the next royalty accounting period.

Subsidiary rights. The foreign-language publisher will acquire subsidiary rights for the territory or language covered by the contract, although certain of these rights may be retained if they are especially valuable. First-serial (and occasionally second-serial) rights to certain books can be worth a great deal of money in certain countries. Book-club rights in

Germany and the Scandinavian countries can be very valuable because of the number of large book clubs in these countries. The splits on the rights granted the foreign publisher are usually 50/50, except that first serial is usually 70/30 (with the foreign publisher keeping the 30 percent).

Copyright and permissions. The foreign publisher will be required to take all necessary steps to protect the copyright in the work, and to print the name of the author and the original American title of the work on the title page or copyright page of its edition. It is usually up to the foreign-language publisher to clear permissions on previously copyrighted text or illustrations. If permissions or production costs for the illustrations are high, the publisher may elect not to use this material in his edition.

What Can You Do About Foreign Rights? The handling of these rights is usually best left to the people who are expert in this field. If you do want to try to sell these rights on your own for some reason, you can find a list of publishers and subagents in *International Literary Market Place*. Keep in mind that this process tends to be slow and that the cost of telephone calls and international mail is high.

Film Rights

In addition to being reprinted in various forms, your book may be used as the basis for a movie, television special or serial, or play. These rights are not normally granted to your book publisher if you have obtained an agent. If you do grant film and performance rights to your publisher, the firm might ask an agent to handle the licensing of these rights for them.

Who Buys Film Rights? Potential buyers include movie studios, major networks (NBC, ABC, CBS), and independent producers. In the old days, the movie studios had a stranglehold on film rights because they owned most of the movie theaters around the country, but in 1948 they were forced to divest themselves of these retail outlets, giving access to these outlets to independent producers. The major studios are now primarily financing and distributing companies. They buy film rights from authors, publishers, and agents and then make individual contracts with producers, directors, and actors, or they buy the rights from producers who have signed up properties on their own.

The Option. The usual procedure is to take an "option" on the work, which will give the potential buyer a period of time (usually a year) to raise money to make the film and/or decide whether he wants to proceed with the project. The option price for a theatrical feature is typically 10 percent of the "pickup" price, so that if this is set at $100,000, the option price will be $10,000; for a made-for-TV movie, one-hour special, 90-minute program, miniseries, or PBS presentation, the fee is usually between $10,000 and $20,000.

The contract will specifically give the purchaser the right to hire various people in connection with the proposed film (scriptwriter, producer, etc.) and to have various kinds of written material developed, such as a "treatment" (a summary that tells the film story in narrative form), scenario, or screenplay. However, the purchaser is under no obligation to exercise the option—or to produce and distribute the film—even if he does buy the rights from you.

Most books that are optioned or bought never make it into the "can." One movie agent estimates that although some one thousand literary properties are optioned each year, only about ninety films are released for theatrical distribution, and a substantial number of these are made from original screenplays rather than from book manuscripts. The same hazards exist in television. The Columbia Pictures Television Writers Workshop estimates that about two thousand ideas for pilots are considered by the networks in any one year. Of these, three hundred to four hundred are written as scripts, one hundred of these scripts are filmed or taped, perhaps twelve are telecast, two or three are reasonably successful, and one series may be renewed for the following season.

Other Terms of a Film Deal. The grant of rights usually includes the following:

• Motion-picture rights, including the rights to sequels and remakes. The grant applies not only to the plot of the book but also to the title and all characters, situations, incidents, events, and themes.

• Television rights, including series, miniseries, made-for-TV movies, cable television, etc. This is important because as the cost of making films escalates (the average cost is $10

million), filmmakers increasingly rely on recouping their investment through a television sale.
- Radio rights.
- Musical rights, including soundtrack-album and music-publishing rights. This applies to an original score written and recorded for the film. This can be very lucrative; the soundtrack for *Saturday Night Fever* reportedly earned more for Paramount than the film did. Most of the major studios have their own record label.
- Merchandising rights (T-shirts, stationery, etc.).

It may also include dramatic rights; the right to publish serializations, synopses, excerpts, and summaries for publicity purposes; the right to license a "tie-in" edition to a mass-market publisher; and various other film rights not explicitly stated or not yet invented. Current film contracts usually include specific references to video cassettes or video discs, for example.

"Pickup" terms. The terms paid to exercise the option (and of course the option terms themselves) will depend on how badly the buyer wants the film rights. United Artists, for example, paid $2.5 million for the rights to Gay Talese's *Thy Neighbor's Wife.* The usual pickup prices are considerably more modest.

The pickup price for a theatrical feature usually ranges between $100,000 and $200,000. A "sequel" uses one or more major characters from your book "participating in different events from those in the present work, whether such events are prior to, concurrent with, or subsequent to the events of the present book, and whose plot is substantially new." *Superman II,* for example, is a sequel. The payment for a sequel is usually one half the amount paid for the first motion picture. A "remake" is based on the plot or story of the present work or a prior motion picture made from the work. *The Blue Lagoon,* for example, a film starring Brooke Shields, is a remake of a movie originally made in 1949 starring Jean Simmons and Donald Houston. Payment for a remake is usually slightly lower than that for the original motion picture.

The agent negotiating the agreement for you will also try to get you a few percentage points of the "gross." Gross is much preferred to net, because film accounting is very complicated and the filmmaker or studio will load as many expenses into the picture as possible, including "third party" distribution fees and expenses, recoupment of the negative cost of the film (the actual production expenses involved in making the film), plus interest on such negative costs. Unless the film is a smash success, a net profit is unlikely. If a television network is involved, the deductions will include overhead costs, production costs in excess of the established budget, and "administrative" costs.

The price for a television movie or one-hour special will be about $25,000; a 90-minute program pays about $35,000 (plus $5,000 for each additional half hour); a miniseries, between $25,000 and $30,000 per two-hour segment. The pay for a regular TV series is between $6,000 and $6,500 for a half-hour segment, about $8,500 for a program running up to an hour, and around $12,000 for a program running up to 90 minutes. For reruns of a series, you are normally paid 20 percent of the above sums each time the program is shown, except that after the fifth rerun a buyout provision goes into effect and you will receive no more money. If the program is being run on a U.S. network, you will be paid for the rerun within sixty days; if it's being run overseas, you may have to wait one hundred and twenty days for payment.

Term and territory. Some film contracts grant the buyer these rights "in perpetuity and throughout the universe," which is a bit extreme. Your representative will probably try to restrict the grant to a limited period of time, say, ten years, and to the North American continent. This latter restriction is important because foreign rights are becoming increasingly lucrative.

Right of control. The filmmaker will retain the right to produce, distribute, and market the motion picture in any way he wishes, including the right to reissue it when and if he wishes, or to withhold or withdraw it from distribution in any country or territory. He also has the right to modify the work by adding, deleting, or rearranging the sequence of events and the characters, and to use any elements he wishes in conjunction with other literary or dramatic material of any kind. (Any "moral rights" you might have in the matter are specifically disavowed.)

Reversion of rights. If the option is exercised but a film is not produced or distributed in the United States within a reasonable period of time, the rights should revert to you. In the case of a TV contract, the rights normally revert to you if the purchaser has not started production five years after the option is exercised.

Author warranties and indemnities. The usual warranties and indemnities apply. However, libel and invasion-of-privacy issues in motion pictures are somewhat different from those in books, and the purchaser will probably have the film vetted by his own attorneys. Furthermore, you should not be required to indemnify the buyer for any materials that have been added to or changed from the original.

Releases. You may be required to obtain releases from any living persons who appear in your book and will be portrayed in the movie, or from anyone who has a prior "interest" in the work or the optioned rights.

Use of author's name or likeness. The purchaser will want the right to use your name, biography, and likeness in advertising and promoting the film. However, your consent must be obtained if a third party (such as a sponsor of a TV show) wishes to claim that you use or endorse a particular product or service.

Credits. The way in which your work will be credited should be specifically spelled out in the agreement. For example, if you have written a novel and the title of the film is the same as the title of your novel, the credit line should read: "Based on the novel by Richard Jones." If the title of the film is different, the credit will be "Based on the novel *Kings and Queens* by Richard Jones."

The credit will appear on a separate frame of the film, or may be combined with the credit for the screenplay, with the stipulation that the type size of your credit will not be smaller than that for the screenplay. The agreement may make reference to the current Writer's Guild of America agreement involving credits.

Recording and Broadcast Rights

Another form of "performance" rights is the right to use all or portions of the book for recording on records, tapes, or discs or for live broadcast over the radio. For example, a company may want the right to record a poet reading his works. And there are several companies that make cassette tapes of books for sale or rental.

A license agreement for recording rights should include the following:

1. The grant of rights will stipulate that the recorder has the right to make a "master" plus multiple reproductions, in whatever form is being contracted for, and to sell or lease the copies in a specified territory. It may further state that the reproduction will be made in a "first-class" manner.

2. No changes should be made in the text without your approval.

3. The recorder will reserve the right to select and pay the performers of his choice.

4. The recorder will agree to display your name and the title of the book on the "jacket" cover, with the credit and copyright line specified by your publisher.

5. The royalty is usually 10 percent of the "gross rental proceeds" from the sale or rental of the master or copies. There may be a small advance against projected royalties.

The company will probably specifically reserve the right to set the retail price and rental charges for the tapes, and to use your name in advertisements and promotion.

6. The usual term is two years, with an automatic renewal until notice is served by either party.

Dramatic Rights

This is the right to adapt your book for presentation on the "regular spoken stage" with living actors "appearing and speaking in person in the actual and immediate presence of the audience." It can include such things as a "first-class" dramatic production on Broadway, an off-Broadway production, a touring performance, a stock-company presentation, or a presentation by a local church group. It can even include a musical adaptation (such as a musical comedy) or an opera based on the book.

A dramatist or producer interested in writing and producing a play based on your book will usually contact your publisher. Most publishers are not very familiar with this type of agreement, however, and will probably have the negotiations handled by an agent. This should not affect your earnings from such a license arrangement, however; the publisher should split his share of the income with the subagent. The usual split of income is 80 percent to you and 20 percent to the publisher.

Cable Television Rights

Cable television is offering interesting new possibilities for the sale of rights (as well as for author promotion). Rodale Press, for example, has formed an electronic publishing division to prepare instructional programs on solar and wood heating, gardening, and other how-to topics. The programs are recorded on videocassette and are sold both by direct mail and through a cable distributor. Since this is such a new field, widely accepted guidelines for the licensing of cable rights and the distribution of materials on video cassette or disc have not been developed yet but the field offers fairly good potential for book material which can be directed to a highly specific audience. However, it should also be noted that some cable programs and operators have done less well than originally expected, and that the industry is presently undergoing a "shakeout" period. Opportunities for subsidiary-rights income from this area are at the moment somewhat uncertain.

Filmstrip, Transparency, Microfilm, and "Mechanical Storage" Rights

This category takes into account many different types of "information storage" rights, such as filmstrip, microfilm, and transparency. In some cases the text of the book will be stored word for word; in others it may be combined with illustrations to create a substantially different work.

Filmstrip rights are of particular interest to educational publishers and to buyers of educational material. The U.S. Government buys a great deal of filmstrip material for use in various educational programs; the characters from the *Peanuts* comic strip, for example, are used in a filmstrip dealing with career education. Sometimes a filmstrip will include sound, sometimes it will not.

The word *transparency* here refers to a large-size transparency to be used with an overhead projector—again, primarily for educational purposes.

Microfilm and microfiche find their greatest use as storage for scholarly, rare, and out-of-print materials. Certain companies buy this right from publishers in order to make books with low levels of demand available to purchasers at a cost generally ranging between $10 and $100, with the price determined by the number of pages involved, type of copy made (photocopy or microfilm), whether cloth binding is included with a "paper copy," and so on. University Microfilms International is one of the larger firms in this field and has a catalog of over 84,000 titles, aimed primarily at the library market. The usual arrangement is to pay a 10 percent royalty on reprint revenues to the publisher.

Electronic Publishing and Computer Software Rights

Electronic publishing is a new and burgeoning area that is imperfectly understood as yet. It can take many forms, from simply converting a finished book into a database source, or into an image that can be transmitted via wire (videotext), or into performances (such as baby care or cooking) that can be recorded on videocassette or videodisc, to converting the material into "software" or creating whole new works specifically for these uses. Some publishers have set up their own electronic publishing or software divisions for these purposes, while others are seeking to license their properties to a third party—or are simply sitting tight and waiting to be approached. A certain number of literary agencies are also very active in the field, seeking to bring together writers and producers of various forms of software.

One of the problems is that the conversion or developmental costs can be substantial. Experienced programmers typically charge between $60 and $150 per hour; computer time for testing and debugging the programs is expensive; there is a vast variety of computer hardware available and many of the systems are not compatible with one another; and so on. However, the income for the author of such materials can be substantial. One agent told me that he had arranged projects carrying advances ranging from $10,000 to $5,000,000. Terms and advances vary enormously, and at this point it's difficult to suggest an "average" range. The best approach is either to have your agent hold onto these rights for you, or grant them to the publisher on the understanding that terms will be negotiated at the time that an offer is made.

Commercial (Merchandising) Rights

These are the rights associated with using elements from a book on other kinds of merchandise, such as posters, greeting cards, beer mugs, towels, and the like. For certain kinds of books—particularly cartoon, humor, or children's books—this can be a lucrative market.

Frankly, few publishers have much experience in licensing these rights because they don't usually have good connections with the manufacturers of such items. Agents try to hold onto these rights for their authors; if the publisher is granted them, they usually try to work through their special sales department or through an intermediary such as the Licensing Corporation of America. Earnings on a per unit basis tend to be low; a greeting card license, for instance, would yield a 1 percent to 2 percent royalty on net income, and an advance of only a few hundred dollars. However, the quantity sold can be substantial, and if the figures or themes used are very popular (such as the *Peanuts* characters or *The Preppy Handbook* gear) the income can be very good indeed.

9

After Publication

Writing is a dog's life, but the only life worth living.
—GUSTAVE FLAUBERT

Is there life after publication? You bet there is! For one
thing, you can continue your efforts to promote and sell the
book for months and even years after publication. But there
are also a number of things that can occur in relation to the
book as literary property. You will start receiving royalty
statements summarizing sales, subsidiary-rights income,
and certain expenses associated with publishing the book.
You will have to report any income from your business as a
writer to the Internal Revenue Service. Your book may go
out of print, in which case you might want to get the rights
back from your publisher. You may want to will, sell, or give
your copyright to someone. And you may write a new book,
in which case you have to honor the option and conflicting-
work clauses in your present contract. This time, you may
even choose to publish the book yourself.

For some suggestions on how to deal with these possibilities, read on.

Decoding Your Royalty Statement

After your book is published, you will begin receiving
statements summarizing the sales made by your publisher
during the preceding royalty period, plus your share of any
subsidiary-rights income from licenses arranged by the publisher, and any expenses charged against your royalty account.

It takes most publishers about four months after the close of a royalty period to prepare statements, so that statements for the period from January 1 to June 30 are usually mailed out in October, and those for the July 1–December 31 period in April. This means that by the time you get the statement, it's already four months out of date. Furthermore, if your book is published early in the royalty period, you can wait as long as eight or nine months before getting a statement. However, you can always ask your editor (or the sales department) for a summary of sales before you actually receive the statement.

Each publisher has its own statement form, and some of them are remarkably difficult to decipher. Furthermore, a statement usually does not show total sales from previous periods, so if you want to know total sales over several periods, you will have to add them up manually.

The Summary Sheet. Most statements come with a top sheet summarizing various kinds of information, such as your total royalty earnings during the period, your share of subsidiary-rights and permissions income during the period, expenses charged to your account, and the total payable. It will probably *not* provide such information as the number of copies in print, number of times the book has been reprinted, total number of free and review copies given out, and so on.

Statement of Sales. Figure 19 is an example of what the portion of the statement showing sales might look like. In order to check and interpret it, you will probably need to refer to the royalty rates specified in your contract, and you will probably need a calculator. Let's "walk through" this particular example to get a better idea of what all the data mean.

The cover price of the book is $15, and that is what the royalty calculations are based on. During the period of July 1 to December 31, 12,000 copies were sold to the trade. The royalty rate changed after the first 5,000 copies were sold, and again after the next 5,000 copies were sold, so the author's earnings at that point were $21,375. There was also a special sale of 150 copies at a discount of 52 percent; in this case, the royalty rate was 10 percent of the amount received by the publisher. Five hundred copies were sold in Canada, and here the rate was two thirds of the prevailing rate; since the author had reached the 15 percent level, the publisher's accounting department multiplied two thirds of this (10 percent) times the cover price times 500 to come up with a total of $750 in royalties for the author. One hundred copies were sold overseas; here the rate was 10 percent of the publisher's income after duty, taxes, etc., had been deducted. The net income on each copy exported may have varied, but in any case, the publisher took in a total of $740, so the author earned $74 in royalties.

Note that although it is not indicated on the statement, the publisher *may* have taken a "reserve for returns." If the publisher is anticipating that a significant number of the copies sold to retailers and wholesalers will be returned for credit, these sales may simply not be shown on the statement; this is what is called a reserve for returns. This usually happens only for the first or second royalty period, when returns are expected to be heavy. Ask your editor if your publisher reserves for returns, and if there was a reserve taken for your book.

Statement of Other Income. If there was subsidiary-rights or permissions income, it may be listed on a separate sheet, such as that shown in Figure 20. In this example, there was quite a lot of income from several sources, including first-

Figure 19
A SAMPLE ROYALTY STATEMENT

AUTHOR: Zelda Jones   PUB DATE: October 5, 1983
TITLE: The Heart Rendeth   PERIOD: July 1 to
                                                          December 31,
                                                          1983

TYPE OF SALE	COPIES SOLD	COVER PRICE	AMOUNT RECEIVED	ROYALTY %	AMT.	PAYMENT TO AUTHOR
Regular	5,000	$15.00	N/A	10	$1.50	$ 7,500.00
Regular	5,000		N/A	12.5	$1.875	9,375.00
Regular	2,000		N/A	15	$2.25	4,500.00
Special (@ 52%)	150		$1,080.00	10	—	108.00
Canadian	500		N/A	2/3rd prevail.		750.00
Export	100		$ 740.00	10% of net		74.00
						$22,307.00

serial and foreign rights (apparently the author did not have an agent who reserved these rights on her behalf). Two things are worth noting in particular:

1. The statement probably will not show the percentage of income you are receiving; it will simply show the results of the calculations by the royalty department. However, it should show which payment it is for those payments that come in installments—on signature of the contract, on distribution, etc. Ask your editor if you are not sure what the payment is for.

2. Foreign-rights sales often involve a subagent whose commission is deducted from your portion of the advance. In addition, there may be other deductions, such as a "value added" tax on income from a British license, bank charges if the money has to be converted into dollars, or taxes withheld by the foreign country.

Charges Against Your Account. There will also be a summary of any charges applied against your royalty account. This can include such things as charges for AA's in proofs that exceeded the percentage allowance provided in the contract, the cost of an index prepared by someone hired by the publisher, the cost of retyping the manuscript, charges for artwork supplied by the house and books purchased by the author (at the discount specified in the contract). If this is your first royalty statement, it will also show the amount of the advance against royalties that you received. Note that:

1. Except for the advance and AA's, it is becoming increasingly common for publishers to bill authors directly for these costs rather than charging them against the royalty account. This is because the income from sales and subsidiary rights is often not enough to pay for these costs or even to retire the cost of the advance.

2. Agents sometimes ask the publisher to provide them with bound galleys or books to use in trying to license the rights they have retained, without telling the author. If puzzling book charges appear on your statement, this may be the reason.

3. If the AA's bill seems high to you, you can ask your editor to verify it, either by checking the compositor's bill or by reviewing the changes on galleys or pages that you made and that were transferred onto the master proofs.

Figure 20
SUMMARY OF OTHER INCOME
ON ROYALTY STATEMENT

		AUTHOR'S SHARE
First serial		
McCall's Magazine ($1,000)		900.00
Chapters 3 and 4 in April 1983 issue		
Book club		
Literary Guild advance ($5,000)		2,500.00
Playboy Book Club advance ($1,000)		500.00
Mass-market paperback edition		
Pocket Books—advance on signature ($2,500)		1,250.00
Foreign rights		
Librairie Dussault Ltee (French-Canadian rights)		
Advance on signature	$500.00	
Less commission to agent	− 50.00	
	$450.00	337.50
Martin Secker & Warburg		
Advance on signature ($1,000)		750.00
Shinchosha Co.—hardcover edition		
Advance on signature	$2,500.00	
Less: Tax withheld	− 250.00	
	$2,250.00	
Less: Commission to agent	− 250.00	
	$2,000.00	1,333.33
Shinchosha Co.—paperback edition		
Advance on signature	$1,000.00	
Less: Tax withheld	− 100.00	
	$ 900.00	
Less: Commission to agent	− 100.00	
	$ 800.00	533.33
Second serial and permissions		
New Woman magazine—excerpt in Oct./		
Nov. issue ($400)		200.00
Oxford University Press		
Permission to use excerpt in anthology, The		
Theme of Romance in Contemporary		
Fiction ($100)		50.00
		$8,354.16

The publisher's royalty department will deduct the expenses chargeable to you from your earnings for that period to determine whether you will receive a check or not. If the total of your advance and expenses exceeds that of your earnings, you will not receive any money during that period. Keep in mind that:

1. The advance applies against *all* earnings, not just the earnings from the trade sales of the book.

2. Even if you have an "early pass-through" clause in your contract with the trade house, you will not receive the specified kinds of rights income until the account has been earned out.

3. If the royalty rates shown on the statement seem peculiar, it may be because sales have fallen below a minimum specified in your contract and the rate has been reduced accordingly.

4. If you did not receive the royalty report when it was due, it may mean that the publisher is late getting the statements out, or the income was below a certain level specified in the contract, or the book has gone out of print, or the publisher is in financial difficulties. If you have an agent, ask her to check for you. If the publisher is in financial straits, you should ask for a statement clarifying the status of your account, with the understanding that the publisher will pay you at the earliest possible time. If the publisher has gone bankrupt, or your contract stipulates that nonpayment of royalties is a breach of contract, you will probably be able to get your rights back. See later in this chapter for details on how to do this.

5. If you suspect that the information shown on a statement is incorrect, try to straighten it out through your agent or editor. It is probably simply a clerical error or an error in interpretation of contract clauses. You may have a clause in your contract allowing you to have a representative check the publisher's records for your book. However, keep in mind that such a royalty examination could involve auditing sales, distribution, returns, and subsidiary-rights reports and a physical check of the publisher's inventory, and can be expensive, running anywhere from $2,500 to $25,000.

Taxes

Making money from writing a book is a very pleasant experience. However, you may have to pay taxes on at least a portion of that income. Uncle Sam says that you must file a federal income tax return if your income from all sources exceeds a certain level. The level in 1983 for a single person under sixty-five years of age was $3,300, with different levels for older writers and married people. However, these levels change from year to year, and you should check current tax regulations for this—and for all tax matters—each year.

The Writing Business. If you regard writing as a business from which you hope to make a profit, you are allowed to deduct certain kinds of expenses related to that business. The Internal Revenue Service defines a business as "a pursuit carried on for livelihood or for profit (as) distinguished from an activity engaged in purely for personal satisfaction." They go on to say that "two characteristic elements of a business are regularity of activities and transactions, and the production of income. If, in a given year, no income or a small amount of income is coupled with expenditures that produce a loss, there may be a question as to whether a business was carried on in that year." However, another regulation states that "an activity is presumed to be engaged in for profit if it produces a profit in any two out of five consecutive years unless the Internal Revenue Service establishes to the contrary." You may take deductions at whatever point your work begins to produce revenue.

This makes life a little difficult for the writer who has just started his business and has little or no income to declare, yet has expenses associated with that business. If you are uncertain about how to proceed, I recommend that you seek the advice of an accountant skilled in current tax laws. Or you may wish to call or visit an IRS office. All states have a toll-free number for the IRS. However, be aware that *you* are ultimately responsible for the forms you turn in, and neither a tax advisor nor an IRS person can be held accountable for advice given to you. The final decision rests with the official who audits your account (if you are unlucky enough to have your return come to the attention of the IRS). To avoid difficulty, be as informed as you reasonably can be about the law, and be honest in reporting the income you have received and the expenses you have incurred in connection with your writing business.

Records. An important element in any business is the keeping of complete and accurate records. The IRS says that these records must be "permanent, accurate, complete, and must clearly establish income, deductions, credits, employee information, etc." and should be retained until the statute of limitations for that return expires. This is ordinarily three years after the return is due to be filed or two years from the date the tax was paid, whichever occurs later. However, it is prudent to hang onto them longer if your income from writing is developing slowly and you want to demonstrate the seriousness of your intention to make money. If you buy any capital equipment such as a typewriter, tape recorder, desk, etc., for which you want to take a depreciation, you should hold onto the receipt for as long as you own the item.

There are many kinds of records, including receipts, canceled checks, a diary or ledger in which you keep track of income and expenses (particularly expenses for which you can't get a receipt, such as the cost of a subway token for a visit to your editor's office), and so on. Remember that the records must be permanent and complete. The ledger or diary should be bound, not looseleaf, and the entries should be made in ink. If you make a mistake, draw a line through it rather than blotting it out. You may want to establish a separate checking account for business transactions; checks are in any case prima facie evidence of an expense, and your check register is an excellent source of information and documentation.

Federal Income Tax Forms. There are several forms that you may utilize in declaring your income and losses from writing.

Form 1040: U.S. Individual Income Tax Return. This is the form you must fill out if your income from any and all sources is above the specified minimum.

Schedule C: Profit or (Loss) from Business or Profession. Here is where you itemize your deductions.

Schedule SE: Computation of Social Security Self-Employment Tax. If you show a net profit on Schedule C of $400 or more, you may have to pay Social Security taxes on it. This depends on whether or not you also have a salaried job from which Social Security taxes are withheld, and you have already paid the maximum tax. (The maximum income subject to Social Security tax in 1983 was $35,700.) Check the current tax law for details.

Form 1040-ES: Declaration of Estimated Tax for Individuals. You are supposed to fill out this form and make quarterly payments if you anticipate that your income tax liability at the end of the year will be more than $300. This can be a complicated and annoying procedure, especially if you don't have a very good idea of what your income is likely to be. It would be wise to consult an experienced tax advisor before getting involved with this.

Filling Out the 1040 Form. Like all of the tax forms, the format of the 1040 form changes from year to year. Furthermore, you have a certain amount of latitude in how you fill the form out, since it is intended primarily as a guideline in reporting your taxable income. However, there are certain entries that you are bound to encounter and that have a close relationship to your business as a writer. They include:

• Wages, salaries, tips, etc. This is the line where you enter the total income from a salaried job (as reported on the W-2 form you receive from your employer), tips, bonuses, and so forth. However, if you are going to fill out a Schedule C, you will probably not want to include income from your work as a writer on this line.

• Business income (or loss) (attach Schedule C). This line on the 1040 is where you would indicate your net profit or loss from your business; the Schedule C form attached will provide the details. If you are showing a loss, enclose the net amount of expenses in excess of income in parentheses.

• Pensions, annuities, rents, royalties, partnerships, etc. (attach Schedule E). This line is used to declare total income from other sources, which can then be itemized in more detail on Schedule E. However, if you are in the writing business, and producing a series of books which produce royalties, you should declare these royalties on Schedule C.

• Payments to an IRA. This stands for Individual Retirement Account, and was originally intended for people employed by companies that did not have a retirement plan. Now anyone can open a tax-sheltered IRA.

• Payments to a Keogh (H.R. 10) retirement plan. The formal name for this plan is the Self-Employed Individuals Tax Retirement Act. It allows a self-employed person to shelter up to 15 percent of his net earned income each year (to a maximum of $30,000, starting in 1984) from taxation until a more convenient time (presumably retirement, when you are in a lower tax bracket). Contributions to such a plan must be made through a financial institution acceptable to the IRS, but can be a great financial benefit to a freelance writer. Again, check with a financial advisor for details.

Filling Out the Top of Schedule C. One of the first questions on Schedule C has to do with your accounting method. Most writers use the "cash" method, in which all income actually received during the year and all expenses actually paid during the year are declared. In the "accrual" method, income and taxes may be declared even though not actually received or paid during that calendar year. This method involves more complicated bookkeeping and is used primarily by businesses where inventory is involved. The cash system is the easiest and most practical for most writers.

The form also has a box that you are to check if you are deducting expenses for an office in your home. This is one of the most volatile issues for a freelancer, and the IRS has been much more stringent in recent years about these kinds of deductions. Such an office must be an area that is used "regularly and exclusively" for your writing business in order for you to deduct a "pro rata portion of the operating and depreciation expense of your home." To figure out the appropriate percentage, you can either divide the total number of square feet in the office area by the total square feet in the house, or if it's an individual room that is relatively similar in size to the other rooms in the house or apartment, you can use this as a basis of your percentage. You can then use this percentage or fraction to deduct the costs of mortgage interest, heat and light, trash collection, and so on. For more information about these deductions, see IRS publication 587, *Business Use of Your Home*. The new tax law passed in 1981, has helped to liberalize this area. You should consult an accountant for advice on the changes.

Income Declared on Schedule C. There is a section on the form to indicate your total income from your writing business, such as advances, royalties, lecture fees, grants, etc. There are certain situations, however, when the income from a prize or grant does not have to be declared. The U.S. government says you do not have to acknowledge an award of cash or merchandise if:

The award is in recognition of past accomplishments in religious, charitable, scientific, educational, artistic, literary, or civic fields.

You were selected as a recipient without any action on your part—that is, you didn't enter a contest, etc.

You are not required, as a condition of receiving the prize, to perform substantial future services, such as giving speeches.

The Nobel and Pulitzer prizes fulfill these requirements, as do a number of others. However, if you enter a literary contest on your own and/or you have to give more than a few readings a year as a condition of receiving the prize, the income is probably taxable. If you are in doubt, check with the organization awarding the prize to find out if the income has been regarded as taxable in the past.

Grants and fellowships are also a slightly different situation. If you receive a grant from a private or public foundation, the income from the grant is tax-free up to $300 a month for each month during the year in which you receive payments under the grant. You can claim this exclusion for a maximum of 36 months during your life (for a total of $10,800), but the months do not have to run consecutively.

If the grant includes an allowance for expenses specifically related to the grant (secretarial help, travel money, etc.), you will not have to pay taxes on this allowance so long as it is specifically used for this purpose and you can prove it by means of receipts.

Expenses Declared on Schedule C. The IRS says that these expenses must be "proximately related" to your business; that is, you had better be able to prove their relationship to your work as a writer. Here are examples of the kinds of things you can include.

Advertising. If you are publishing your own book and/or have contributed to the cost of ads run by your publisher, you can enter the cost here. If you run an ad in a periodical to let people know that your manuscript is available for publication, this cost is also deductible.

Bank charges. If you have a separate bank account for income and expenses related to your business, the bank charges for this account can be deducted.

Motor vehicle expenses. Many freelancers use their own vehicles in the course of researching, traveling to interview people, etc. Operating costs, parking fees, and other related expenses are deductible either as a ratio of business use to total use or on a cost-per-business-mile basis as established annually by the IRS.

Commissions. The commissions you pay your literary agent can be deducted; so are the commissions paid to subagents for handling various kinds of subsidiary-rights sales.

Depreciation. Most expenses listed on Schedule C relate to costs that occur during that year and are limited to a one-year period. But if you purchase equipment or furnishings that can be expected to have a useful life of more than one year, the cost of those purchases can be recovered in small annual increments. There are various ways of calculating this depreciation, including straight-line, declining-balance, and sum-of-the-years. If the equipment has a useful life of three years or longer, you may also be entitled to an investment credit as well as a deduction. See the IRS *Tax Guide for Small Businesses* for details. For property acquired after 1981, you should consult the new rules on depreciation.

Dues and publications. Most writers belong to professional associations and writers' groups of various kinds, and also buy books and periodicals related to their field and to their writing. The cost of dues and of publications can be deducted on Schedule C.

Employee benefit programs. If you are working on such a large project that you have had to hire a full-time secretary or researcher, you may wish to provide that employee with various kinds of "benefits" such as health insurance, etc. The premiums for such benefits can be deducted from your taxes. You can perhaps take this deduction for yourself if you have incorporated under Subchapter S; see the discussion of corporations below.

Freight. Usually not applicable for a writer, unless you are self-publishing and are paying for shipments of your book by freight to book dealers.

Insurance. If you are carrying homeowner's insurance on equipment or furnishings necessary to your business, the cost of the insurance can be deducted. Fire and theft insurance on these items, plus an appropriate proportion of your car insurance, can also be deducted, as can libel insurance.

Interest on business indebtedness. If you have had to buy equipment or furniture for your business on "time" (that is, using a credit arrangement of some sort), you can deduct the interest you are paying on that loan. (You can also deduct the interest on a personal loan you have taken to support yourself while writing your book. However, this deduction must be itemized in the section listing personal, itemized deductions.)

Laundry and cleaning. This item is intended primarily for businesses where uniforms are necessary, such as performing artists who must have their costumes cleaned. However, it may also apply to payments that you make to have your office cleaned.

Legal and professional services. If you have hired an attorney to review your contract, or to help in a lawsuit over copyright infringement or other matters, you can write this expense off. Professional services might also include hiring a professional typist to type your manuscript, or a freelance editor to help you with your work. You can also deduct your accountant's fee for preparing your taxes, but only for the work related to your business expenses.

Office supplies. Here you would lump the cost of materials you would normally use up in the course of a year, such as typing paper, paperclips, etc. You can also include the cost of having your manuscript duplicated for submissions to publishers. If you buy a relatively inexpensive piece of office equipment that you don't want to depreciate, you can enter that here as well.

Pension and profit-sharing plans. If you are offering employees a pension or profit-sharing plan, you can deduct the cost.

Postage. The cost of postage for sending query letters, proposals, and manuscripts to agents and publishers is deductible. So are postage costs for mailing letters to people you wish to interview for your book, etc.

Rent on business property. If you are renting your home or apartment, and have set part of it aside for use as an office, you can deduct the appropriate portion of the rent here. If you have had to rent space in a building that is not your residence, you can deduct the cost of the rental. Rental fees for special equipment, such as a word processor, can be deducted.

Repairs. The cost of repairs on equipment or furnishings used in your business is deductible. So are repairs to office space that you have rented, if you are liable for these costs, plus the cost of repairs to your home in proportion to the percentage you are declaring as office space. However, under the new tax law, if you sell your house, you might lose some tax advantage by taking these deductions. It is advisable to consult an accountant or attorney on this matter.

Taxes. If you have employees, you are responsible for contributing a share to taxes such as Social Security. These taxes, plus other taxes related to your business, such as sales tax, can be deducted.

Telephone. If you are maintaining a separate office and telephone for your writing business, you can deduct the cost of the telephone service. If you use the same telephone for personal and business calls, you can write off only that portion of your bill related to business calls. To provide evidence of these expenses, you should keep your itemized bills from the telephone company.

Travel and entertainment. There may also be certain necessary expenses related to research, selling the rights to your book, lecturing or making publicity appearances, and so on that can be included under the category of travel and entertainment. If you need to interview someone who is only available during the lunch hour, for example, you can deduct the cost of that luncheon from your taxes. If you entertain someone in your home who is performing a service related to your writing business, this is also a legitimate deduction.

Travel expenses related to your writing can be deducted so long as they do not fall into the category of "commutation"—that is, travel from your home to "work," rather than from one place of work to another. If you take a taxi to meet your editor at her place of business, for example, the fare from your home can be deducted only if your office is in your home.

The IRS has strict rules regarding travel and entertainment deductions. For more information, consult their Publication 463. Note that if you are attending some sort of meeting and have received a per diem allowance, this allowance must be declared as part of your income if you are deducting expenses.

Utilities. If you have an office in your home, or are renting outside space for this purpose, you can deduct an appropriate proportion of the cost of utilities (electricity, gas, etc.).

Wages, job credits, etc. The wages you pay people for helping you with your writing business, such as typists and researchers, can be fully deducted. In addition, you may qualify for certain types of credits.

A "Jobs Credit" is part of a government program to encourage employment of the "hard to hire," such as a vocational rehabilitation referral, an "economically disadvantaged" youth, and so on. If you hire such an individual, you may be entitled to a "targeted jobs credit" of 50 percent of the first $6,000 of first-year wages and 25 percent of the first $6,000 of second-year wages.

WIN stands for Work Incentive Program. If you employ an individual whom the secretary of labor has certified as having been placed in employment under a WIN program or who is a welfare recipient eligible for AFDC (Aid for Dependent Children) payments, this also qualifies as a targeted jobs credit.

Note that a credit against taxes is more valuable than a deduction, because it is a "dollar for dollar" reduction rather than simply reducing the amount of your taxable income.

Other expenses. Miscellaneous expenses could include such items as:

Fees charged for the use of copyrighted material (permissions fees).

The cost of hiring an illustrator or photographer to prepare illustrations for your book (unless this is included under fees for professional services).

The cost of classes necessary to maintaining or improving your skills as a writer.

The cost of admission to museums, movies, or other places or events related to the book you have written.

Business gifts, up to $25 per business associate per year. If someone has granted you an interview for several hours, for example, you may express your gratitude by sending that individual a bouquet of flowers. The cost of the bouquet can be deducted.

State and Local Taxes. In addition to paying the federal government, the money you make from your writing business may be subject to certain state and city taxes. In New York City, for example, writers with high incomes may have to pay the New York City Unincorporated Business Tax, plus New York State taxes. Your accountant should know the requirements in your area; otherwise, check with your state and city income-tax bureaus.

Foreign Income and Foreign Tax Credits. In the example of a royalty statement shown earlier in this chapter (Figure 19), the Japanese government withheld taxes on some subsidiary-rights licenses. You still have to pay taxes on the money received from a foreign license, but the amount of taxes you have already paid abroad may reduce the amount you owe at home. Check with your accountant for the appropriate information.

Income Averaging. If your income takes a substantial jump from one year to the next, you may be able to reduce your liability by a technique called income averaging. You will need your tax records for the previous five years, plus a form called Schedule G, which has detailed instructions on the back. For more information, get IRS Publication 506. Be especially aware that the use of income averaging can be affected by a change in your personal status, such as getting married or divorced.

Limitation on Income. One way to limit your tax burden is to deduct absolutely everything you legitimately can. But there are also other strategies you can employ in order to limit Uncle Sam's bite on your income. One option is to make an arrangement with your publisher to limit the amount of money you will receive in any given year. This can be done by means of a "limitation on income" clause in your contract, which will limit the amount of royalties and subsidiary-rights income you will receive in any given year to a specified amount. This does not have to be the same amount each year; you can set different limits for specified years. And if the publisher has published more than one of your books, this limit can apply to all of the contracts in force. The limitation can remain in effect until you are in a lower tax bracket, at which point the deferred amounts can finally be paid.

However, having your publisher hold back portions of your income has distinct disadvantages. For one thing, you will not be earning any interest on the money being held by the publisher—although the publisher certainly will be. For another, it is doubtful that you would be given access to these monies if you suddenly needed a large amount of cash (although you might be able to get a loan using the amount due you for collateral). And you also run the risk of having the publisher suddenly go bankrupt. Be sure to seek professional advice on this matter.

Forming a Corporation or Partnership. Another possibility you might want to consider is forming a corporation or partnership. The purpose of these business arrangements is to gain advantages in terms of the amount of taxes payable on income or the "losses" that can be written off.

A corporation is an artificial legal entity that has certain business advantages. For example, the income of a "regular" corporation is taxed at a considerably lower rate than that of an individual and can be reduced even further through the payment of a salary to you, which creates a deduction for the corporation but which constitutes taxable income to you as an employee of the corporation. A "Subchapter S" corporation is not taxed at the corporate level; instead, income is credited directly to stockholders' accounts and they are taxed as individuals. Life insurance policies can be a deductible business expense, and you may be able to set up an advantageous pension plan.

However, the legal costs of the initial forming of the corporation may be expensive, and more complex records have to be maintained. Furthermore, you may be subject to double taxation for corporate and personal taxes. Most accountants think that this alternative is probably not practical for anyone grossing less than $100,000 a year. Since the tax considerations are sophisticated, you should seek counsel from a tax attorney before undertaking such measures.

Partnership arrangements are even rarer for writers. The basic idea here is that individual partners are taxed on their share of partnership income, so that if you know one or more people who need some sort of tax shelter, you can form a partnership whereby the "investors" are allocated a larger proportion of the business loss. (This is much more usual in the theater than in writing.) Again, this is a complicated procedure, and should be undertaken with the assistance of an excellent lawyer.

Moving to a "Tax Haven." Some writers think that if they start earning a lot of money from their writing, they can protect their income by moving to a "tax haven" such as Ireland, where writers are not required to pay income taxes. Unfortunately, this works best for English writers like Frederick Forsyth and Len Deighton, since their own country does not tax them if they live abroad (English income taxes are very high). This is not true for Americans, alas; if you retain your American citizenship, you have to pay U.S. taxes on all income from anywhere in the world, whether or not you live abroad.

You *may* be able to exclude up to a certain amount in income from foreign sources if you fulfill requirements regarding the amount of time spent abroad and if the IRS agrees to regard this income as "earned," but that may not be worth all the trouble to you. If you do decide to live abroad, you should check the consulate in that country for any treaties affecting taxation on your income. Some writers and other celebrities with large incomes have settled in Monte Carlo, where there are virtually no taxes.

Copyright as Literary Property

Registration. Although a copyright is less tangible than a castle in Spain or a Mercedes in your driveway, it is a form of property that you can buy, sell, lease, mortgage, license, bequeath by will, or give away. The copyright is created when you create the work, but to provide positive evidence of your claim to that work (and to gain certain advantages in the event of a copyright infringement suit), the copyright should be registered with the U.S. Copyright Office in Washington, D.C. Your publisher will normally take care of this for you. There is no particular advantage in registering your manuscript before it has been published, but if you wish to do so, obtain and fill out Form TX from the Copyright Office and return it to that office with a duplicate of the manuscript and the filing fee (presently $10).

Regaining Rights. When you make a contract with a publisher, you are essentially yielding specific rights for the term of copyright. However, there are various circumstances under which you (or your heirs) can get these rights back. Under the old copyright law, the heirs could get the rights for the renewal period if the author died before the renewal period began; this is still true for works published before January 1, 1978, and in fact, under the new copyright law, there are certain circumstances which the author (or the author's heirs) may terminate contracts entered into before January 1, 1978, in order to recapture up to the last nineteen years of a book's copyright. Under the new copyright law, you or your heirs can demand the rights back either thirty-five years from the date of publication or forty years from the date of the publishing contract, whichever is earliest; this applies to works published on or after January 1, 1978.

You can also get the rights back if the publisher fails to keep the work in print. Check the specific wording in your contract. "In print" may be defined as being available in any edition (including that of another publisher) or under license or under option.

If you think your book is out of print, write your editor a letter asking that the publisher either put the work back in print or revert the rights to you. (If you have an agent, the agent should write the letter.) The letter will probably be passed on to the contracts manager, who will check the status of the book with the sales and subsidiary-rights departments. If the publisher wants to keep the rights, he can order a small reprinting or arrange a license with a reprinter, and there is not much you can do about it. In fact, some contracts stipulate that the writer cannot "unreasonably withhold" consent to a reprint license in order to cause reversion of the rights.

If the publisher agrees to revert the rights, he will write you a letter stating that the rights are being returned. He may give you the option of purchasing any remaining bound books, unbound sheets, dies, printing plates, or film, but may retain the rights to reproduce the book from the materials prepared by the house. If you are given the right to reproduce the book from these materials, you probably won't want the printing plates because they are large and heavy, but you may want to buy the film.

If you do not want to buy all of the remaining stock of books, the publisher will probably want the right to sell them off. Any royalties due you will be paid, and you will also continue to receive your share of any subsidiary-rights income from licenses that have already been granted. If the term of any of the licenses has expired, you may be able to have these rights terminated as well. You or your new publisher can then try to arrange a new license.

It will not be necessary to notify the Copyright Office of this reversion if the copyright notice in the book bears your name; if the notice has the publisher's name, you will have to get a copyright assignment from the publisher which you will then send to the Copyright Office for recording, along with the necessary fee. You should not change the notice in future copies until after the assignment is recorded by the Copyright Office.

The reversion letter from the publisher will probably state that the warranties and indemnities originally specified in the contract will survive the termination. This is because someone can still bring suit for invasion of rights, and the publisher wants to continue to be protected by the warranty and indemnity clauses.

You may also be able to get your rights back if the publisher goes bankrupt. However, your specific rights in the matter will depend on the wording of the bankruptcy clause in your contract and on the current bankruptcy laws. Consult an attorney to determine your rights in the matter. If the publisher is bought out by another firm, you probably will not be able to get your rights back, because contracts usually give publishers the right to assign the publishing rights to someone else, at least as part of a sale of their business assets.

Making a Will. If you die without leaving a will with specific instructions for the disposal of your literary property, the laws of the state of your domicile will govern how your property is distributed. The probate court will appoint an administrator for your estate (this is usually a person who expects to receive a substantial part of your estate, such as your spouse or one of your children). The assets of your estate will be gathered by the administrator, and the value set by expert appraisers, if necessary. To determine the value of your copyright, the administrator will probably ask your publisher for sales data, in order to estimate the probable worth of the copyright in the future. The physical manuscript itself, any unpublished manuscripts, your personal papers, and your library may also have value and should be appraised. After outstanding debts have been paid, an "estate tax" will be levied on the taxable estate, and the remaining assets will be distributed according to the laws of the state.

Making a will in advance of this melancholy event has several advantages:

1. Your property will be distributed as you wish—after the requirements of the state have been fulfilled. In some states, your spouse or surviving children may have an elective right to a considerable portion of your estate. In some states your spouse may also have a community property interest.

2. You can name a specific person to act as executor. You may wish to appoint someone skilled in the handling of literary property, such as your editor or a "literary lawyer." Or you might appoint two executors: one for your literary property and one for the remainder of your assets. Acting as an executor can be a demanding job, particularly if your literary property is extensive. Make sure that your executor understands the different kinds of problems he or she may face.

3. You can take steps to protect your heirs from onerous estate taxes on your literary property. You may arrange to sell your copyrights, or give them away more than three years before your death, or set up a trust, or have your manuscripts and other personal papers donated to an institution after your death. A donation after your death is valued at the "fair market value" of the work, which can be considerable if you have become well-known; if the donation is made before your death, the deduction is limited to the cost of the materials in the work (paper, etc.).

I recommend that you draw up your will with the aid of an attorney, to deal with sophisticated questions of taxation and property rights, and to reduce the chance of having it challenged in court.

Selling Your Copyright. As in the case of any form of property, the copyright to a work—or individual exclusive rights to the use of that work—can be sold. The principal problem is determining the value of the rights being sold.

One common formula used for *textbooks* is to take the average of sales over the past five years and multiply by a factor of three. Trade books are more difficult to assess, because the trade-sales and subsidiary-rights potentials are more volatile. The price negotiated will depend on the perceived potential for future exploitation. Dashiell Hammett's heirs sold the copyrights to all his novels and stories for $5,000 because at that time there was little interest in Hammett's works. Now, of course, they are worth a great deal of money.

The price will also depend on whether you are selling the whole copyright, or only exclusive rights. Obviously, if any of these rights is currently held by someone, you cannot transfer ownership. If you wish, you can limit the right of the purchaser to modify the work, or set certain conditions in regard to author credit line. You may insist that you *always* be given credit as author of the work; conversely, you may not want to be credited at all if your original work is substantially changed by a movie company or some other type of buyer. In any case, the copyright law requires that such a transfer of exclusive rights be accompanied by "an instrument of conveyance or a note or memorandum of the transfer . . . in writing and signed by the owner of the rights conveyed or such owner's duly authorized representative."

Giving Your Copyright or Exclusive Rights Away. You can also *give* your copyright or certain of the exclusive rights associated with that copyright to someone. The basic procedure is to notify your publisher that you have transferred to someone else your "right, title and interest" to the copyright, specific rights, or the royalties and other sums received under the contract with the publisher. The person to whom you have transferred this interest will then be entitled to receive income from it and will have to pay taxes on the income. However, the tax laws relating to such a gift are complex and subject to change, and you should seek the advice and assistance of an attorney in such a transfer. Some attorneys recommend that you make such arrangements *be-*

fore you sign a contract with a publisher to reduce the risk of a challenge by the Internal Revenue Service.

Setting Up a Trust. You may wish to consider setting up one or more trusts. In a trust, property is transferred to a "trustee" (usually a bank or trust company) that holds and manages the property for the benefit of beneficiaries named by you. This may have tax advantages for you, and in the event of your death may prevent delays due to probate of the will, claims of creditors, and so on. The trust can be set up to suit your particular needs, but again, this is a complex matter and should be undertaken only with the aid of an experienced attorney.

Your Continued Relationship with Your Publisher

Your editor will continue to be one of your best friends in the publishing house for a long time after publication. It will be his or her responsibility to pass along reviews and news stories that come in, to let you know about new rights sales or requests for you to appear in the media, and to answer any questions you have about sales and the overall status of the book.

Be sure to get back the "dead matter" to the book—that is, your original manuscript, artwork, and any proofs that you marked up. You may be a famous writer some day, and this material could be valuable. If you don't get it back, the publisher will eventually dispose of it.

After publication, requests to reprint all or portions of your book will be handled by the publisher's permissions department. If the copyright for artwork or photographs is held by the artist or photographer, the reprint request will be forwarded to that person if the publishing house has an up-to-date address; otherwise, you may be contacted for this information.

A Revised Edition. If your book is successful and becomes a backlist item, you may eventually be asked to revise it. A number of questions will arise here:

• If you have the time and the desire to make the revisions, will you receive additional compensation for this work? The answer is generally no. The old edition will be phased out and you will receive royalty payments on the new edition.

• What if you don't have the time or desire to make these revisions? In this case, the publisher will probably hire somebody else to update the book. You and the publisher will have to settle on how the "reviser" will be paid and how he will be credited. Most times, a rewriter is granted a certain percentage of the royalties on the books, perhaps one fourth or one third. If you are extremely well-known, the rewriter will probably *not* be credited on the book, because the publisher will want to retain the market value of your authorship. However, if the book is substantially revised in a way that does not meet with your approval, you have the right *not* to have your name used in association with it.

• What if *you* want the book revised and your publisher does not want to incur the expenses of a new edition? You usually can't do much about this. The publisher will balance the projected costs of making the revisions versus the anticipated sales of the revised edition. If the projected sales won't offset the revision costs, you will have to learn to live with a book that is not as up-to-date as you would like.

The Option Clause. If you are planning on writing a new book, you should check the wording in the option clause of your present contract to see whether you are obliged to offer the work to your present publisher. If the clause applies to "your next work of nonfiction," for example, and you are planning on writing a novel, you are not obliged to submit the book to your present publisher. If the clause does apply to your new book, check to see when you can submit the material and what form it must be in (can it be a proposal, or must it be a complete manuscript?).

Whatever the case, you may be obliged to honor this option in "good faith"—legal language that is vague but can be used in court. If you turn in a proposal for a book that is completely inappropriate for the house (such as submitting a proposal for a novel to a house that publishes only nonfiction), the publisher may refuse to release you from the option. However, if your first book did not sell well and the publisher does not see much hope for your second one, you will probably be released from the option, by means of a letter stating that you have met the requirements of the option clause and are under no further obligation to submit a new book.

The Conflicting-Work Clause. This could also be called a no-competition clause because it restricts you from contracting with another publishing house to bring out a book similar to that covered by your present contract—even though your present publisher has declined to exercise its option for it. This is rarely an issue in the case of fiction, but can be troublesome in the case of nonfiction.

You should try to get this clause stricken from your contract before you sign it. If that is not possible, either try to get a release from your original publisher before approaching a new house with a similar project, or make the new book different enough that the original publisher is unlikely to try to enforce the conflicting work clause.

Publishing Your Own Book

Although you may never have given serious consideration to this possibility before, you might want to give some thought now to publishing a book on your own, either a new book or one for which the publishing rights have reverted to you. Publishing your own book has a number of advantages. It means that you have control over the whole process, and can be more completely involved in whether the book is a success or not. However, it also means a considerable financial investment and a fair amount of work. For further information on the hazards and opportunities, consult the several books on self-publishing listed in the Bibliography of this manual. Good luck!

10

Having Your Book Published as a Mass-Market Paperback Original

One of the most common complaints and questions I've heard over the years is why paperbacks aren't marketed like soap—and it seems as if the second most common complaint I've heard is that paperbacks are marketed like soap and shouldn't be.

—OSCAR DYSTEL, *former chairman; Bantam Books*

As suggested earlier in this manual, having your book published as a mass-market original is a good possibility for genre fiction, and is an increasingly viable alternative for many other kinds of books as well. As mass-market houses compete more aggressively with trade publishers for authors, they are expanding their lists and publishing a greater range of works as "originals" than ever before.

Initial publication in this format has numerous advantages. For one thing, it may simply be the best format for your book in that it will permit the book to reach its widest possible audience. Mass-market paperbacks are distributed to many more outlets than trade books are, and the lower cover price makes them affordable for many more people. The royalty per copy is substantially lower than that for a trade hardcover, but the larger number of copies sold can end up netting you an equivalent amount of money, and the advance money can be as attractive as that offered by trade publishers. Review attention may be less than that devoted to most hardcovers, but mass-market houses are excellent at promoting their books, and will continue to support and re-issue a book if it does well the first time around and/or you continue to write successful books of this type. And finally, publishing originally in paperback may be a good way of building up an audience for your work. Many writers, such as John D. Macdonald, Louis L'Amour, et al, have started in the paperback field and are now being published in hard-cover editions as well. And if a paperback original does un-usually well, the hardcover rights may be sold "backwards" to a trade house, or the mass-market house may do a trade hardcover edition as well.

Negative factors include the potentially less review atten-tion already mentioned, plus the fact that the average mass-market paperback does not stay out in the stores as long as trade hardcovers or paperbacks. Furthermore, mass-market paperbacks are less durable than trade hardcovers and may carry slightly less prestige.

Who Are the Publishers?

Looking for a mass-market publisher can be simpler than looking for a trade publisher, because the possibilities are more limited. There are only nine large houses that publish general fiction and nonfiction titles, and another seven or so that are well-known but smaller or more specialized. Figure 21 (page 244) lists and briefly describes these mass-market publishers. In addition there is a smattering of smaller houses that publish only genre paperbacks or erotica; a few of these houses are listed at the bottom of Figure 21. Note especially the following:

1. Each of these houses publishes mass-market paper-backs on a monthly basis. The big houses typically publish between thirty and forty mass-market titles a month; the smaller houses, considerably fewer. This means that there are about four hundred new releases coming from the mass-market houses each month, and roughly five thousand mass-market paperbacks published each year. In addition, most of the major paperback houses are publishing trade paper-backs, and some are publishing trade hardcovers.

2. Most of the nine large general publishers publish both originals and reprints. However, Berkley and Jove are both

Figure 21
THE MASS-MARKET PUBLISHERS

Large general houses

NAME	1983 TITLES	COMMENTS
Avon Books	300	Particularly well known for high quality literary fiction. Several imprints including Band, Discus, and Flare. Owned by the Hearst Corporation.
Ballantine Books	300	General fiction and nonfiction, including Fawcett lines. Owned by Random House.
Bantam Books	675	The largest house, with broad range including religious, educational, and hardcover. Imprints include New Age, Windstone, Bantam Classics.
Berkley Publishing Co.	235	Mostly reprints. Part of Berkley-Jove books owned by Putnam's.
Dell Publishing Co.	575	General plus Candlelight romances. Delta is trade paperback. Delacorte publishes hardcover in association with Dell.
Jove Publications	154	Mostly originals. Part of Berkley-Jove books owned by Putnam's.
New American Library (NAL)	510	First to publish hardcovers. Several imprints including Plume, Mentor, Meridian, and Signet for general fiction/nonfiction.
Pocket Books	350	Owned by Simon & Schuster. Washington Square Press imprint for high quality mass market. Also publishes trade hardcovers.
Warner Books	232	Strongest on commercial fiction. Includes Popular Library backlist. Also publishes trade hardcovers. Owned by Warner Communications.

Smaller or more specialized general publishers

NAME	TITLES	COMMENTS
Ace Books	242	Originally science fiction; now also action/adventure, western, romance, juvenile. Owned by Putnam's.
DAW Books	72	Science fiction. Distributed by NAL.
Del-Ray	75	Science fiction. Owned by Random House.

Figure 21—*Continued*
THE MASS-MARKET PUBLISHERS

Smaller or more specialized general publishers—Continued

NAME	1983 TITLES	COMMENTS
Harlequin Books	614	Canadian company that publishes 22 contemporary romances per month in five lines: Harlequin, Harlequin Presents, Harlequin Romances, Harlequin Superromances, and Harlequin Temptations (March 1984).
Penguin Books	268	Originally literary/scholarly; expanding into more commercial.
Pinnacle Books	150	"Fast-moving escape reading" and romances.
Silhouette Romances	292	Adult & young adult contemporary romances. Owned by Simon & Schuster. Publishes 28 titles per month in six lines: Silhouette Romances, First Love (for teens), Silhouette Special Edition, Silhouette Desire, Silhouette Intimate Moments, and Silhouette Inspirations (Feb. 1984).

Others: Condor, Leisure, Macfadden, Major Books, Nordon, Tempo Books, Tower, Zebra, publishers of erotica.

owned by Putnam's, and Berkley concentrates on reprints while Jove publishes primarily originals.

3. Many of the series published by mass-market houses are produced by packagers, with the authors working on a "for-hire" basis. The income is usually split 50/50 between the packager and writer. Not all series are written by one author, incidentally. Frequently they are written by a "syndicate" of writers who follow a "Bible" developed by the lead writer for the series; Jove's "Longarm" series of westerns, for example, was produced this way.

4. Harlequin is a Canadian-based firm that is largely responsible for the explosive growth of contemporary romances in the last several years. It launched its drive by carefully controlling the editorial content of the books, then packaging them in a standard format and at a low cover price, and distributing them through nonbookstore outlets.

A strong brand identification was developed, and women began asking for "Harlequin Romances" rather than individual titles or authors. The concept was very successful and has been imitated by other publishers, notably Silhouette Books, which is owned jointly by Simon & Schuster and Pocket Books. (In fact, S&S used to distribute the Harlequin line.)

How Do You Find a Publisher?

In deciding to approach a publisher you will obviously do best to select those houses that bring out books of the type you have written. This is reasonably easy to determine by spending an afternoon in a well-stocked paperback bookstore noting the publisher's imprints. If you are writing science fiction, for example, there are several publishers specializing in this area. Figure 22 (page 247) lists many well-known publishers and series of category fiction. If you are writing a more general type of book, you will probably direct it to one of the large general houses.

Should You Use an Agent? Although agents used to be rare in mass-market publishing, they now play an important role. If you want to deal with one of the major mass-market houses, it's advisable to have an agent, and in fact, some of the big houses will not consider material that does not come in from an agent or packager.

To find an agent, you can check some of the listings mentioned in Chapter 2, although many agents do not handle paperback originals, and the ones that specialize in this area may not be identified in the listing you consult. You might try calling a few of the agencies to see if they handle paperback originals or if they can give you the names of agents who do. Other tactics include attending a writers' conference, consulting a writers' organization, or contacting the Society of Author's Representatives or the Independent Literary Agents Association.

To find out whether a publisher accepts "unsolicited" material directly from writers, you can check the listings in *Writer's Market;* otherwise, you may have to call the publisher to find out.

Figure 22
SOME WELL-KNOWN PUBLISHERS AND LINES
OF CATEGORY FICTION

Romances	Avon "Finding Mr. Right," NAL "Rapture Romance," Harlequin, Silhouette, Pinnacle, Dell Candlelight, Jove "Second Chance at Love," Zebra "Hourglass Romances," Romances for young adults, Scholastic "Wildfire" and "Wishing Star," Bantam's "Sweet Dreams" and "Loveswept"
Science fiction	Ballantine Del-Ray, Pocket Books, DAW, Ace, Berkley
Western	Bantam, Dell, Jove, Pinnacle, Warner
Male adventure/ suspense	Warner, Pinnacle, Charter, Ballantine ("Espionage/Intelligence Library")
Mysteries	Harlequin Raven House Mysteries, Dell Murder Ink and Scene of the Crime, Penguin Crime Monthly, Pocket Books

Writing Genre Fiction. "Genre" or "category" fiction can be defined as fiction that has very specific plot and language requirements. Publishers of contemporary romances, for example, usually want clearly defined plot and character types, and provide a "tip sheet" for writers interested in writing for the line. Be sure to obtain this tip sheet from the publisher if you want to write for a specific line.

Study the requirements of any genre you are interested in writing for *carefully.* The competition for a spot in these fields is growing more fierce, and it's no longer possible to approach this in an amateurish way. Study examples in the genre you wish to work in, and also check any guides available. (Some of them are listed in the Bibliography.) One thing to be particularly aware of is that fashions in genre fiction tend to change quite dramatically. For a long time, for example, gothic romances were the brightest star in the romance firmament. Then in 1971 Avon Books published an original paperback called *The Flame and the Flower,* and the historical romance genre was born. Historical romances were very much in the ascendancy until the rise of contemporary and "sensual" romances in the last few years.

There has been a certain amount of backlash in the face of this floodtide of romances. Some publishers began to feel that the male reader was being neglected, and several "male action" series and lines have been launched recently. But there are always the hardy perennials: mysteries, traditional and modern westerns, science fiction, and so on.

The point in terms of trends is that once a particular genre gets "hot," many of the professional writers immediately start writing for it, and publishers' inventories fill up quickly. If you are trying to break into the field, it's important to be alert to what's going on, so that you have time to get on the bandwagon. Keep up with what's going on by reading *PW* and other review media covering mass-market paperbacks and by joining a professional writer's association if possible; word of mouth probably travels faster in the mass-market field than anywhere else.

Some General Tips About
Paperback Originals

1. In the genre field, paperback editors are particularly fond of books that have the potential for becoming a series. A series has the great merit that once it is established, there is a readership just waiting for the next book to come out. And as other readers discover the series, this generates sales for the books published earlier in the series. If you're writing genre fiction, it's a good idea to try to create a strong and appealing central character (or group of characters, if you're creating a multigenerational family saga) that can sustain a series of books.

2. Pay particular attention to the length conventions of paperback fiction. With the exception of historical or "big" commercial novels, most original mass-market fiction runs around sixty thousand words—considerably shorter than the average trade novel. The books are meant to be read in one sitting, and they also have to be relatively short to keep the cover price down.

3. Observe the submission requirements of the particular house you are submitting to. Try to find out in advance if the house prefers to receive proposals rather than complete manuscripts, by calling the publishing house or by checking

Writer's Market to see if its submission policies are indicated. Type the material neatly, following the suggestions given in Chapter 4. And remember, you have to *sell* the book as well as write it—at least the first one. Make the presentation material as well-written and attractive as you possibly can.

What Happens
in the Publishing House?

Mass-market paperback houses publish a list of books every month. The large houses publish between thirty and forty mass-market titles a month, the smaller houses somewhat fewer.

The List. The mass-market titles are usually listed in the monthly catalog in groups, reflecting the audience to which they are directed and the number of copies the house anticipates selling. Each list will have one or two "lead" titles—books that appear first in the catalog and on the order form and have the largest printing. A lead book will have a first printing of 500,000 to 800,000 copies, but it can be higher. This book is frequently a reprint of a best-selling trade book, but can also be a strong paperback original—almost always a long novel. Sometimes the publisher has two leads—one fiction and one nonfiction.

Next on the list is a selection of "midlist" titles: fiction or nonfiction titles that should sell well to the bookstore trade. A first printing can be as low as 15,000 to 25,000 copies for a literary novel, but the usual level for a fairly commercial novel or work of nonfiction is 75,000 to 100,000 copies.

Next come the genre titles—romances, mysteries, westerns, science fiction, etc. The first printing for a genre book by a relatively unknown writer is 45,000 to 60,000 copies; a book by a very popular writer may have a printing of 125,000 to 150,000.

There may also be miscellaneous kinds of titles, such as movie or television tie-in editions, young adult and juvenile books, titles aimed primarily at the educational market, and trade paperbacks.

An Editor's Considerations. When an editor evaluates a submission, she asks such questions as: Is this book strong enough to be a lead title, or is it a midlist or genre title? Furthermore, is it the type of book that we do well with? How many copies are we likely to be able to sell? Have we published too many books of this type recently? Does the author have promotion potential? Does the book have a new and fresh idea? Does it have the potential for launching a series? Does the author intend to write more books, and is he or she a writer we would like to have on our list? When will the final manuscript be available, and when will we be able to publish the book? The editor may also do a formal cost projection or P&L but this is much less common for a mass-market house than a trade house.

If the editor wants to make a publishing offer, s/he will present the book at the weekly editorial meeting attended by all of the editors, the editor-in-chief, representatives from the marketing staff, and perhaps the publisher. The book will be discussed by everyone concerned, and if the consensus is favorable, the editor will be authorized to make a publishing offer. In some houses, the procedure is less formal, and an editor can get approval directly from the editor-in-chief.

The Advance and Royalties. The item of primary consideration will be the advance against royalties. A paperback house might offer as much as $25,000 for a book whose first printing would be around 100,000 copies. However, a genre paperback by a new writer usually fetches about $3,500 to $5,000 from one of the larger houses, and perhaps less from one of the small publishers. If you are represented by an established agent and/or the house is very keen to have the book, the ante can go higher, and if the house is thinking about making the book a lead, the money can be substantial indeed. If the book has potential for being published as a trade book and the paperback house is acquiring "volume" rights with the intention of bringing out or licensing a trade edition, the advance may also be higher than average.

The royalty rate for a new writer is typically 6 to 8 percent of the cover price, with an increase to 9 or 10 percent after a substantial number of copies have been sold. For an established writer, the rate may start at 8 or even 10 percent, eventually escalating to 12½ percent after a very large number of copies have been sold.

There is generally not much room for negotiation by a new writer, particularly if you are not represented by an agent. In this case, it's probably more useful to concentrate on establishing a good relationship with an editor and publisher and on generating more books—particularly if you hope to make a living at this kind of writing.

The Contract

Mass-market contracts are similar to those used by trade publishers. There are some variations, reflecting differences in the way the different firms do business, but most of the terms in the contract you receive can be understood by referring to the discussion of contracts in Chapter 3 of this manual. Here are the areas that are likely to be different:

Advance and Royalties. I have already discussed the probable advance and royalty rates on domestic sales. Note that some of the smaller publishers may not be able to afford an advance, while others buy the copyright to a work outright. This discussion assumes that you will be dealing with a royalty contract.

The usual payout schedule for an advance is in halves or thirds, with the first portion due on signing the contract, the next on delivery and acceptance of the final manuscript, and the last (if this is in thirds) on publication; for larger amounts of money, the house may want to break the payments into fourths, fifths, and even sixths, with the last payments on publication and six months (or even longer) after publication.

For copies sold outside the United States, the royalty rate is usually 5 percent of the *amount received*. The same rate will apply to special and premium sales, to copies sold at an unusually high discount (say, 60 percent or more), to copies sold by mail order, or to copies sold in bulk to book clubs (where there is normally a low printing and low income). The royalty on copies sold as remainders is usually 4 to 5 percent of the amount received. However, the contract may specify that no royalty will be paid if the books are sold at or below cost (the unit cost of the most recent printing), and that copies sold at or below 85 percent of the retail price of the edition will be deemed sold below cost. No royalty will be paid on copies used for promotional purposes, or copies that are damaged or destroyed.

The contract may define "amount received" as the sum remaining after "allowances" and "return credits." This is a reference to the custom of allowing dealers to return unsold copies (or covers stripped from books) for credit. It should *not* include items normally regarded as the cost of doing business, such as postage, insurance, taxes, etc.

The contract may also specify royalties for a trade paperback or hardcover edition. The rates should be the same as those paid by a trade publisher; see Chapter 3 for guidelines.

Revisions. The contract may specifically require you to make any revisions requested by the publisher "as promptly as possible after the publisher's request," and without any additional payments. (This may include changes deemed necessary by the publisher's lawyers, although making these changes will not relieve you of your liability under the indemnity clause of the contract.) The contract may also give the publisher the right to make revisions in the manuscript without consulting you, including changing the title or subtitle, and omitting portions of the original manuscript.

These clauses are holdovers from the days when mass-market editors were dealing strictly with genre paperbacks and wanted the freedom to change the material in any way they saw fit. This same sort of latitude may not be appropriate for the type of book you have written, and you may wish these clauses modified to give you more "say" in the matter of editorial revisions.

Subsidiary Rights. Subsidiary rights for trade books are discussed extensively in Chapter 8 of this book. The activity for mass-market paperbacks is usually limited, and is discussed in detail at the end of this chapter (Chapter 10). But note that if the mass-market house is owned by another publishing house (Pocket Books is owned by Simon & Schuster, for example), there may be a clause in the contract allowing the mass-market publisher to grant *any of the subsidiary rights for the book to its parent company,* provided the royalty rate is no lower than what might, in the *publisher's* judgment, be paid by a third party. In other words, this clause would allow the mass-market house (Pocket Books, in this case) to grant the hardcover rights to Simon & Schuster and the movie rights to Paramount Pictures, another subsidiary of S&S's owner, Gulf & Western. This clause should be clarified *before* you sign the contract.

If the movie rights to the work were retained on your behalf, the contract with the mass-market house may stipulate that the publisher has the right to publish a tie-in edition if you license the film rights to a movie producer, and to make use of the motion-picture title, logos, stills, and so forth. You may also be required to obtain all necessary permissions and other materials for the publisher's use.

Accounting and Royalty Statements. The language relating to royalty statements will be similar to that found in a trade-book contract. However, there may be an additional statement to the effect that the publisher is "relying on" reports from his distributors in computing sales and amounts received. Essentially, what this clause does is put the responsibility for the accuracy of sales reports on the national distributor dealing with regional wholesalers. (These dealers are described in more detail later in this chapter.)

Out-of-Print/Termination Procedures. Most mass-market paperbacks have a relatively short shelf life although the publisher may want to "reissue" the book from time to time. The contract should spell out what your options are if the book is out of print for a specified period of time, and should give you the right to purchase any remaining copies and the production materials if you wish to do so.

Miscellaneous Clauses. Additional clauses will spell out the publisher's liability in case of loss of or damage to the materials you have furnished (e.g., the manuscript), what happens in case of bankruptcy, the right of the publisher to assign the contract to a third party, and the state laws under which the contract will be interpreted. You should be given at least ten free copies of the book, with the right to buy more at a 40 percent discount. You *may* be specifically prohibited from reselling these books.

If the book was published previously and the rights have reverted to you, you may be required to supply the publisher with written evidence that the agreement with the previous publisher has been terminated, with copies of any licenses granted, and with copies of the copyright registration certificates.

Production

Scheduling. Once the contract has been signed, the book title will be added to inventory by the managing editor, and a tentative decision about the publication month will be made, depending on the delivery date of the final manuscript and the needs of the house. In most cases, the final manuscript should be available at least nine to ten months before publication so that normal schedules can be followed. Occasionally, however, the publisher will "crash" a book if the subject is particularly timely (as in the case of "instant" books or "extras" produced by mass-market houses in connection with news events) or if the book is particularly important for revenue or to fill a hole on the list. After you have delivered the final manuscript to your editor and it has been approved for release, a production schedule will be set and work on the monthly catalog can begin.

Copyediting. Copyediting usually takes from three to five weeks. The copyedited manuscript will be given to your editor, who will try to resolve all of the queries on his or her own initiative or in a telephone conversation with you. It is unlikely that you will see the copyedited manuscript before it is sent out for typesetting. If you do, refer to Chapter 5 for guidance on how to proceed.

Design. Design of a mass-market paperback original is somewhat simpler than that for a trade book, because the trim size (usually 4½″ × 7″) and paper stock are standardized. However, the advent of phototypesetting has made it possible to have much greater variety in the typefaces used (as for example in books containing computer instructions). Books in a series will also be carefully designed to have a "family" appearance.

Typesetting and Printing. Typesetting and printing will be done at one of the two or three firms that specialize in mass-market paperback books. It will probably take about three weeks to one month to get galley proofs of the book after the copyedited manuscript has been released to the typesetter. One or two sets of galley proofs will be given to your editor;

you *may* be given a set to read as well. (See Chapter 5 for suggestions on how to proofread galleys.) One set of galley proofs will also be used to make up bound galleys for reviewers and for use in obtaining "quotes" or endorsements for the book.

Any corrections that you or your editor make on the galleys will be transferred to a set of master galleys. After corrections in type have been made, the galleys will be broken into pages, and headings and footings will be added. If an index needs to be made, the publisher will probably have this done by an indexing service.

After the pages have been proofread and all necessary corrections made, printing plates (made of photopolymer) will be made from repros and the book will be printed on a high-speed press. If it is a Cameron press, printing and binding can be done in the same run; otherwise, folded signatures will be taken from the press to a binding machine, where the covers will be attached. The finished books will then be boxed and shipped according to orders forwarded from the publisher's sales department.

The Cover. One of the most important elements in selling a mass-market paperback is the cover. Since paperbacks generally get little review attention, they rely heavily on the attractiveness of the cover art and on the advertising copy on the front and back of the book (and sometimes on the first one or two inside pages) to convince the impulse buyer to pick up the book and buy it.

Most mass-market houses have an art director who works with freelance artists to produce the cover art for the front of the book. Genre titles are usually packaged according to established conventions. Historical romances and family sagas typically have a painting of significant characters and events that takes up the whole front cover and extends onto the back. Action/adventure books usually show the hero's face in a sketchy scene of violent action; mysteries typically use an evocative piece of spot art, frequently the murder weapon.

A lead book will get particularly careful attention, because the house has a lot of money riding on this book and because the artwork will be used repeatedly in advertisements and promotion for the book. What the publisher wants is a strong and memorable cover that will reproduce well and that people will remember easily. The usual approach is to use large, impressive type, flattering quotes from important people, and spot art on a white or light background. Various other techniques may be used, such as foil stamping, several different covers for the same book, and so on.

The artwork for the cover is discussed at a "cover conference" attended by the editors, the editor-in-chief, the publisher, and representatives from the marketing staff. They will discuss what they think should be on the cover, and at a later meeting, they will evaluate comps prepared by the artist to determine whether the art "works" for that particular book. Finished art will then be prepared, although if the sales reps strongly dislike the cover for an important book it may be redone.

Advertising, Promotion, and Publicity

The primary tool used to sell the monthly list is a catalog showing the cover of each book and briefly describing the book's contents, physical dimensions, price, and any special promotional plans. Midlist and genre titles generally do not receive special promotion beyond mention in the catalog, but lead books and midlist books by important authors do.

Promotion can include extensive advertising on radio, television, and in the print media; special merchandising kits containing such things as four-color posters, bookmarks, and paper bags; a counter pack or floor display (usually called a dump); contests for dealers and readers; networking and so on. A full-scale campaign is often given a name such as a "Super Release." The amount of money spent and the kind of effort expended on behalf of a book will of course depend on the kinds of sales the publisher is hoping to generate as a result.

Publicity is also becoming an important tool for paperback originals. Until fairly recently, not much review space was given to original paperbacks because so many of them were strictly category titles. But as publishers are bringing out more originals as midlist and lead titles, the review space given paperbacks is increasing. *Publishers Weekly* and the *New York Times Book Review* are giving quite a bit of review space to trade and mass-market paperbacks (as well as running paperback bestseller lists), and many other publications are also giving them more review space, so if your book is likely to benefit from reviews, the publisher's publicity department will probably send out bound galleys or advance copies to trade and consumer publications. If you think there are any publications that might be particularly interested in reviewing your book, be sure to let your editor know.

Publicity appearances or tours by authors of original paperbacks are also becoming more common, particularly if the author is well-known, or if it's a nonfiction title that is selling extremely well. If your publisher suggests a tour, seize the opportunity if you can; it's a terrific way to spread the word about your book and sell a lot of copies. But don't *expect* this to happen; it is still much more the exception than the rule. You can also set up appearances on your own, either in conjunction with the tour arranged by your publisher or after the tour is over. But keep in mind that paperbacks usually don't stay out on the racks very long, so such appearances usually have to be scheduled close to publication date. See Chapter 6 for further information on author tours.

Sales

ID Sales and Direct Sales. Mass-market paperbacks are distributed to retail outlets through two main channels—to bookstores and book wholesalers through a "direct" sales force, and to nonbookstore outlets such as newsstands and drugstores through a network of about five hundred regional wholesalers called ID's (independent distributors). The ID's distribute magazines and newspapers as well as paperbacks (in fact, paperbacks represent only 15 to 20 percent of most IDs' business), and have virtual monopolies in the regions where they are located. These distribution monopolies used to be protected by law, but now other distributors are allowed to compete with the ID's.

Distribution to the ID's is usually handled through an intermediary organization called a national distributor. The national distributor evaluates the books being offered by the publisher, then uses its own group of sales reps to call on the ID's and solicit orders. Some national distributors represent more than one paperback publisher, and most of them represent magazine publishers as well. A few of the biggest mass-market houses have their own national distributor organization (including Bantam).

The distribution process begins four or five months before publication month. Representatives from the "direct" sales force and from the national distributor (if the publisher isn't its own national distributor) meet with the publisher's marketing staff to set final printings for the books on that list. A month or two later, the publisher's and national distributors' reps receive the monthly catalog and other sales tools, such as offprints of jackets, a cassette tape describing the books on the list, and so forth, and set off to sell their accounts.

Sales to the ID's. Only the larger ID's may be called on regularly by the national distributors' reps; smaller accounts will receive the catalog and other sales materials by mail, and may be called on occasionally by a rep. In some cases, the books sent to an ID will be selected by the national distributor rather than the ID; this is called "forced" distribution.

After a rep has presented the list to the ID's paperback buyer, the order will be sent back to the national distributor's headquarters. Orders from key accounts are checked to see whether sales are running as predicted or whether the first printing for particular titles should be raised or lowered. The orders are then passed on to the publisher for fulfillment and shipping. Books will be shipped directly from the printer to the ID warehouses, with the overprint going to the publisher's warehouse to fill reorders.

As books and magazines from the different publishers pour into an ID's warehouse, they are sorted into groups according to the accounts on each truck driver's route. (Unlike paperback jobbers, who use the mails or "common carriers" to deliver books to their customers, ID's own their own fleet of trucks.) Accounts can include such businesses as variety stores, drugstores, supermarkets, terminals, gift shops, hotels and motels, restaurants, hospitals, military bases, schools, libraries, and even small bookstores, but will probably not include large retail chains (such as Sears, etc.) that can get better discounts by buying directly from the publisher.

Paperbacks are delivered weekly. In some cases, the retailers maintain the racks themselves, pulling certain books off and rearranging others to make room for new arrivals; in other cases, the truck driver will decide which books should be pulled and how the books should be arranged on the racks. Most outlets have fewer than two hundred pockets to crowd books into, and since about four hundred new titles come out each month, competition for space is fierce. An outlet usually sets aside a certain number of pockets for each publisher; the better the publisher's track record, the more pockets. Position is also important. Books are usually bunched together by category, with bestsellers near the top and center (where most customers look first). Or they may go into a "new releases" section, or be displayed over multiple pockets.

About ten days after distribution of the monthly list, the national distributor's sales reps will check retail outlets to see how many copies and dumps were distributed, and how many copies were sold to consumers. If 40 percent of the copies distributed have been sold, a book is considered to be selling well. If a book is not selling well, it will be "moved down the rack" quickly, or pulled off altogether after a few weeks.

After a book is removed, it goes back to the ID's warehouse, where the cover is ripped off for return to the publisher for credit (it's too expensive to return whole books) and the rest of the book is consigned to the shredder. The ID is required to prepare an affidavit guaranteeing that these copies have been destroyed.

Returns from ID wholesalers have been averaging about 45 percent while returns from bookstores are averaging about 25 percent, probably reflecting greater expertise in ordering by bookstore owners as well as the results of competition for the wholesalers' customers by other kinds of dealers—including the paperback publishers themselves.

Sales to Retail Bookstores. The retail bookstore trade is an increasingly important source of revenue for mass-market publishers. It is estimated that by 1990, up to 70 percent of all bookstore sales will be either trade or mass-market paperbacks. Large publishers like Bantam and Pocket Books may have as many as one hundred salespersons calling on bookstore chains, independents, large retail chains, and wholesalers to push their wares, efforts that are supplemented by other techniques such as telephone sales and mail-order sales.

Educational Sales. Another very important source of revenue for both trade and mass-market paperbacks is the educational market. Trade paperbacks pioneered in this field about thirty years ago, and many of the mass-market and trade publishers have lines or imprints directed specifically to the educational market. Some of these books have special study aids provided, and are listed in "thematic" or "graded" catalogs addressed to educators. The publishers attend educational conventions, advertise their books in the trade journals (*Library Journal, School Library Journal, Wilson Quarterly,* etc.), put on and/or attend book fairs, and so on. Several of the publishers have educational sales managers who work closely with schools and libraries, as well as with wholesalers who specialize in selling paperbacks to schools.

Export Sales. Export sales are also extremely important in the paperback field. Inexpensive English-language paperbacks sell very well in other countries throughout the world, and the mass-market publishers compete vigorously for this market (if the rights in that particular market have not been licensed to a British publisher). In countries that are defined as the open market, there may in fact be several editions of the same book—the American edition, the English edition, and editions in other languages. This can even happen in Canada. Be aware, incidentally, that the royalty on foreign sales is usually half of the normal royalty.

Special Sales. Finally, there is the area of "special" sales, which is basically any sale to a customer outside of the regular book-trade or ID channels. A yogurt manufacturer, for example, might want to buy copies of a yogurt cookbook as part of a special promotion for his product (in which case the manufacturer will probably ask the publisher to change the cover of the book and delete the publisher's logo). Bulk sales of this sort are usually not very profitable for either the author or the publisher, but they are a good way of moving a lot of copies without the hassle of returns. Another possible avenue of sales is jobbers who specialize in putting on book fairs. A big jobber might buy thousands of copies of a title to package with other titles for sale directly to students at book fairs staged in schools.

Reprint, Reissue, or Revert? While the books are actively being sold, the sales manager will keep a close eye on stock and will advise the publisher to go back to press as needed. The whole list of books will also be reviewed periodically by the sales manager and publisher to determine which books should be reissued, which ones should remain dormant for the time being, and which ones can be reverted to the copyright owner. As a general rule, publishers are not eager to revert the rights, since keeping the rights gives them the option of reissuing a book at a later date, perhaps to tie in with the publication of a new book by the same author. (If you look at the copyright pages of books by some of the popular mystery writers, for example, you will notice that many of them have copyright dates from the 1960s and '70s and even earlier.)

Subsidiary Rights

Subsidiary rights for original paperbacks have been somewhat less lucrative than that for trade books, but there are some definite possibilities, and the situation is likely to improve in the future as more and more books are published as originals.

One promising area is that of foreign rights. French publishers, for example, are actively buying French-language rights to some of the best-selling romances in this country, and German publishers have been buying quite a bit of nonfiction. Spanish rights are also beginning to look more lucrative, especially as more and more Spanish-speaking people are becoming citizens of this country, and many publishers are exploring this area actively. The prices paid for the rights vary widely, depending on the type of book, the reputation of the author, and so on, and can run from as low as a few hundred dollars to a $15,000 or $20,000 advance against royalties.

Serial and syndication rights also occasionally sell, especially for nonfiction books that are easily excerptable, such as diet and celebrity books. *Good Housekeeping* magazine, for example, is a good potential market for historical and contemporary romances.

Book clubs have not shown much interest in taking original paperbacks, with the exception of Book-of-the-Month Club's Quality Paperback Book Service. But Preferred Choice Book Plan occasionally buys book-club rights to a number of romances, then offers them in shrink-wrapped groups of five to their members. A few of the publishers are starting their own romance book clubs, such as Doubleday's Romance Library. Scholastic Book Club takes paperbacks for children and young adults, but purchases them in bulk (as a special sale) rather than buying them on a license basis.

There is also the possibility of selling hardcover rights "backwards" to a trade house. This happened frequently in the past, but will probably be less frequent as the mass-market houses develop their own hardcover lines. A backwards sale is conducted similarly to the sale of paperback rights by a trade house; that is, it may be a single submission to one house or a multiple submission, or the hardcover rights may be auctioned. The hardcover house may acquire certain subsidiary rights, such as the right to license the hardcover edition to a book club.

Postscript

The writing and publishing of books is an absorbing and satisfying activity. Unfortunately, it can be difficult to make a living at it. Surveys by both the Author's Guild and P.E.N. have convincingly demonstrated that writing is a tough way to keep bread on the table if it is your only source of income. According to the Guild's survey, the median income for a writer is about $5,000—and that median is much higher than it would be if the incomes of several highly successful writers had not been included in the totals. So if you are thinking of throwing off the shackles of the work-a-day world to assume the garland of the writer, you had better wait until you have sold a few books, or have made so much money from a bestseller that you are secure for the rest of your life.

It's difficult to predict what the future is likely to bring to the world of books and writers. However, there are some developments I think we can look forward to.

One obvious area of change will be that of technology. Word processors will undoubtedly be more widely used, as authors become more familiar with them and the prices for them drop. Use of this equipment not only speeds up and simplifies preparation of the final text; it can also eliminate rekeyboarding for typesetting if the writer's equipment is compatible with that of the publisher's. This can probably be done via telephone lines, so that the first draft could be printed out in your editor's office, edited there, and the suggested changes transmitted back to you. After you have reworked the material, the text could be transmitted back to the editor's office for final editing and copyediting. When all queries have been resolved, the manuscript could be coded by the copyeditor or designer for the desired typefaces and other design characteristics.

The storage, transmittal, and sale of finished books may also change radically. It seems likely that specialized books with limited audiences will no longer be produced in printed form, but will instead be stored on microfilm or on some type of electronic medium, either in the publisher's office or at a large reference center or library. Someone wishing to obtain a copy of the book would then ask to have a single copy printed out. This is usually referred to as "on demand" publishing. As home computers and word processors become more widespread, this type of book purchasing could be done from your own home; you could simply dial up a centralized book-ordering source, select the particular book you are interested in, and have it printed out on your own printer. Billing would also be computerized.

Such a change in how books are produced could have a substantial impact on how they are distributed. While I think that the majority of books—certainly the more "popular" books—will continue to be published in the conventional way, specialized publishing will be largely computerized, and library holdings will expand to include storage of computerized information. Computer terminals will become common in libraries, and may also become a standard feature in bookstores, both as a source of centralized information about the in-print status of books and as a source of single copies of certain titles. Wholesalers may ultimately play a somewhat smaller role in the distribution of books.

Cable television also presents interesting possibilities. Right now some cable stations offer subscribers a "magazine" format, in which articles and stories in printed form are shown on the screen for reading. This may possibly be extended to books as well. This form of "narrowcasting" is a promising additional source of subsidiary-rights income for writers.

The traditional relationship between authors, agents, editors, and publishers may also be in for some changes. Right now, the function of most publishers extends from editing through distribution and promotion, and the rights are held for the term of copyright. In the future, some authors may wish to retain more of the rights to their books, and grant limited rights to a publisher for a fixed term. Furthermore, it may become more usual for authors to work with freelance editors, and then sell the distribution rights only, perhaps even retaining the right to control the promotion activities for the book. Agents and packagers would play a somewhat larger role in this type of arrangement.

Who will buy the books in the future? It seems certain that the international market for books will become more important, as literacy becomes more widespread and the world increasingly resembles Marshall McLuhan's "global village." Paperbacks will play an increasingly important role, as the costs of publishing a book—and the resultant cover price—continue to escalate.

One thing is certain, though, and that is that the book as we know it will never disappear. It still remains the least expensive and the most portable mode of communicating information and providing entertainment, and the possibilities for writers seem better than ever.

Appendix A

How a Trade-Book Editor Prepares a Precontract Estimate

Every publishing house has its own method of projecting costs and income for a potential book project. In this section I will describe the way in which a trade house might project the costs and profits for a hardcover book. The editor making these projections is named Jack Sprat, and the name of the firm is the Speedo Publishing Company.

The book being estimated is titled *Making Do* by Jeremy Weatherbottom. It is a serious study of the coming scarcities in foodstuffs and other commodities and is aimed at a highly educated readership.

Some Initial Numbers. In order to make an estimate, Jack Sprat has to have certain kinds of information available. To start with, he needs to know the projected word count in the final book (assuming he doesn't have the final manuscript) and whether illustrations will be included. He can then use this information to estimate the final page count of the book, and whether it should have a small, medium, or large trim size.

Chapter 5 of this book described how books are designed. In the Speedo Publishing Company, three basic trim sizes are used for hardcover books. (The trims for trade paperbacks are much less limited.) To help the editors make cost estimates, the production department has made up grids showing the relationship between word count, trim size, number of pages in the finished book, and costs. Figure 23 (page 268) shows these grids.

The author has indicated that the book will contain a few charts but no other illustrations, and will run about 85,000 words. Jack thinks that the medium trim would be most suitable for this particular book and when he checks the Word Count Averages grid, he sees that a book with 88,000 words will run about 256 pages in the medium trim. (These figures are, of course, simply guidelines and can vary considerably, depending on the final design of the book.) With this basic information in hand, Jack can now proceed to fill out an estimate form.

The Estimate Form. Figure 24 (page 270) shows the form filled out by Jack for this book. (In some companies, this calculation can now be done by a computer.) The estimated first printing is the first figure entered, and is relatively low because Jack believes that the audience for the book will be fairly limited.

Next Jack indicates the estimated net sale. This is less than the estimated first printing, because a certain number of the books will probably be returned and a certain number will be used for advertising and promotion.

Next comes the cover price, which Jack thinks will be about $17.95, based on the length of the book, current market conditions, and so on. Then he applies a discount to see how much money the company will take in on each book sold. Books are sold to dealers at discounts ranging from 40 to 50 percent; the Speedo editors use an average discount of 44 percent in calculating estimated net income per book sold. On a $17.95 cover price, Speedo would take in a little over $10 if the book is sold at a 44 percent discount; if 4,500 copies are sold at this discount, the net income would be $45,234.00.

Next Jack indicates a number of costs that are sometimes referred to as operating costs. "Plant cost" is the cost of setting the book in type, making printing plates, and so on; it is a one-time cost. To get the figure for this particular book, Jack refers to his grids again and sees that a 256-page book in the medium trim at 1984 prices (these prices increase by about 7 percent to 10 percent each year) will run about $7,187.00 in plant costs.

Figure 23
CHART OF AVERAGE PRODUCTION COSTS
AS OF 1984

WORD COUNT AVERAGES

	192 pp	256 pp	320 pp	384 pp	448 pp	512 pp
5⅜ × 8	60,000	75,000	90,000	100,000	115,000	130,000
5½ × 8⅜	70,000	88,000	110,000	130,000	145,000	160,000
6⅛ × 9¼	80,000	100,000	130,000	150,000	165,000	180,000

PLANT COST AVERAGES

	192 pp	256 pp	320 pp	384 pp	448 pp	512 pp
5⅜ × 8	$5,000	$5,750	$6,875	$ 7,750	$ 8,750	$ 9,375
5½ × 8⅜	6,000	7,187	7,750	9,250	10,000	11,250
6⅛ × 9¼	7,187	7,750	9,250	10,000	11,250	12,250

UNIT COST AVERAGES

	192 pp	256 pp	320 pp	384 pp	448 pp	512 pp
5⅜ × 8	1.35	1.45	1.60	1.75	1.95	2.15
5½ × 8⅜	1.45	1.60	1.75	1.95	2.15	2.35
6⅛ × 9¼	1.60	1.75	1.95	2.15	2.35	2.50

Then he determines the "unit cost" figure. This is also often called PP&B (for paper, printing, and binding) and represents the cost of manufacturing one copy of the book. The chart indicates that a hardcover book with these dimensions will cost about $1.60 each. When Jack multiplies this figure by the number of copies to be printed, he obtains a total PP&B cost of $8,000, and when he adds this to the plant cost, he ends up with a total production cost of $15,187.00.

The next operating cost is the royalties payable to the author for each copy sold. The rate they are using for this book is 10 percent of the cover price, so that if they sell 4,500 copies at a cover price of $17.95, they will owe Mr. Weatherbottom $8,077.50.

Jack also decides to add in some figures for the cost of advertising and promoting the book. Since the first printing is small, he has set aside only a small amount of money for advertising (perhaps covering a small space ad in a specialized magazine), plus enough money to cover the cost of sending out a few hundred free copies of the book and some bound galleys. An author tour is unlikely, so his final promotion cost would be $2,000—which is considerably lower than what he would have available if he applied the usual formula of 10 percent of net income for these expenses. (This would have yielded a budget of $4,523.40.)

His next step is to add up all of the projected costs for the book, including production, royalties, and promotion. His total is $25,264.50. Then he subtracts this number from his estimated net revenue from sales ($45,234.00) to obtain a gross margin of $19,969.50.

Unfortunately, there are a number of other costs that Jack hasn't taken into account yet. Running a business costs money, and some of the income from the publishing program has to go for the costs of space (rental, heat, lights, etc.), staff salaries, benefits programs, taxes, and so on. Furthermore, a publisher has to maintain a warehouse, a shipping and billing department, and a customer-service department. All of these costs can be included under the heading of overhead. Publishing companies calculate this factor different ways. The Speedo Company uses a flat formula of $10,000 for every title published, plus $1.50 for each copy printed. This means an assessment of $17,500.00 against *Making Do*, and net earnings of about $2,500.

There is also the possibility of subsidiary-rights income. A conservative publisher does not include this in his projections because such income is speculative for most books, but some publishers do include it for obviously commercial titles. In this particular example, the possibility of rights income is limited because of the nature of the subject.

Figure 24
PRECONTRACT ESTIMATE FORM
FOR A NONFICTION BOOK

Book Title *Making Do*

Author *Jeremy Weatherbottom*

Editor *Jack Sprat*   Date Prepared *7/22/83*

Trim *Medium* Est. page count *256*   Illus. *none*

1. Estimated first printing *5,000*
2. Estimated net sale *4,500*
3. Probable cover price *$17.95*
4. Net income @ 44% dis. *$10,052*
5. Estimated net revenue *$45,234.00*
   (#2 × #4)
6. Plant cost *$7,187.00*
7. Unit cost (PP & B) *$1.60*
8. Total PP & B *$8,000.00*
   (#7 × #1)
9. Total production cost *$15,187.00*
   (#6 × #8)
10. Royalties
    a. 4,500 @ 10%   ($1.795) *$8,077.50*
    b.   @ 12½%   ————
    c.   @ 15%
         Total *$8,077.50*
11. Advertising/promotion *$1,000.00*
12. Publicity *$1,000.00*
13. Author tour *none*
14. Total promo. *$2,000.00*

15. Miscellaneous costs   *none*
16. Total Costs   # 25,264.50
    (#9 + #10 + #14
    + #15)
17. Gross Margin   # 19,969.50
    (#5 − #16)
18. Overhead   # 17,500.00
19. Net Margin   # 2,469.50
    (#17 − #18)

Projected Other

Income

    First serial (10%)   _____

    Book club (50%)   _____

    Mass reprint (50%)   _____

    Movie/TV (10%)   _____

    British (33⅓%)   _____

    Translation (33⅓%)   _____

    Other (50%)   _____

       TOTAL   _____

Comments: _____

_____

_____

Appendix B

Example of a Trade-Book Contract

This form (Figure 25) is used by Random House for contracts with authors of trade books. I have included it because it is representative of the forms used by the large trade houses, is relatively easy to understand, and is slightly more favorable to authors than many such contracts. After the "variable" terms such as the advance and royalty rates have been negotiated with the author or agent, these data will be typed in on the form.

Figure 25
SAMPLE BOOK CONTRACT

RANDOM HOUSE, INC.

AGREEMENT made this   day of   , 19   between RANDOM HOUSE, INC of 201 East 50th Street, New York, 10022 (referred to as the Publisher), and

whose address is

who is a citizen of   and resident of (state)
(referred to as the Author and designated by the masculine singular pronoun)

     WHEREAS the parties wish respectively to publish and have published a work (referred to as the work) of   provisionally titled

     NOW, THEREFORE, they mutually agree as follows:

     1. The author grants to the Publisher during the term of copyright, including renewals and extensions thereof:

Grants of Rights

     a. Exclusive right in the English language, in the United States of America, the Philippine Republic, and Canada, and non-exclusive right in all other countries except the British Commonwealth (other than Canada), the Republic of South Africa, and the Irish Republic, to:

     i. Print, publish and sell the work in book form;

     ii. License publication of the work (in complete, condensed or abridged versions) by book clubs, including subsidiaries of the Publisher;

     iii. License publication of a reprint edition by another publisher with the consent of the Author. The Author shall be deemed to have given consent if within twenty (20) days after the forwarding of written request he fails to notify the Publisher in writing of his refusal to consent;

     iv. License publication of the work (in complete, condensed, adapted or abridged versions) or selections from the work in anthologies and other publications, in mail-order and schoolbook editions, as premiums and other special editions and through microfilm and with the Author's consent Xerox or other forms of copying;

     v. License periodical publication including magazines, newspapers and digests prior to book publication;

     vi. License periodical publication after book publication to the extent that any such right is available;

     vii. License, subject to the approval of the Author, adaptation of the work for filmstrips, printed cartoon versions and mechanical reproduction;

     viii. License, without charge, transcription or publication of the work in Braille or in other forms, for the physically handicapped;

     ix. For publicity purposes, publish or permit others to publish or broadcast (but not dramatize) by radio or television, without charge, such selections from the work as in the opinion of the Publisher may benefit its sale.

     b. Exclusive right to license in the English language throughout the British Commonwealth (other than Canada), the Republic of South Africa, and the Irish Republic, the rights granted in subdivision a. above, revocable by the Author with respect to any country for which no license or option has been given within eighteen (18) months after first publication in the United States.

     c. Exclusive right to license in all foreign languages and all countries, the rights granted in subdivision a. above, revocable by the Author with respect to each language or country for which no license or option has been given within three (3) years after first publication in the United States.

     d. Exclusive right to use or license others to use, subject to the approval of the Author, the name and likeness of the Author, the work and the title of the work, in whole or in part, or any adaptation thereof as the basis for trademark or trade name for other products or for any other commercial use in connection with such other products.

Delivery of Satisfactory Copy

     2. The Author agrees to deliver two complete copies (original and clean copy) of the manuscript of the work in the English language of approximately   words in length, satisfactory to the Publisher, together with any permission required pursuant to Paragraph 3, and all photographs, illustrations, drawings, charts, maps and indexes suitable for reproduction and necessary to the completion of the manuscript not later than

If he fails to do so the Publisher shall have the right to supply them and charge the cost against any sums accruing to the Author. The complete manuscript shall include the following additional items

If the Author fails to deliver the manuscript within ninety (90) days after the above date, or if any manuscript that is delivered is not, in the Publisher's judgment, satisfactory, the Publisher may terminate this agreement by giving written notice, whereupon the Author agrees to repay forthwith all amounts which may have been advanced hereunder.

Permission for Copyrighted Material

     3. If the Author incorporates in the work any copyrighted material, he shall procure, at his expense, written permission to reprint it.

4. a. The Author warrants that he is the sole author of the work; that he is the sole owner of all the rights granted to the Publisher; that he has not previously assigned, pledged or otherwise encumbered the same; that he has full power to enter into this agreement; that except for the material obtained pursuant to Paragraph 3 the work is original, has not been published before, and is not in the public domain; that it does not violate any right of privacy; that it is not libelous or obscene; that it does not infringe upon any statutory or common law copyright; and that any recipe, formula or instruction contained in the work is not injurious to the user.

b. In the event of any claim, action or proceeding based upon an alleged violation of any of these warranties (i) the Publisher shall have the right to defend the same through counsel of its own choosing, and (ii) no settlement shall be effected without the prior written consent of the Author, which consent shall not unreasonably be withheld, and (iii) the Author shall hold harmless the Publisher, any seller of the work, and any licensee of a subsidiary right in the work, against any damages finally sustained. If such claim, action or proceeding is successfully defended or settled, the Author's indemnity hereunder shall be limited to fifty per cent (50%) of the expense (including reasonable counsel fees) attributable to such defense or settlement; however, such limitation of liability shall not apply if the claim, action or proceeding is based on copyright infringement.

c. If any such claim, action or proceeding is instituted, the Publisher shall promptly notify the Author, who shall fully cooperate in the defense thereof, and the Publisher may withhold payments of reasonable amounts due him under this or any other agreement between the parties.

d. These warranties and indemnities shall survive the termination of this agreement.

5. The Author agrees that during the term of this agreement he will not, without the written permission of the Publisher, publish or permit to be published any material, in book or pamphlet form, based on material in the work.

6. Within one year after the Author has delivered the manuscript in conformity with Paragraph 2, the Publisher shall publish the work at its own expense, in such style and manner, under such imprint and at such price as it deems suitable. The Publisher shall not be responsible for delays caused by any circumstance beyond its control. No changes in the manuscript or the provisional title shall be made without the consent of the Author. However, in no event shall the Publisher be obligated to publish a work which in its opinion violates the common law or statutory copyright or the right of privacy of any person or contains libelous or obscene matter.

7. The Author agrees to read, revise, correct and return promptly all proofs of the work and to pay in cash or, at the option of the Publisher, to have charged against him, the cost of alterations, in type or in plates, required by the Author, other than those due to printer's errors, in excess of ten per cent (10%) of the cost of setting type, provided a statement of these charges is sent to the Author within thirty (30) days of the receipt of the printer's bills and the corrected proofs are presented upon request for his inspection.

8. The Publisher shall copyright the work in the name of the Author, in the United States, in compliance with the Universal Copyright Convention, and apply for renewals of such copyright. If copyright should be in the name of the Publisher, it shall assign such copyright upon request of the Author. The Publisher agrees to arrange for the sale of the work in Canada. If the Publisher adds illustrations or other material, and if copyright is in the Author's name, he agrees, upon request, to assign the copyright of such material. If the Author retains the right to periodical or foreign publication before publication by the Publisher, he shall notify the Publisher promptly of any arrangement of such publication or any postponement thereof. In the event of a periodical publication, if the copyright shall be in the name of any person other than the Author, he shall promptly deliver to the Publisher a legally recordable assignment of such copyright or of the rights granted. In the event of a publication outside the United States, promptly thereafter, he shall furnish to the Publisher three copies of the first published work and the date of such publication.

9. The Publisher shall pay to the Author as an advance against and on account of all moneys accruing to him under this agreement, the sum of
dollars ($), payable

Any such advance shall not be repayable, provided that the Author has delivered the manuscript in conformity with Paragraph 2 and is not otherwise in default under this agreement.

10. The Publisher shall pay to the Author a royalty on the retail price of every copy sold by the Publisher, less actual returns and a reasonable reserve for returns (except as set forth below):

a.   per cent (%) up to and including   copies;
          per cent (%) in excess of   copies up to and including
          copies; and   per cent (%) in excess of   copies.

Where the discount in the United States is forty-eight per cent (48%) or more from the retail price, the rate provided in this subdivision a. shall be reduced by one-half the difference between forty-four per cent (44%) and the discount granted. In no event, however, shall such royalty be less than one-half of the rate provided herein. If the semi-annual sales aggregate fewer than 400 copies, the royalty shall be two-thirds (⅔) of the rate provided in this subdivision a. if such copies are sold from a second or subsequent printing. Copies covered by any other subdivision of this Paragraph shall not be included in such computation.

b. Five percent (5%) of the amount received for copies sold directly to the consumer through the medium of mail-order or coupon advertising, or radio or television advertising.

c. Five per cent (5%) of the amount received for copies sold by the Publisher's Premium or Subscription Books Wholesale Department.

d. Ten per cent (10%) for hard-cover copies and five per cent (5%) for soft-cover copies sold with a lower retail price as college textbooks.

e. For a School edition the royalty provided in subdivision a. of this Paragraph but no more than:
i. Ten per cent (10%) of the amount received for a Senior High School edition;
ii. Eight per cent (8%) of the amount received for a Junior High School edition;
iii. Six per cent (6%) of the amount received for an Elementary School edition.

Lower-price Editions

    f. Five per cent (5%) for an edition published at a lower retail price or for an edition in the Modern Library (regular or giant size) or in Vintage Books; and two per cent (2%) or two cents (2¢) per copy, whichever is greater, for an edition in the Modern Library College Editions.

Export Sales

    g. Ten per cent (10%) of the amount received for the original edition and five per cent (5%) of the amount received for any lower-price edition for copies sold for export.

Special Sales

    h. For copies sold outside normal wholesale and retail trade channels, ten per cent (10%) of the amount received for the original edition and five per cent (5%) of the amount received for any lower-price edition for copies sold at a discount between fifty per cent (50%) and sixty per cent (60%) from the retail price and five per cent (5%) of the amount received for copies sold at a discount of sixty per cent (60%) or more from the retail price, or for the use of the plates by any governmental agency.

No Royalty Copies

    i. No royalty shall be paid on copies sold below or at cost including expenses incurred, or furnished gratis to the Author, or for review, advertising, sample or like purposes.

Receipts From Other Rights

    j. Fifty per cent (50%) of the amount received from the disposition of licenses granted pursuant to Paragraph 1, subdivision a., ii, iii, iv, vi and vii. At the Author's request his share from book club and reprint licensing, less any unearned advances, shall be paid to him within two weeks after the receipt thereof by the Publisher. If the Publisher rebates to booksellers for unsold copies due to the publication of a lower-price or reprint edition, the royalty on such copies shall be the same as for such lower-price edition.

First Serial

    k. Ninety per cent (90%) of the amount received from the disposition of licenses in the United States and Canada granted pursuant to Paragraph 1, subdivision a., v.

British

    l. Eighty per cent (80%) of the amount received from the disposition of licenses granted pursuant to Paragraph 1, subdivision b.

Translation

    m. Seventy-five per cent (75%) of the amount received from the disposition of licenses granted pursuant to Paragraph 1, subdivision c.

Commercial

    n. Fifty per cent (50%) of the amount received from the disposition of licenses granted pursuant to Paragraph 1, subdivision d., provided that all expenses in connection therewith shall be borne by the Publisher.

Share to Other Authors

    o. If any license granted by the Publisher pursuant to Paragraph 1 shall include material of others, the amount payable to the Author shall be inclusive of royalty to other authors.

Performance Rights

    11. The Author appoints the Publisher as his exclusive agent to dispose of the performance rights including dramatic, musical, radio, television, motion picture and allied rights, subject to the Author's consent, and the Publisher shall receive a commission of ten per cent (10%) of the amount received.

    In the event of the disposition of performance rights, the Publisher may grant to the purchaser the privilege to publish excerpts and summaries of the work in the aggregate not to exceed 7,500 words, for advertising and exploiting such rights, provided, however, that such grant shall require the purchaser to take all steps which may be necessary to protect the copyright of the work.

Rights Retained by Author

    12. The Author agrees to notify the Publisher promptly of the disposition of any right which the Author has retained for himself.

Reports and Payments

    13. The Publisher shall render semi-annual statements of account to the first day of April and the first day of October, and shall mail such statements during the July and January following, together with checks in payment of the amounts due thereon.

    Should the Author receive an overpayment of royalty arising from copies reported sold but subsequently returned, the Publisher may deduct such overpayment from any further sums due the Author.

    Upon his written request, the Author may examine or cause to be examined through certified public accountants the books of account of the Publisher in so far as they relate to the sale or licensing of the work.

    Notwithstanding anything to the contrary in this or any prior agreement between the parties, the Author shall in no event be entitled to receive under this and all prior agreements with the Publisher more than $ during any one calendar year. If in any one calendar year the total of the sums accruing to the Author under this and all prior agreements with the Publisher shall exceed such amount, he shall be entitled to receive the excess amount in any succeeding calendar year in which the sums accruing to him under this and all prior agreements with the Publisher do not exceed the maximum herein stated, provided that the total amount to which the Author may be entitled under this and all prior agreements with the Publisher in any succeeding calendar year shall not exceed the maximum herein stated.

Option for Next Work

    14. The Author agrees to submit to the Publisher his next book-length work before submitting the same to any other publisher. The Publisher shall be entitled to a period of six weeks after the submission of the completed manuscript, which period shall not commence to run prior to one month after the publication of the work covered by this agreement, within which to notify the Author of its decision. If within that time the Publisher shall notify the Author of its desire to publish the manuscript, it shall thereupon negotiate with him with respect to the terms of such publication. If within thirty (30) days thereafter the parties are unable in good faith to arrive at a mutually satisfactory agreement for such publication, the Author shall be free to submit his manuscript elsewhere, provided, however, that he shall not enter into a contract for the publication of such manuscript with any other publisher upon terms less favorable than those offered by the Publisher.

Copies to Author

    15. On publication the Publisher shall give ten (10) free copies to the Author, who may purchase further copies for personal use at a discount of forty per cent (40%) from the retail price.

Discontinuance of Publication

    16. If the Publisher fails to keep the work in print and the Author makes written demand to reprint it, the Publisher shall, within sixty (60) days after the receipt of such demand, notify the Author in writing if it intends to comply. Within six (6) months thereafter, the Publisher shall reprint the work unless prevented from doing so by circumstances beyond its control. If the Publisher fails to notify the Author within sixty (60) days that it intends to comply, or, within six (6) months after such notification, the Publisher declines or neglects to reprint the work, then this agreement shall terminate and all rights granted hereunder except those deriving from the option in Paragraph 14 shall revert to the Author, subject to licenses previously granted, provided the Author is not indebted to the Publisher for any sum owing to it under this agreement. After such reversion, the Publisher shall continue to participate to the extent set forth in this agreement in moneys received from any license previously granted by it. Upon such termination, the Author shall have the right for thirty (30) days thereafter to purchase the plates, if any, at one-fourth of the cost (including type setting).

If the work is under contract for publication or on sale in any edition in the United States, it shall be considered to be in print. A work shall not be deemed in print by reason of a license granted by the Publisher for the reproduction of single copies of the work. If the Publisher should determine that there is not sufficient sale for the work to enable it to continue its publication and sale profitably, the Publisher may dispose of the copies remaining on hand as it deems best, subject to the royalty provisions of Paragraph 10. In such event, the Author shall have the right, within two (2) weeks of the forwarding of a written notice from the Publisher, to a single purchase of copies at the "remainder" price.

17. Except for loss or damage due to its own negligence, the Publisher shall not be responsible for loss of or damage to any property of the Author.

18. In the absence of written request from the Author prior to publication for their return, the Publisher, after publication of the work, may dispose of the original manuscript and proofs.

19. If the copyright of the work is infringed, and if the parties proceed jointly, the expenses and recoveries, if any, shall be shared equally, and if they do not proceed jointly, either party shall have the right to prosecute such action, and such party shall bear the expenses thereof, and any recoveries shall belong to such party; and if such party shall not hold the record title of the copyright, the other party hereby consents that the action be brought in his or its name.

20. If (a) a petition in bankruptcy is filed by the Publisher, or (b) a petition in bankruptcy is filed against the Publisher and such petition is finally sustained, or (c) a petition for arrangement is filed by the Publisher or a petition for reorganization is filed by or against the Publisher, and an order is entered directing the liquidation of the Publisher as in bankruptcy, or (d) the Publisher makes an assignment for the benefit of creditors, or (e) the Publisher liquidates its business for any cause whatever, the Author may terminate this agreement by written notice and thereupon all rights granted by him hereunder shall revert to him. Upon such termination, the Author, at his option, may purchase the plates as provided in Paragraph 16 and the remaining copies at one-half of the manufacturing cost, exclusive of overhead. If he fails to exercise such option within sixty (60) days after the happening of any one of the events above referred to, the Trustee, Receiver, or Assignee may destroy the plates and sell the copies remaining on hand, subject to the royalty provisions of Paragraph 10.

21. Any sums due and owing from the Author to the Publisher, whether or not arising out of this agreement, may be deducted from any sum due or to become due from the Publisher to the Author pursuant to this agreement. For the purposes of this Paragraph a non-repayable unearned advance made to the Author pursuant to another agreement shall not be construed as being a sum due and owing, unless the Author is in default under such other agreement.

22. This agreement shall be interpreted according to the law of the State of New York.

23. It is a condition of the rights granted hereby that the Publisher agrees that all copies of the work that are distributed to the public shall bear the copyright notice prescribed by the applicable copyright laws of the United States of America. The Author hereby appoints the Publisher as his attorney-in-fact in his name and in his stead to execute all documents for recording in the Copyright Office evidencing transfer of ownership in the exclusive rights granted to the Publisher hereunder.

24. This agreement shall be binding upon the heirs, executors, administrators and assigns of the Author, and upon the successors and assigns of the Publisher, but no assignment except to an affiliate of the Publisher, shall be binding on either of the parties without the written consent of the other.

25. This agreement constitutes the complete understanding of the parties. No modification or waiver of any provision shall be valid unless in writing and signed by both parties.

IN WITNESS WHEREOF the parties have duly executed this agreement the day and year first above written.

RANDOM HOUSE, Inc.

In the presence of

.... By ....
The Publisher

In the presence of

....
The Author

....
Social Security Number

Appendix C

Working with a Collaborator or as an Author-for-Hire

Collaboration

Since many books require specialized kinds of expertise (and also take a great deal of time and energy to write), many writers choose to work with one or more collaborators, to share the labor and make the process more fun.

The partnership can be set up in different ways, depending on the talents and contributions of the people involved. For example, you may decide to do the research and the rough draft yourself and have your collaborator do the rewrite. Or you may want to work through the manuscript together, each partner contributing equally to the development of the material. Or you can divide the book up, with one partner responsible for the first half and the other responsible for the second half.

Whatever your arrangement, it's a good idea to spell out the responsibilities of each collaborator in *writing*. The agreement should cover the following points:

The nature of each person's contribution to the collaboration. Be clear not only about your role in research and writing, but also about who will be responsible for typing the final manuscript, arranging for illustrations and copyright permissions, preparing the index, and so on. Also decide who will have "artistic control" over the work. How will you decide when the work is ready for submission to a publisher or agent, or whether something needs to be rewritten or not?

The tentative schedule for the book. In what order is work to be done, and when is each portion to be completed?

Expenses. Will you establish a "slush" fund to which each of you has access, or will you pay your expenses out of your own pockets and then even things up later? Will part of the advance against royalties be set aside for expenses? How will you decide which expenses are legitimately connected with writing the book and which are not?

Earnings. Will each of you share equally in the income, or will one receive a larger percentage because of a greater contribution to the creation and development of the book?

Copyright. Will you share equally in the copyright to the work, or will the copyright be only in one person's name? If you share equally in the copyright, you are also jointly responsible in case of a lawsuit for invasion of someone else's rights; if you are only one of several contributors to a book and your contribution is clearly separate from other contributions (as in an anthology), then you are legally responsible only for the material you wrote. As a co-owner, you are legally entitled to make use of the work so long as you account to the others for the profits; and you are also permitted to sell, give away, or otherwise transfer your ownership interest to others. However, if the entire copyright or any of the exclusive rights are to be sold or transferred, consent must be obtained from all the co-owners.

Credit. This is closely connected with the question of copyright. Will you all be credited equally on the book, or will one person be identified as playing a larger role? Also decide the order in which your names will appear on the book.

Procedures for dissolution of the agreement. Specify what will happen if one partner dies or quits the project before it is completed. Who has the rights to the material produced to date? This usually depends on how the idea for the book was conceived. If the book was your idea and you asked someone else to work with you, for example, you will probably want the right either to purchase the materials he contributed or return them to him with the stipulation that he may not use his material in another book without your consent.

Revisions. Decide what will happen if the book is successfully published and the publisher wants the material revised for a new edition. Who will be responsible for making these revisions, and how will the income from the revised edition be shared?

Working as an Author-for-Hire

A collaboration agreement usually implies an equal partnership. However, it's also possible that you will be hired as a writer for a project in which you will not share in the copyright, that is, as an author-for-hire. According to our copyright law, a work is defined as a "work made for hire" if it is "prepared by an employee within the scope of his or her employment" or if it is "specially ordered and commissioned for use as a contribution to a collective work, as part of a motion picture or other audiovisual work, as a translation, as a supplementary work, as a compilation, as an instructional text, as a test, as answer material for a test, or as an atlas, if the parties expressly agree in a written instrument signed by them that the work shall be considered a work made for hire." In other words, it is unlikely that a full-length trade book would ever be a work-for-hire, but it is common for chapters in a book (or similar material) to be so.

In working as an author-for-hire, it is essential that you have an agreement clearly spelling out what your responsibilities are and what the method of payment will be. The best arrangement usually is to get a flat fee plus a share of the royalties, so that you are protected if the book doesn't do well, but will reap the benefits if it is enormously successful.

Crediting is also important. Find out whether you are going to remain a true "ghost," with no mention at all on the book, or whether there will be some sort of phrase crediting you, such as "with (you)" or "by (principal author) and (you)."

Appendix D

Writers' Aids

The days when a writer had to slave away alone in his garret without anyone else to talk to or render assistance are largely gone—if they did in fact ever exist. Now there are many places you can turn to for help and advice in your writing career, or for companionship with other writers, or even financial support. Here are some possibilities to consider:

Writing Help

Courses. If you're interested in taking a course on writing, check the universities in your area to see what courses they have available during the day or in their extension (nightschool) division. Writing courses are also occasionally held in high schools in the evening; check with your local school district, or perhaps at one of the larger local libraries.

Another possibility is to take a correspondence course in writing. Courses on writing for children, writing mystery stories, and other kinds of writing are frequently advertised in *The Writer* and *Writer's Digest* magazines. For a brief commentary on correspondence courses and writing courses in general, see "So You're Going to Take a Writing Course" by Hayes B. Jacobs in the May 1981 issue of *Writer's Digest*.

If you are interested in a degree program in writing, you can either contact local colleges or get in touch with an organization called Associated Writing Programs (AWP), c/o Department of English, Old Dominion University, Norfolk, VA 23508 (804) 440-3000. AWP sells a catalog with a descriptive listing of college and university workshops and degree programs in creative writing, plus a review of writers' colonies. The fourth edition, published in 1984, lists over 250 such programs and sells for $10.

There are also courses in book publishing. See the Bibliography of this manual for a reference.

Conferences. You might also want to consider a one- or two-day seminar, or perhaps a conference running a week or more. Seminars are frequently sponsored by professional writers' associations, or by for-profit companies such as *Writer's Digest*. For news about such seminars, watch the writers' magazines and keep an eye on the "Calendar" column in *Publishers Weekly*.

A writers' conference typically runs a week or more, is held in some pleasant spa or on a college campus during the summer, and features lectures, workshops, and private conferences with writer-instructors. This is not only a good way to get away from your family and learn something about writing, it can be fruitful in terms of professional contacts. More than one writer has found his editor or agent at such a conference. For a listing of conferences, check *Literary Market Place*, *Writer's Market*, or the May issue of *Writer's Digest*.

Editorial Help. If you want more direct help with a particular project you are working on, there are a few possibilities you can explore.

One is to turn to another writer who has already published a book and is willing to help you with yours. Many writers are understandably reluctant to do this; in fact, Arthur C. Clarke has a mimeographed form that he returns to writers stating, "UNDER NO CIRCUMSTANCES will I comment on manuscripts," and suggesting that you "read at least one book a day and write as much as you can." However, other writers may be willing to help you, with or without a fee. You can try to find such a writer through a writers' association, or perhaps at a seminar or conference. Another possibility is to contact one of the writers listed in *A Directory of American Poets & Fiction Writers* put out by Poets & Writers Inc.

Perhaps a better idea is to work with a professional editor, such as those listed under "Editorial Services" in *LMP*. Services offered include such things as manuscript analysis, substantive editing, research, rewriting, and copyediting. No fees are specified and it's difficult to know how good the people offering these services are. But it may be worth investigating; one writer I admire very much insists that any new writer should have his material evaluated by a professional editor *before* submitting it to a publisher. What you probably should do is interview the editor first, to find out exactly what kinds of services he can provide you and to get the names of other writers who have been able to sell their books as a result of his help.

Paid evaluation by an agent. Another possibility is to send your manuscript to a literary agent who charges a "reading fee" for manuscript evaluation. Some of these agents advertise in the writers' magazines, and a few of those listed in *LMP* and *Writer's Market* also charge fees (although that fact isn't always indicated). An article in the June 1980 issue of *Writer's Digest* identifies some of the established agents who charge reading fees (and Chapter 2 of this book indicates some typical fees). Writer's Digest, Inc., also offers a manuscript criticism service; the evaluation is done by a professional writer in your field, and the rate for books or outlines with sample chapters is $125 minimum for up to 20,000 words, plus $5 for each additional 1,000 words or fraction thereof.

The pros and cons of this type of service are hotly debated. Some people feel that it is essentially worthless, since the report is simply the opinion of someone who is not in the position to buy the rights to manuscripts. Others feel that such an evaluation can help a writer who doesn't know anyone qualified to give him a professional opinion. Some of the agencies do refund the fee if they take you on as a client and succeed in getting a book contract for you. I should caution you, however, that some of the agencies that charge reading fees have few contacts with the larger publishing houses and probably haven't made a significant sale for many years. So proceed with care.

Writers' Groups and Associations

There are many different types of groups and associations that offer aid and companionship to writers. *The Writer's New York City Source Book* (see Bibliography, "miscellaneous") lists many of the most important and well-known. *LMP* also has a quite complete listing of writers' associations, but does not provide a detailed description of any of them; for more information, you have to write the association itself. There may also be some sort of writers' group in your town.

One of the most important active associations on behalf of writers is Poets & Writers Inc., a nonprofit organization funded by grants from the National Endowment for the Arts and by private donations. It runs an information service at 201 W. 54th St., New York, NY 10019 (212) 757-1766, and publishes booklets on subjects of interest to writers (literary agents, sponsors of workshops and readings, etc.) and a newsletter, *Coda,* which comes out five times a year. Your local library probably has a subscription to *Coda*, and I recommend that you become acquainted with this publication.

Two articles that ran in *Coda* are particularly relevant here. One is a listing of twelve groups that provide information and service to writers, which ran in the November/December 1980 issue; the other is a "Guide to Writers' Resources" that ran in the June/July 1981 issue. Both of these articles are available as reprints for $1.00 each plus a stamped, self-addressed envelope.

Funding Organizations and Other Sources of Financial Support

Making a living as a writer is extremely difficult, but there are many places that you can turn to for financial help.

One is the Literature Program of the National Endowment for the Arts (NEA), which is a federal agency empowered to provide fellowships for published writers and translators, plus grants to various kinds of organizations (such as Poets & Writers) that provide support to writers. The fellowships from NEA are very generous ($12,000 a year) and are fiercely contended for. For further information write the Literature Program, National Endowment for the Arts, 2401 E St. NW, Washington, DC 20506. The telephone number is (202) 634-6044.

There is also an arts council in every state that provides funding and assistance to writers. You can find out about the arts council in your state by writing your state capital or by purchasing the *Sponsors List* from Poets & Writers at a cost of $3.95 ($2.95 for writers listed with P&W). This publication lists all of the state arts councils, plus 550 or so other national organizations that sponsor programs employing fiction writers and poets. Poets & Writers also publishes a list of writing workshops in New York City three times a year; the listing costs $1 plus a stamped, self-addressed envelope. And every issue of *Coda* has news about grants and foundations. For further information about jobs for writers, contact Poets & Writers for a reprint titled "Jobs for Writers and Where to Find Them" which ran in the June/July 1978 issue of *Coda*. You also might want to take a look at an article titled "Is Academia the Writer's Best Friend?" in *Coda's* June/July 1981 issue.

A grant is basically a gift from a governmental agency or private organization. There are many foundations that sponsor grants and fellowships for writers. One of the best sources for information on grants is an organization called the Foundation Center, which offers information and help to grant-seekers. It operates libraries in New York, Washington, San Francisco, and Cleveland, and also has arrangements with seventy-five cooperating libraries. For the name and address of the collection nearest you, call (800) 424-9836, toll free. There are also a number of publications available on "grantsmanship"; I have listed several in the Bibliography of this book (see "Guides to Literary Contests, Prizes, and Grants"). And *LMP* has a brief listing of literary fellowships and grants.

Another strategy to keep the wolf away from the door is to enter prize contests. An astonishing number of these contests are open to writers each year, some of them with substantial cash prizes, others offering an award (it's good for prestige) and/or publication for the prizewinners. For a listing, check *LMP* under "Literary Awards" and "Prize Contests Open," or *Writer's Market* under "Contests and Awards." Other publications dealing with contests are listed in the Bibliography of this book in the section referred to above.

A writers' colony is a retreat where writers and other artists can go for a period ranging from one week to one year, with expenses paid and occasionally a small stipend. The best-known colonies are probably the McDowell Colony in

Peterborough, New Hampshire, and Yaddo at Saratoga Springs, New York. For an excellent article on such colonies, see "Fifteen Heavens for Writers" in the June/July 1978 issue of *Coda;* contact Poets & Writers for further information. The fourth edition of the Associated Writing Programs publication (mentioned earlier in this Appendix) also has a review of writers' colonies.

Bibliography

Following is a selected list of books and periodicals relating to writing and publishing. Where possible, I have indicated the most recent edition and whether the book is out of print or not. I have not indicated prices in most cases, since these often change when a book is reprinted. For other books on these topics, consult the *Subject Guide to Books in Print,* published by the R. R. Bowker Co., or the bibliographies of some of the books indicated. To find an out-of-print book, check to see whether a library in your area has a copy (or can get one through an interlibrary loan), check a second-hand bookstore, or use an out-of-print search service.

Periodicals

Any writer of trade books should be familiar with the major review media, such as the *New York Times Book Review, Saturday Review, New York Review of Books, West Coast Review of Books,* and so forth. In addition, you should also become familiar with *Publishers Weekly* and with the two magazines for writers—*Writer's Digest* and *The Writer*—mentioned several times in the text. In addition, there is a bimonthly newsletter called *Freelancer's Market* that provides news of what magazines and book editors are currently looking for; it can be obtained from Riverhouse Publications, 20 Waterside Plaza, New York, NY 10010. For news about the small-press scene, consult *Coda,* published by Poets & Writers Inc., 201 W. 54th St., New York, NY 10019, and/or *Small Press: The Magazine of Independent Book Publishing,* published bimonthly by the R. R. Bowker

Company, 205 E. 42nd St., New York, N.Y. 10003 ($18.00/year).

There are also several directories of periodicals. The most important and useful for a writer include:

Ayer Directory of Publications. Fort Washington, Pa.: IMS Press, rev. ed., 1983. Annual. A complete listing of American and Canadian newspapers and periodicals.

Magazine Industry Market Place 1984. New York: R. R. Bowker Co., 1983. A guide to some 2,800 consumer, professional, literary, and scholarly publications.

The Standard Periodical Directory: 1983–84. New York: Oxbridge Communications, 8th ed., 1982. Revised biennially. A listing of 65,000 U.S. and Canadian periodicals, arranged by subject.

Ulrich's International Periodicals Directory, 1983. New York: R. R. Bowker Co., 22nd ed., 1983. Two volumes, revised biennially. A subject-arranged list of over 67,000 periodicals published throughout the world.

Directories and Guides to Book Publishing

Books in Print. This is a series of books published by the R. R. Bowker Company that lists books currently available from their publishers. The basic listing consists of a two-volume compilation by author's name and another two-volume compilation by book title (which includes three indexes to publishers). The 1983–84 edition lists over 618,000 books from 15,200 U.S. publishers; the listing is revised annually in October. The *Subject Guide* lists nearly 575,000 nonfiction titles under 62,300 different Library of Congress subject classifications, and is revised annually in October. *Forthcoming Books in Print* lists books to be published during the upcoming five-month period; there are also a *Subject Guide* and bimonthly cumulative updates. In addition, there are separate listings of *Paperbound Books in Print, Children's Books in Print, Religious Books and Serials in Print, Business and Economics Books & Serials in Print, Large Type Books in*

Print, Law Books in Print, Medical Books & Serials in Print, and *Scientific and Technical Books & Serials in Print.*

Book Publishers Directory. Detroit, Mich.: Gale Research Co., 4th ed., 1983. A guide to 7,134 "new and established, private and special interest, avant-garde and alternative, organization and association, government and institution presses." Includes subject and geographical indexes. A supplement lists additional publishers, plus 126 distributors, bringing the total number of listings to 8,472.

Book Trade of the World. New York: R. R. Bowker Co., 4 vols. A survey of bookselling and publishing throughout the world.

International Directory of Little Magazines & Small Presses: 19th Annual. Paradise, Calif.: Dustbooks, 1983. Hardcover and paperback. A listing of about 3,000 little magazines and small presses throughout the world. Includes subject and geographical indexes and a list of small-press distributors.

International Literary Market Place, 1983–84. New York: R. R. Bowker Co., 18th ed., 1983. A directory of the book trade outside of the United States and Canada. Covers 9,000 publishers in over 160 countries.

Literary Market Place with Names & Numbers/The Directory of American Book Publishing. New York: R. R. Bowker Co., 45th ed., 1983. The single best and most useful guide to American book publishing with some 2,000 U.S. and Canadian publishers listed in the 1984 edition. Seventy-nine different sections relating to all aspects of book publishing, plus a Yellow Pages section with names, affiliations, and telephone numbers. The "Reference Books of the Trade" section lists many other valuable publications related to book publishing.

Publishers, Distributors & Wholesalers of the United States: A Directory. New York: R. R. Bowker Co., 5th ed., 1983. Lists over 37,500 book publishers and distributors (wholesalers, etc.).

Publishers' Trade List Annual, 1983. New York: R. R. Bowker Co. Five volumes revised annually. A compilation of the annual catalogs of over 1,800 publishers. About 7,000 sets are made up each year, and can be found in the larger libraries and bookstores. Subject index.

Religious Writers Marketplace. William Gentz and Elaine Colvin, eds. Philadelphia: Running Press, 1980. A directory of U.S. and Canadian publishers of religious materials.

A Writer's Guide to Chicago-Area Publishers & Other Freelance Markets. Jerold L. Kellman, ed. Skokie, Ill.: Gabriel House, 1979. Paperback. A list of more than 300 firms in the Chicago area that buy book manuscripts and other materials.

Writer's Handbook. Sylvia K. Burack, ed. Boston, Mass.: The Writer, Inc., 1981. Contains 100 chapters of advice on freelance writing by well-known authors and editors, plus a list of about 200 hardcover publishers, 50 paperback publishers, 15 publishers of romance novels, and 40 university presses.

Writer's Market, 1984. Bernadine Clark, ed. Cincinnati, Ohio: Writer's Digest, annual. Directory of magazine and book publishers. The 1984 edition lists about 800 book publishers. Includes information and tips for writers. The same company publishes a *Writer's Yearbook* in magazine format that contains similar information, in January.

Books About Book Publishing

General

Adler, Bill. *Inside Publishing*. Indianapolis/New York: Bobbs-Merrill, 1982. A chatty, informative, and highly idiosyncratic discussion about what *really* goes on in trade-book publishing, by an agent/author.

Benjamin, Curtis G. *A Candid Critique of Book Publishing*. New York: R. R. Bowker Co., 1977. A discussion of the problems facing the book industry today, by the former chairman of McGraw-Hill. (Out of print.)

Coser, Lewis A., Charles Kadushin, and Walter W. Powell. *Books: The Culture and Commerce of Publishing*. New York: Basic Books, 1982. A comprehensive examination of book publishing in America by a team of distinguished sociologists.

Dessauer, John P. *Book Publishing: What It Is, What It Does*. New York: R. R. Bowker Co., 1974, 2nd ed., 1981. The first book to describe the book publishing business clearly from one man's point of view. Dessauer is a well-known statistician and publishing consultant.

Grannis, Chandler. *What Happens in Book Publishing*. New York: Columbia University Press, 2nd ed., 1967. Now out of print, but one of the standard guides to book publishing by twenty experts in their fields.

Greenfield, Howard. *Books: From Writer to Reader*. New York: Crown Publishers, 1976. An introduction to how books are published, with drawings, black-and-white photographs, color illustrations, and a glossary.

Gross, Gerald, ed. *Publishers on Publishing*. New York: Grosset & Dunlap, 1961. Paperbound. A compendium of essays by some of the most influential book publishers in America. Out of print.

Henderson, Bill, ed. *The Art of Literary Publishing*. New York: Pushcart Press, 1980. A collection of essays by editors from trade houses, small presses, and literary magazines about the joys and perils of literary publishing.

Jovanovich, William. *Now, Barabbas*. New York: Harper & Row, 1964. A collection of essays on publishing by the present chairman of Harcourt Brace Jovanovich, Inc. (Out of print.)

Kujoth, Jean, ed. *Book Publishing: Inside Views*. Metuchen, N.J.: Scarecrow Press, 1971. Essays on many aspects of book publishing. Still relevant today. (Out of print.)

Madison, Charles. *Irving to Irving: Author-Publisher Relations, 1800–1974*. New York: R. R. Bowker Co., 1974.

The changing relations between authors and publishers, from Washington Irving to Clifford Irving.

Shatzkin, Leonard. *In Cold Type: Overcoming the Book Crisis*. Boston: Houghton Mifflin, 1982. A publisher's controversial prescription for curing book publishing's ills.

Tebbel, John. *A History of Book Publishing in the United States*. New York: R. R. Bowker Co., 4 vols. Ranging from the years 1630 to 1980, this is the definitive historical study of the book-publishing industry.

Unwin, Sir Stanley. *The Truth About Publishing*. 8th edition revised and partly rewritten by Philip Unwin. Chicago: Academy Chicago, 1976. Trade paperback. One of the classics in the field, it was first published in 1926. Updated and softened somewhat by his son, it is still acerbic, dogmatic, and a wonderful discussion of book publishing by an old English pro.

Mass-Market Paperbacks

Bonn, Thomas L. *Under Cover: An Illustrated History of American Mass-Market Paperbacks*. New York: Penguin, 1982. One of the few guides to the history of mass-market paperbacks.

Dans, Kenneth C. *Two-Bit Culture: The Paperbacking of America*. Boston: Houghton-Mifflin, 1984. This intelligently written book examines the social and cultural contributions made by paperbacks in America.

O'Brien, Geoffrey. *Hardboiled America: The Lurid Years of Paperbacks*. New York: Van Nostrand Reinhold, 1981. An entertaining study of the "hardboiled fiction of the 1930's and 1940's by Chandler, Hammett, and the like, with examples of some covers.

Peterson, Clarence. *The Bantam Story: Thirty Years of Paperback Publishing*. New York: Bantam Books, 1975. In the course of discussing the history of Bantam, Peterson also tells a great deal about the evolution of mass-market paperbacks. (Out of print.)

Smith, Roger. *Paperback Parnassus*. Boulder, Colo.: Westview Press, 1976. A survey of the mass-market industry. (Out of print.)

University Presses

Association of American University Presses, ed. *One Book/ Five Ways: The Publishing Procedures of Five University Presses*. Los Altos, Calif.: William Kaufmann, 1978. Five university presses describe in detail how they would go about publishing a book, providing an opportunity to see how many options there really are.

Bailey, Herbert S., Jr. *The Art and Science of Book Publishing*. Austin, Texas: University of Texas Press, 1980. Paperback. A thorough discussion of the way a publisher goes about his business, by the director of the Princeton University Press. Focuses on general trade publishing and scholarly publishing.

Hawes, Gene R. *To Advance Knowledge: A Handbook of American University Press Publishing*. New York: American University Press Services for the AAUP, 1967. A guide for people planning to enter scholarly publishing. (Out of print.)

Self-Publishing

Chickadel, Charles J. *Publish It Yourself: The Complete Guide to Self-Publishing Your Book*. Aurora, Ill.: Caroline House Publishers, 2nd ed., 1980. Paperback. Aimed primarily at a West Coast audience, this book concentrates on the production aspects of self-publishing. (Out of print.)

Hasselstrom, L. M. *The Book Book: A Publishing Handbook for Beginners and Others*. Herman, S.D.: Lame Johnny Press, 1979. A brief discussion of the steps involved in publishing a book, followed by an extensive glossary and lists of various types of services. Bibliography. Again, the emphasis is on production.

Henderson, Bill, ed. *The Publish It Yourself Handbook: Pushcart Press's Revised Edition*. New York: Pushcart Press/Harper & Row, rev. ed., 1980. Paperback. Probably the best-known book in the field. Includes several essays by famous and not-so-famous self-publishers, plus how-to tips by Henderson, publisher of Pushcart Press.

Mathieu, Aaron. *The Book Market: How to Write, Publish and Market Your Book.* New York: Andover Press, 1981. A somewhat oversimplified guide to publishing your own book.

Nicholas, Ted. *How to Self-publish Your Own Book and Make It a Bestseller.* Wilmington, Del.: Enterprise Publishing, 3rd ed., 1980. Paperback. A fairly good if somewhat thin guide to self-publishing. The Appendix provides lists of book manufacturers, direct-mail specialists, and other suppliers.

Poynter, Dan. *The Self-Publishing Manual: How to Write, Print and Sell Your Own Book.* Santa Barbara, Calif.: Para Publishing, 2nd ed., 1980. Far and away the most detailed and best book on the subject. Poynter knows what he's talking about and gives very detailed and useful information.

See also the tips on self-publishing in Appelbaum and Evans, next listing.

Books for Writers About the Publishing Process

The distinctions between this category and other books dealing more with writing are foggy at best; nonetheless, the books listed here put more emphasis on the *business* of being a writer.

Appelbaum, Judith, and Nancy Evans. *How to Get Happily Published.* New York: NAL, 1982. Paperback. A chatty, informative guide for the new writer, with considerable emphasis on self-publishing and an extensive list of resources.

Balkin, Richard. *Writer's Guide to Book Publishing.* New York: E. P. Dutton, 1977, 1981. Paperback. A solid, well-thought-out guide to trade publishing, with additional information on academic publishing and on small presses.

Cassill, Kay. *The Complete Book for Freelance Writers*. Cincinnati, Ohio: Writer's Digest Books, 1981. Intended for both magazine and book writers, this guide provides very detailed and useful advice for freelance writers who want to make a living from their work.

Gearing, Philip J., and Evelyn V. Brunson. *Breaking into Print: How to Get Your Work Published*. Englewood Cliffs, N.J.: Prentice-Hall, 1977. Paperback. An oversimplified discussion of the publishing process, including lengthy lists of the contents of reference books.

Hill, Mary, and Wendell Cochran. *Into Print: A Practical Guide to Writing, Illustrating and Publishing*. Los Altos, Calif.: William Kaufmann, 1977. Primarily concerned with the preparation and publication of technical materials, but detailed and informative.

Martindale, David. *How to Be a Freelance Writer: A Guide to Building a Full-time Career*. Crown, 1982. Expert advice from an expert, for both book and magazine writers.

Mau, Ernest E. *The Free-lance Writer's Survival Book*. Chicago: Contemporary Books, 1981. A discussion of the business of being a writer. Gives specific advice on how to structure your business, keep records, prepare taxes, etc., especially for writers doing work for corporations.

Thomas, David St. John, and Hubert Bermant. *Getting Published*. New York: Harper & Row, 1974. Paperback. A general look at how a writer should prepare his book for publication and approach a publisher.

Books About Writing

Although this is not a book about how to write a book, there are a number of books on the subject that I have found helpful and pertinent. The following are among the best. Writer's Digest, Inc., publishes a large number of books on writing; they are advertised in each edition of *Writer's Digest* magazine.

Barzun, Jacques. *On Writing, Editing and Publishing*. Chicago: University of Chicago Press, 1971. Several bracing essays by the distinguished writer and scholar.

Brady, John, ed. *Fiction Writer's Market*. Cincinnati, Ohio: Writer's Digest, 1980. An excellent collection of essays on the art of writing fiction. Includes lists of small presses and commercial publishers; contests and awards, writers' organizations, a glossary, and an index of publishers by category.

Braine, John. *Writing a Novel*. New York: McGraw-Hill, 1975. Excellent advice and examples by the author of *Room at the Top* and other novels.

Brittain, Vera. *On Being an Author*. New York: Macmillan Publishing Co., 1948. An oldie but goodie, this is both the autobiography of a distinguished English writer and a succinct, pungent commentary on the art and craft of writing and publishing. (Out of print.)

Burnett, Hallie and Whit. *Fiction Writer's Handbook*. New York: Harper & Row, 1975. Vivid, useful advice by the coeditors of *Story* magazine, who also taught creative writing and wrote and edited numerous books.

Daigh, Ralph. *Maybe You Should Write a Book*. Englewood Cliffs, N.J.: Prentice-Hall, 1977. By a founding publisher of Fawcett Books, this is somewhat awkwardly written but filled with fascinating anecdotes by many well-known writers.

Falk, Kathryn. *How to Write a Romance and Get It Published*. New York: Crown, 1983. There are several books on writing romances currently available; this seems to be the best. Has contributions from 65 writers, editors, and other people connected with the field, plus lists of romance lines.

Forster, E. M. *Aspects of the Novel*. New York: Harcourt Brace Jovanovich, 1956. Paperback; original ed. 1927. A classic, and well worth reading for the pleasure of the style alone. But Forster's comments on story, plot, characterization, and language are as much on the mark today as they were fifty years ago.

Gardner, John. *On Becoming a Novelist*. New York: Harper & Row, 1983. The late, gifted author discusses three main questions young writers frequently have: Am I talented enough? How should I educate myself? Can I make a living from writing fiction? Absorbing and valuable.

Gunther, Max. *Writing and Selling a Nonfiction Book*. Boston: The Writer, 1973. One of the best of the few guides available on writing nonfiction.

Hersey, John, ed. *The Writer's Craft*. New York: Alfred A. Knopf, 1974. An extraordinary collection of essays on writing by most of the masters of the modern novel. To be read for the sheer pleasure of it.

Jacobs, Hayes B. *A Complete Guide to Writing and Selling Nonfiction*. Cincinnati, Ohio: Writer's Digest, 1975. A very workmanlike guide to writing and publishing nonfiction.

MacCampbell, Donald. *The Writing Business*. New York: Crown Publishers, 1978. About writers, agents, and publishers. Somewhat overopinionated for my taste, but there are a few gems here and there.

Maugham, Somerset. *A Writer's Notebook*. New York: Penguin Books. Notes and reminiscences by the famous writer.

Meredith, Scott. *Writing to Sell*. New York: Harper & Row, 2nd ed., 1974. Advice on how to plot and write conventional commercial novels, by a well-known literary agent.

O'Connor, Flannery. *Mystery and Manners: Occasional Prose*. Robert and Sally Fitzgerald, eds. New York: Farrar, Straus & Giroux, 1969. Another classic, with stunning language, wit, and precision of thought. O'Connor knew a great deal about the art—and mystery—of writing well.

Porter, Roy E., et al. *The Writer's Manual*. Palm Springs, Calif.: ETC Publications, rev. ed., 1979. A compendium of articles on writing different kinds of materials for different kinds of publications.

Reynolds, Paul. *The Writing and Selling of Fiction*. New York: William Morrow & Co., 1965, 1980. Another guide to writing conventional novels by a well-known literary agent. It begins: "Anyone of reasonable intelligence can learn to write publishable nonfiction. About fiction no such statement can be made."

Wallace, Irving. *The Writing of One Novel*. New York: Simon & Schuster, 1968. An anatomy of how one book, *The Prize*, was written and what happened afterward.

Woolf, Virginia. *A Writer's Diary: Being Extracts from the Diary of Virginia Woolf*. New York: Harcourt Brace Jovanovich, 1973. Paperback. One of the classics, edited by Leonard Woolf from diaries that his wife kept from 1918 to 1941.

Directories of and Interviews with Writers

There are many different types of directories of writers listed in the "Reference Books of the Trade" section of *Literary Market Place*. One of the best-known is *A Directory of American Poets & Fiction Writers*, published by Poets & Writers Inc. Another directory not listed in *LMP* is *The Writer's Directory*, published by St. Martin's Press, which lists 12,000 living writers with their addresses and a summary of their work.

There are also a number of interview series with authors. Probably the best-known is titled *Writers at Work: The Paris Review Interviews*, which is presently being published by the Viking Press. There are four series (volumes) to date, some edited by Malcolm Cowley and others by George Plimpton. Here are a few others you might want to locate:

The Author Speaks: Selected PW Interviews 1967–1976. New York: R. R. Bowker Co., 1977. Over 160 *PW* interviews with authors, arranged in sections by type of book.

Bruccoli, Matthew, ed. *Conversations with Writers.* Vols. 1 and 2. Detroit: Gale Research Co., 1977, 1978. Interviews with well-known writers.

Tooker, Dan, and Roger Hofheims. *Fiction! Interviews with Northern California Novelists.* New York: Harcourt Brace Jovanovich/William Kaufmann, 1976. Interviews with twelve well-known West Coast novelists.

Contracts, Copyright, and Other Legal Matters

Bunnin, Brod, and Peter Beren. *Author Law and Strategies: A Legal Guide for the Working Writer.* Berkeley, Calif.: Nolo Press, 1983. Trade paperback. Thorough, pleasantly written, and entertaining, with hilarious cartoons.

Crawford, Tad. *The Writer's Legal Guide.* New York: Hawthorn/Dutton, 1977. Written by a lawyer, this guide provides excellent information on various legal aspects of publishing, but is sometimes awkwardly written and difficult to understand.

Herron, Caroline, ed. *Writer's Guide to Copyright.* New York: Poets & Writers, 1979. An excellent, clear guide to the copyright law as it particularly affects writers.

Johnston, Donald F. *Copyright Handbook.* New York: R. R. Bowker Co., 1st ed., 1978. A guide to the U.S. copyright law which went into effect on January 1, 1978.

Norwick, Kenneth P., and Jerry Simon Chasen, with Henry R. Kaufman. *The Rights of Authors and Artists.* New York: Bantam, 1984. An excellent guide to all aspects of literary law.

Polking, Kirk, and Leonard S. Meranus. *Law and the Writer.* Cincinnati, Ohio: Writer's Digest Books, rev. ed., 1981. A somewhat superficial guide to various aspects of the law that might concern a writer. Includes the complete text of the 1978 copyright law, a list of small-claims courts, and a glossary of terms.

Rembar, Charles. *The End of Obscenity: The Trials of Lady Chatterley, Tropic of Cancer and Fanny Hill*. New York: Random House, 1968. A fascinating account by the lawyer who defended these books, resulting in a landmark change in the obscenity laws.

Strong, William G. *The Copyright Book: A Practical Guide*. Cambridge, Mass.: The MIT Press, 1981. A cogent guide to the new copyright law.

Wincor, Richard. *Literary Rights Contracts: A Handbook for Professionals*. New York: Law & Business/Harcourt Brace Jovanovich, 1979. Written for lawyers, this is a surprisingly entertaining guide to the transfer of various kinds of literary rights.

Wittenberg, Charles. *The Protection of Literary Property*. Boston: The Writer, rev. ed., 1978. An informative discussion of legal problems affecting the writing and publication of literary property.

Editors and Editing

Surprisingly, there are very few how-to books on the subject of editing. However, here are several interesting collections of essays and correspondence and a few biographies and autobiographies that will give you a closer look at the mind of an editor.

Berg, Scott. *Maxwell Perkins: Editor of Genius*. New York: E. P. Dutton, 1978. A fascinating biography of the most famous editor in America.

Commins, Dorothy. *What Is an Editor? Saxe Commins at Work*. Chicago: University of Chicago Press, 1978. Commins was an editor at Random House for many years and worked with some of the most famous writers in America. This biography is by his wife.

Gross, Gerald, ed. *Editors on Editing*. New York: Grosset & Dunlap, 1962. A collection of essays covering all aspects of editing books and magazines, this is a valuable discussion of the role of the editor. (Out of print.)

Haydn, Hiram. *Words and Faces*. New York: Harcourt Brace Jovanovich, 1974. Haydn edited *The American Scholar* for many years, then became a book editor and worked at several houses, the last being HBJ. His autobiography discloses much about the world of publishing and editing.

Judd, Karen. *Copyediting: A Practical Guide*. Los Altos, Calif.: William Kaufmann, 1982. As billed, a good, practical guide to the ins and outs of copyediting general-interest books.

Kuehl, John, and Jackson R. Bryer. *Dear Scott, Dear Max: The Fitzgerald-Perkins Correspondence*. New York: Charles Scribner's Sons, 1971. A selection of letters written by F. Scott Fitzgerald and Maxwell Perkins from 1915 to 1940 provides an illuminating look at the relationship between a famous author and his famous editor. (Out of print.)

Mitchell, Burroughs. *The Education of an Editor*. Garden City, N.Y.: Doubleday, 1980. A small (literally) reminiscence by an editor who had Maxwell Perkins as his mentor, with particular emphasis on Mitchell's relationship with James Jones.

Plotnik, Arthur. *The Elements of Editing: A Modern Guide for Editors and Journalists*. New York: Macmillan, 1982. Mainly for journalists, but has an interesting chapter on book editors.

Targ, William. *Indecent Pleasures*. New York: Macmillan Publishing Co., 1975. Some terrific anecdotes by the former editor-in-chief of Putnam's. (Out of print.)

Wheelock, John Hall. *Editor to Author: The Letters of Maxwell E. Perkins*. New York: Charles Scribner's Sons, 1950.

An editor's letters to some of the most famous writers in America. (Out of print.)

Literary Agents

Curtis, Richard. *How to Be Your Own Literary Agent.* Boston: Houghton Mifflin, 1983. A good description of the ways an agent can help you, particularly in negotiating a contract. An Appendix gives a "quick guide to deal points for authors in the midst of negotiations."

Literary Agents of North America: Marketplace 1983–84. Ed. by Author Aid-Research Asso. Intl., 1983. A listing of over 450 U.S. and Canadian literary agencies with a brief discussion of their specialties, cross-indexed by subjects handled and geographical location. I don't agree with some of the statements in the Introduction, but the listing itself seems reasonably sound.

Mayer, Debbie. *Literary Agents: A Writer's Guide.* New York: Poets & Writers, 1983. A discussion of what agents are and what they do, plus the names and addresses of agents who will consider work from new writers. Also discusses fee-charging agents, lecture agents, and publicity agents.

Reynolds, Paul R. *The Middle Man: The Adventures of a Literary Agent.* New York: William Morrow, 1972. Reminiscences of the writer and his father, who established the first literary agency in the United States.

Strauss, Helen M. *A Talent for Luck: An Autobiography.* New York: Random House, 1979. An entertaining account by one of the doyens of the agency business. (Out of print.)

See also the June 1980 issue of *Writer's Digest* magazine for an article titled "All About Agents" and the January 1, 1981, issue of *Publishers Weekly* for an article about literary agents in the San Francisco Bay area.

Style Manuals

A Manual of Style. Chicago: University of Chicago Press, 13th ed., 1982. One of the standards, albeit addressed to academic writers.

Nicholson, Margaret. *A Practical Style Guide for Authors and Editors*. New York: Holt, Rinehart & Winston, 1970. Paperback. A somewhat less technical style guide.

Skillin, Marjorie E., Robert M. Gay, et al. *Words into Type*. Englewood Cliffs, N.J.: Prentice-Hall, 3rd ed., 1974. Another one of the standards, heavily used by copy editors.

Strunk, William, Jr., and E. B. White. *The Elements of Style*. New York: Macmillan Publishing Co., 3rd ed., 1973. The famous collection of "rules" about style and usage.

Book Production and Design

Lee, Marshall. *Bookmaking: The Illustrated Guide to Design/Production/Editing*. New York: R. R. Bowker Co., new and enlarged ed., 1980. A complete guide to designing and producing a book, with some words about editing.

Pocket Pal: A Graphic Arts Production Handbook. New York: International Paper Co., 12th ed., 1979. A beginner's guide to book design, production, and the graphic arts.

Strauss, Victor. *The Printing Industry: An Introduction to Its Many Branches, Processes and Products*. New York: R. R. Bowker Co./Printing Industries of America, 1967. An encyclopedia of all phases of the printing industry.

See also various books for self-publishers struggling with these problems.

Guides to Literary Contests,
Prizes, and Grants

Appendix D of this manual provides a brief discussion of grants and prize contests. In addition to the listings mentioned in *Literary Market Place* and *Writer's Market,* you may want to consult the following:

Awards, Honors and Prizes: United States and Canada, Vol. I. Detroit, Mich.: Gale Research Co., Paul Wasserman, ed. Volume I of this two-volume set (5th ed., 1982) has listings for the United States and Canada. Volume II (5th ed., 1982) covers international and foreign prizes.

Gadney, Alan. *How to Enter and Win Fiction Writing Contests* and *How to Enter and Win Non-fiction and Journalism Contests.* New York: Facts on File, 1981. Paperback. These two guides provide details on different types of contests, broken down by types of books and including a description of the rules, amount of award, entry fee, judging methods, and deadlines.

Grants and Awards Available to American Writers. New York: PEN American Center, 12th rev. ed., 1982. Paperback. An excellent guide for writers.

Literary and Library Prizes. New York: R. R. Bowker Co., 10th ed., 1980. A guide to the history, rules, and conditions of literary prizes, awards, fellowships, and grants in the United States, Canada, and Great Britain.

Smith, Craig, and Erick Skjei. *Getting Grants: A Creative Guide to the Grants System—How to Find Funders, Write Convincing Proposals, and Make Your Grants Work.* New York: Harper & Row, 1980. The subtitle says it all. An excellent how-to guide.

Guides to Publicity and Promotion

There are many types of reference tools available to professional publicists who want to keep up with changes in different types of media. A number of these are listed in *LMP* ("Reference Books of the Trade"), and some may be available in libraries. In addition, the Public Relations Society of America maintains an information center at 845 Third Ave., New York, NY 10022, which is open to the public.

In addition, you may wish to consult the following:

Bodian, Nat G. *Book Marketing Handbook*. New York: R. R. Bowker Co., 1980. A guide to publicity, advertising, marketing, and promotion. The emphasis is on academic books, but you may be able to use these ideas in helping market your own book.

Carter, Robert A., ed. *Trade Book Marketing: A Practical Guide*. New York: R. R. Bowker Co., 1983. An overview of all aspects of trade-book marketing and distribution by top experts in the field.

Lendt, David L., ed. *The Publicity Process*. Ames, Iowa: Iowa State University Press, 2nd ed., 1975. A beginner's guide to the publicity process.

Guides to and Books About Bookselling

American Book Trade Directory, 1983. New York: R. R. Bowker Co., 29th ed., 1983. Annual. A comprehensive directory of booksellers in the United States and Canada, arranged by city and state. Includes wholesalers.

Bliven, Bruce. *Book Traveler*. New York: Dodd Mead, 1975. A brief but charming and informative account of how a traveling book salesman does his job. (Out of print.)

Egan, Robert. *The Bookstore Book: A Guide to Manhattan Booksellers*. New York: Avon Books, 1979. A listing of general, remainder, specialty, used, and antiquarian book-sellers, with maps and with cross-indexes by subject and geographic area.

Fulton, Len, with Ellen Ferber. *American Odyssey: A Book-selling Travelogue*. Paradise, Calif.: Dustbooks, 1975. The author, publisher of Dustbooks, tells of a book-selling trip he took across the United States.

Literary Bookstores in the U.S. New York: Poets & Writers, 1980. A list of 344 bookstores specializing in contemporary fiction and poetry, with notes on biases such as feminism, and an appendix listing 34 literary bars and coffeehouses.

Guides to Libraries

American Library Directory. New York: R. R. Bowker Co., 36th ed., 1983. Revised biennially. Detailed listing of U.S., Canadian, and selected overseas libraries and library schools.

Subject Collections. New York: R. R. Bowker Co., 5th ed., 1978. A guide to the subject emphases of 16,000 American and Canadian libraries, plus 70,000 special collections (includes books and other materials).

Miscellaneous

Charlton, James, ed. *The Writer's Quotation Book: A Literary Companion*. New York: Penguin Books, 1981. Amusing, entertaining, and instructive quotes from literary folks.

City of New York, Department of Cultural Affairs. *The Writer's New York City Source Book*. New York: The Groundwater Press, 1981. A descriptive guide to the many services available to writers in the New York area.

Encyclopedia of Associations. Detroit, Mich.: Gale Research Co., 16th ed., 1981. A three-volume guide to over

15,000 national associations in the United States. May be useful in trying to make special sales.

Fear of Filing: A Beginner's Guide to Tax Preparation and Record Keeping for Artists, Performers, Writers and Freelance Professionals. New York: Volunteer Lawyers for the Arts, annual. A guide for writers in filling out their income taxes.

Gregory, Mollie. *Making Films Your Business*. New York: Schocken Books, 1979. An excellent guide to the motion-picture and television industries.

Information Industry Marketplace 1984. New York: R. R. Bowker Co., 1984. A guide to more than 1,400 suppliers of publicly available on-line data bases, including publishers, telecommunication and library networks, and the like.

Poynter, Dan. *Word Processors and Information Processing: How to Buy and How to Use*. Englewood Cliffs, N.J.: Prentice-Hall, 1983. This is aimed at people working in offices, but includes one section on using a word processor at home.

Shaffer, Susan E., in cooperation with the Education for Publishing Committee of the Association of American Publishers. *Guide to Book Publishing Courses: Academic and Professional Programs*. Princeton, N.J.: Peterson's Guides, 1st ed., 1979. A guide to over 200 courses at more than 100 institutions.

Index

ABOUT THE AUTHOR

CAROL J. MEYER is a native of Grand Rapids, Minnesota. After graduating from the University of Minnesota in 1960, she went to California to warm up, and spent the next ten years there as a technical writer in electronics and computers. In 1971 she came to New York to work in trade book publishing, where she subsequently worked as a subsidiary-rights assistant at Random House and then as assistant to the director, managing editor, and editor for Harcourt Brace Jovanovich's trade book division. She is now a free-lance writer, editor, and consultant, and director of the Rice University Publishing Program in Houston, Texas.

LEARNING TO WRITE AND ENJOYING IT

Books that can help you improve your ability to communicate. The interested beginning writer will find valuable direction and hints about how to write more efficiently and creatively.

☐ 24108	**THE WRITER'S SURVIVAL MANUAL** Carol Meyer		$3.95
☐ 24109	**HOW TO BE A FREE LANCE WRITER** David Martindale		$3.95
☐ 14344	**BUSINESS WRITING HANDBOOK**	Paxson	$3.95
☐ 20957	**IT PAYS TO INCREASE YOUR WORD POWER** P. Funk		$2.95
☐ 23326	**SOULE'S DICTIONARY OF ENGLISH SYNONYMS** Soule/Sheffield		$3.50
☐ 23393	**SCRIBNER/BANTAM ENGLISH DICTIONARY** E. Williams		$2.95
☐ 24066	**HOW TO ACHIEVE COMPETENCE IN ENGLISH** Eric W. Johnson		$3.50
☐ 24145	**BANTAM BOOK OF CORRECT LETTER WRITING** Lillian Eichler Watson		$3.95
☐ 24073	**30 WAYS TO HELP YOU WRITE** Fran Shaw		$2.95
☐ 22695	**WRITING IN GENERAL AND THE SHORT STORY IN PARTICULAR** Rust Hills		$2.95
☐ 22975	**WRITING AND RESEARCHING TERM PAPERS** Ehrlich & Murphy		$2.95

Prices and availability subject to change without notice.

Buy them at your local bookstore or use this handy coupon for ordering:

Bantam Books, Inc., Dept. WR, 414 East Golf Road, Des Plaines, Ill. 60016

Please send me the books I have checked above. I am enclosing $_____
(please add $1.25 to cover postage and handling). Send check or money order
—no cash or C.O.D.'s please.

Mr/Mrs/Miss _____

Address _____

City_____ State/Zip_____

WR—8/84

Please allow four to six weeks for delivery. This offer expires 3/85.